Ethnicity, Inc.

CHICAGO STUDIES IN PRACTICES OF MEANING

Edited by Jean Comaroff, Andreas Glaeser, William Sewell, and Lisa Wedeen

ALSO IN THE SERIES

Ethnicity, Inc.

JOHN L. COMAROFF AND JEAN COMAROFF

The University of Chicago Press   Chicago and London

JOHN L. COMAROFF is the Harold M. Swift Distinguished Service
Professor of Anthropology at the University of Chicago, Honorary Pro-
fessor, University of Cape Town, and Research Professor, American Bar
Foundation.
JEAN COMAROFF is the Bernard E. and Ellen C. Sunny Distin-
guished Service Professor of Anthropology at the University of Chicago,
Director, Chicago Center for Contemporary Theory, and Honorary Pro-
fessor, University of Cape Town.

The University of Chicago Press, Chicago 60637
The University of Chicago Press, Ltd., London
© 2009 by The University of Chicago
All rights reserved. Published 2009
Printed in the United States of America
Photographs are by John Comaroff unless otherwise noted.
17 16 15 14 13 12 11 10   4 5
ISBN-13: 978-0-226-11471-2 (cloth)
ISBN-13: 978-0-226-11472-9 (paper)
ISBN-10: 0-226-11471-6 (cloth)
ISBN-10: 0-226-11472-4 (paper)

Library of Congress Cataloging-in-Publication Data
Comaroff, John L., 1945–
    Ethnicity, Inc. / John L. Comaroff and Jean Comaroff.
      p. cm. — (Chicago studies in practices of meaning)
    Includes bibliographical references and index.
    ISBN-13: 978-0-226-11471-2 (cloth: alk. paper)
    ISBN-13: 978-0-226-11472-9 (pbk.: alk. paper)
    ISBN-10: 0-226-11471-6 (cloth: alk. paper)
    ISBN-10: 0-226-11472-4 (pbk.: alk. paper) 1. Ethnicity. 2. Ethnicity—
Economic aspects. 3. Ethnicity—Economic aspects—South Africa. I.
Comaroff, Jean. II. Title. III. Series.
GN495.6.C6454 2009
305.8—dc22   2008040972

♾ The paper used in this publication meets the minimum requirements
of the American National Standard for Information Sciences—
Permanence of Paper for Printed Library Materials, ANSI Z39.48-1992.

Contents

ONE

Prologue

Something strange is happening to the thing we call "ethnicity," the taken-for-granted species of collective subjectivity that lies at the intersection of identity and culture. Our ethno-episteme—the sum of ethno-consciousness, ethno-politics, ethno-practice, and the terms in which we apprehend them—appears to be morphing into exactly the opposite of what the orthodox social sciences would once have had us believe. Or rather, the *opposites*. Ethnicity is, has always been, both one thing and many, the same yet infinitely diverse. It is not just that there is a lot of it about these days, a lot of ethnic awareness, ethnic assertion, ethnic sentiment, ethno-talk; this despite the fact that it was supposed to wither away with the rise of modernity, with disenchantment, and with the incursion of the market. What is at issue is more its quality than its quantity, more its disposition than its demography. While it is increasingly the stuff of existential passion, of the self-conscious fashioning of meaningful, morally anchored selfhood, ethnicity is *also* becoming more corporate, more commodified, more implicated than ever before in the economics of everyday life. To this doubling—to the inscription of things ethnic, simultaneously, in affect and interest, emotion and utility—is added yet another. Cultural identity, in the here-and-now, represents itself ever more as two things at once: the object of choice and self-construction, typically through the act of consumption, *and* the manifest product of biology, genetics, human essence.

Herewith a few initial clues to what we are talking about, a few texts from different fronts opening up in the domain of cultural difference.

The North Catalan Economy: The Inspiration of Identity

The "identity" sector of the North Catalonian[1] economy represents a new open-mindedness [that] will see an expansion based on the culture of the region . . . as an alternative to globalisation.

The "identity" economy signifies a return to the formerly popular products which were abandoned in the 20th Century . . . The rediscovery of the natural potentials of the land, the advantage of ancestral experience and the added value of "identity" as a synonym of quality represents a welcome possibility in a region missing a productive economy . . . The "identity" economy . . . induces an obvious closeness [among Catalonians] . . .

The Catalan identity is a collective sentiment, a vision of the communal world, a language, a culture, a lifestyle . . . Becoming less local, [it] can now rediscover itself and find new forms of expression.

The Catalan social reality demonstrates its power of integration and its modernity, and thus it assures the survival of a culture threatened but living.

CATALOGNE-NORD HOME PAGE[2]

Note the reference to the "identity economy." Under its sign, several inimical things are conjoined: 'ancestral experience' is linked to 'open-mindedness,' 'closeness' to becoming 'less local,' 'modernity' to 'cultural survival,' 'natural potentials' to the 'rediscovery' of 'collective sentiment.' The objectification of identity, in short, appears here to have produced a new sensibility, an explicitly new awareness of its essence, its affective, material, and expressive potential. In the process, North Catalonian ethnicity is *both* commodified, made into the basis of *value-added* corporate collectivity, and claimed as the basis of shared emotion, shared lifestyle, shared imaginings for the future.

Two Angles on the Amazon, Peru

Frame 1: Welcome to the Land and Life-Ways of the Shipibo

Experience the Shipibo[3] Way of Life for yourself in the heart of the Amazon Basin with our Peru Eco-Tourism adventure! Learn how to make Shipibo ceramic artwork, go spear fishing in the Amazon river and much, much more.

Find ancient Shipibo remedies for various illness ranging from the common cold to cancer and receive visionary consultation from licensed Shipibo Shamans.
Meet New Friends.
Chat with a Shipibo in Peru via Email, Instant Message, or Phone.
SHIPIBO HOME PAGE[4]

FRAME 2: On Tourism and Traditional Healing

Mateo Arevalo, 43, was born into a family of traditional healers, or *curanderos*, in the Shipibo community of San Francisco de Yarinacocha in Peru . . . While Arevalo's fore-fathers put [their] knowledge to local use, generally treating their neighbors on a pro bono basis, Arevalo is proud to apply it to a wider audience . . . He now leads posh retreats in jungle lodges for foreigners, and hosts shamanism students in his home for three- or six-month courses.

"I am an innovator, adding to my ancestral knowledge," he explains. "We, the Shipibos, are like any other human community—we need to grow and change. We can't just stay the same so that the tourists can stare at the naked Indians in feath-ers and anthropologists can treat us like a living museum." . . . Ayahuasca ceremonies [ayahuasca is a powerful hallucinogen used in shamanic practices—JLC/JC] can be pur-chased in most major tourist destinations in Peru, and numerous jungle lodges now offer ceremonies or retreats, the latter costing in the neighborhood of $700–$1,500 a week. RACHEL PROCTOR, *CULTURAL SURVIVAL*, 2001

Once more, tradition is offered in alienable form, here as indigenous knowledge that inheres in Shipibo identity: 'ceramics,' 'remedies for ill-nesses' both trivial and dire, 'licensed shamanism,' even a 'way of life.' In this case, though, cultural products and practices are directed explicitly at consumers of the exotic, of spiritual reclamation, of jungle adventure. Their transaction conjures a curious mix of the intimate and the remote ('chat with a Shipibo . . . via Email'); it bespeaks the close distance charac-teristic of mass-mediated difference where the promise of self-discovery is the flip side of self-estrangement.[5] Once more, as well, the 'ancestral' ap-pears as a creative source of innovation, a view at odds with conventional understandings of "culture" as "heritage" or "custom." Culture, now, is also intellectual property, displaced from the 'museum' and the 'anthro-pological' gaze, no longer 'naked' nor available to just anyone pro bono.

Kenyan Chronicles, 2005

The First: Letter from the Field

An interesting development on the Ethnicity, Inc. front here: the defunct GEMA—Gikuyu, Embu, Meru Association—is being reconstituted. Since the new president is Gikuyu, they seem to feel that it is time to assert their interests again. What is interest-ing is that there is now a financial wing that will be involved in "venture capital," . . . turning tribe into corporation. The new GEMA is called MEGA.

ROB BLUNT, UNIVERSITY OF CHICAGO, 8 AUGUST 2005

The Second: Notes on the MEGA Initiative Welfare Society

MEGA Initiative Welfare Society is a community organisation formed to foster social/cultural and economic development of Ameru, Aembu and Agikuyu people of Kenya. It . . . is driven by the desire to demonstrate how a community or a region can bring about prosperity by exploiting the cultural richness and entrepreneurial skills and resources of its people . . .

MEGA Holding Initiative Ltd. Intends to be a major Vehicle for economic developments in this Country and in the Region by: . . . [d]eveloping projects and offloading the investment to its members as individuals or a group of individuals . . . [and] [w]orking as incubators of projects and of mobilisers of Venture capital.

MEGA WELFARE SOCIETY HOME PAGE[6]

In this instance it is less the marketing of ethnicity-as-substance that stands out than its deployment as a means of 'turning tribes into corporations'; literally, that is—into 'holding companies,' 'venture capitalists,' and the like—not in the analogical sense intended by an older generation of British anthropologists, for whom descent in Africa gave rise to what they called "corporate" lineages (see below). In Kenya, ethnic federations are becoming commercial enterprises, sole stakeholders in identity-based businesses. At times, contrary to the universal rationality of market ideology, these companies trade on claims to distinctive, 'culturally rich' forms of 'entrepreneurial skill.' Thus does identity-as-difference carve out specific niches of value production.

Scotland, the Brand

Step One: Developing the Brand

Currently, research is being undertaken by the official body, Scotland the Brand, into "Scottishness" and its exploitability in advertising and the packaging of Scottish goods. The country's new official marketing device, unveiled in November 1997, is the word "Scotland", in signature style, in which the Saltire blue of the national flag blends into tartan. The logo is to be used across the range of products and services—food, drink, textiles, financial and medical services, engineering, the universities . . . It seems that consumer nationalism of a kind will now be inescapable.

PHILIP SCHLESINGER, *LE MONDE DIPLOMATIQUE*, 1998[7]

Step Two: Enterprising Scotland

Scotland's growing life sciences sector has been given a . . . boost with the launch of a new national identity. The new Life Sciences Scotland brand will be used to demonstrate Scotland's approach to developing the sector and for marketing to global investors and potential overseas partners. The identity was unveiled by life sciences community body the Life Sciences Alliance at the world's biggest industry show, BIO 2006 . . . [Said] Mr. Snowden [Scottish Enterprise's director of life sciences], "It makes perfect sense to use this event to launch what will be Scotland's new face to the international life science community. Having a single brand will go a long way to focusing international attention on what we have to offer.

CRAIG COWBROUGH, *SCOTTISH ENTERPRISE*, 2006[8]

Identity incorporated, patently, can extend to populations beyond the scale of ethnic groups—at least, as conventionally understood—interpolating a cultural imagining of an 'exploitable' collective self (*Scottishness*) into civic nationhood, on which Scotland has long prided itself. In the process, a 'new national identity' is ostensibly fashioned. In the process, too, the relationship between the ethnic and the national is called into question, dissolved even, as 'consumer nationalism' sets out to 'brand' itself. And to place an ethnic logo on that most universal of human qualities: *life* itself.

––––––––

Southern Europeans, Latin Americans from the remote reaches of the Peruvian Amazon, East Africans, Scots. It could as well have been others. Many others. All pointing the way, in various ways, to the future of ethnicity. The keywords that index that future?

Identity economy, corporate identity, identity as value-added
Collective sentiment, emotion, closeness, close distance
Culture-for-sale, culture-as-innovation, cultural survival
Intellectual property, brand, ethno–logo
Tribe-into-corporation, new (national) identity, consumer nationhood
Modernity, rediscovery, venture capitalism, alternative to globalization

Nouns, adjectives, verbs: scattered clues that talk, in many tongues, of a world being patterned anew of elements both familiar and unfamiliar. Let us look deeper into that world from the vantage of the global south.

TWO

Three or Four Things about Ethno-futures

In October 2000, *Business Day,* South Africa's newspaper for the corporate sector, posted an extraordinary story on its Web site. Its title read: "Traditional Leaders to Form Private Firm for Investment."[1] The Congress of Traditional Leaders of South Africa (Contralesa) is the representative voice of ethnicity in the country. It speaks for culture, customary law, and the collective rights of indigenous peoples. Also for the authority of their chiefs and kings, past and present. Contralesa has long been committed to bringing about a change in the national constitution. Its ultimate objective is a nation-state that accords to traditional leaders sovereign autonomy over their realms, a nation-state that puts the dictates of culture at least on a par with, if not above, the universal rights of citizens. At times it has felt close to achieving its objective: most notably in late 2000, in the wake of a conference held by the Ministry of Provincial and Local Government[2] with a view to producing a parliamentary white paper and, eventually, new legislation on "traditional leadership and institutions." At other times, the organization has declared that it had "reached the end of the road," that "there was never an intention to accommodate [chiefly authority in] the making of the new South Africa"; these being the words of Chief (a.k.a. Prince, Doctor) Mangosuthu Gatsha Buthelezi, head of the Inkatha Freedom Party, former chief minister of the apartheid homeland of KwaZulu, and sometime minister of home affairs in the national government.[3]

Meanwhile, Contralesa seeks, by whatever political means possible, to privilege the kingdom of custom. And the customary privileges of kings.

According to *Business Day,* the traditional leaders had decided to move the politics of ethnicity into the marketplace. Having established a business trust a year earlier in order to join a mining consortium, they were about to create a *for*-profit corporation to pursue investment opportunities in minerals, forestry, and tourism; formal application had been made to register the company. The chiefs already had a share in a conglomerate then tendering for the license to open Cell C, a new mobile phone service.[4] Seeking to "capitalise on the 'Africanist' value of [their] constituency" (Oomen 2005:143, 97), they now planned to bid for parastatals up for private ownership. Said Patekile Holomisa, the powerful Xhosa head of Contralesa: "We have concentrated for too long on the political fight for . . . constitutional recognition." It had become more important to "empower their people" by venturing out from their traditional capitals into the realm of venture capital.

And venture they did. Over the next five or so years, Contralesa began to appear all over the financial landscape of South Africa, headlining the business sections of local newspapers, mentioned in state documents covering commercial deals, and so on. Thus, for example, when the Competition Tribunal heard a case involving a corporate takeover in September 2004, Contralesa Investment Holdings (Pty.) Ltd. was a part of the black economic empowerment group that held 25 percent of the shares in the acquiring syndicate.[5] Similarly, all of the nation's major media announced on 16 November 2004 that "[t]he Congress of Traditional Leaders of SA (Contralesa) had bought just over twenty-five per cent of UWP Consulting, a Johannesburg-based engineering consulting firm." *South African Business* went on:[6]

Prince Mpumalanga Gwadiso, chief executive of Contralesa Investment Holdings, the body's investment arm, said the acquisition was in line with its intention to achieve good returns for Contralesa members and the largely rural constituencies it represents. "In rural areas traditional leaders have always taken responsibility for their own community resources. Contralesa Investment Holdings aims to add value . . . [B]y investing in a stable, established company with proven competence in rural infrastructure development, this requirement is met," said Gwadiso.

Less than a year later, Contralesa bought from Howden Africa Holdings Ltd. its 42 percent share of Pump Brands, an enterprise involved in the design, manufacture, marketing, and selling of pumps and related products into the local and African markets. The deal cost the chiefs over R25m, approximately $4 million.[7]

Chief Setumo Montshiwa of the Tshidi-Rolong, the Tswana people among whom we were living at the time, had alerted us to all this before he died in July 2000. The chief had made his own private fortune in a gambling venture; ironic this, since, elsewhere in the world, as in Native America (Cattelino 2004, 2008), casino capitalism has long been connected to ethno-enterprise (see below, p. 64).[8] Setumo had said, more than once, that the (then) impending decision of the chiefs to enter the world of finance was "the way of the future." Ethnic groups, he often added, had to become like "pty's." Pty. abbreviates "proprietary" in South African financial English: "(Pty.) Ltd." is a private, limited company ("Inc." in its American translation, "Plc." in the UK equivalent). *Merafe* like his own— perhaps the closest translation from Setswana is "ethno-nations"—had to "join the modern world, " to "become business-like," to "market" themselves, to "manage" their symbolic and material assets. Not surprisingly perhaps, we were questioned closely by him about the profits that might accrue from our own work on *setswana*, "things Tswana"; he hoped to established an archive and cultural resource center that itself might be part of a new local enterprise. Futurity for this African chief, as for Contralesa, depended on turning finance capital into cultural capital and vice versa. For them, in fact, the line between the two had become porous to the point of dissolving.

Could it be, *contra* much of social science orthodoxy (see, e.g., Chabal and Daloz 2006:113–15), that one possible future—perhaps *the* future— of ethnicity lies, metaphorically and materially alike, in ethno-futures? In taking it into the marketplace? In hitching it, overtly, to the world of franchising and finance capital? In vesting it in an "identity economy"? Echoing the Catalonians, the Kenyans, the Shipibo, and the Scots, Leruo Molotlegi, king of the Bafokeng, South Africa's wealthiest people, intimated as much in an address to an American ivy-league university in 2002. The wealth of ethno-nations is a topic about which Leruo knows a great deal. So did his late predecessors, his father, Lebone Molotlegi I, and his brother, Lebone Molotlegi II. In September 1999, just before he died, Lebone Molotlegi II fronted a special supplement in *Enterprise* magazine devoted to the lucrative platinum mining partnership for which the Bafokeng are famous. Under his photograph was the caption "Kgosi Lebone II: CEO of Bafokeng Inc." (see plate 1).[9] Thirteen months later, soon after he took over the kingship, Leruo himself was featured on the cover of *Mining Weekly*. Its banner headline read: "Meet the New CEO of BAFOKENG INC" (plate 2).[10]

Cut away to another time, another optic, another part of South Africa.

In 1994, in the North West Province, there appeared an op-ed piece in *The Mail,* a local weekly newspaper. Titled "Searching for Tswana Heritage," it was signed by one Tswagare Namane.[11] "I [cannot] claim to be [an] . . . expert," it began, but "I . . . deserve to be heard." The point of the piece was to argue that the future of the region, of its ethnic Tswana population, and of Africa at large lay in tourism. But, Namane said, to attract visitors to this corner of the country would demand more than just fine hotels and well-stocked game parks. It would require "uncovering" and putting forth "what is authentically Tswana." Recourse to the cargo of cultural tourism, which has a long history, has become a universal panacea, an autonomic reflex almost, for those with no work and little to sell (cf. Castile 1996);[12] this in spite of the fact that it seldom yields what it seems to promise. But Namane had in mind something more than simply the foreign dollar. The commercialization of identity, he insisted, does *not* necessarily cheapen it or reduce it to a brute commodity. Quite the opposite: marketing what is "authentically Tswana" is also a mode of reflection, of self-construction, of *producing* and *feeling* Tswana-ness. This claim, we shall see, also lies behind another growth industry: genealogical tourism, founded on recreational genomics, a business rising up in the fecund spaces of the identity economy wherein the corporeal meets the corporate, where essence becomes enterprise.

Tswagare Namane's point has also been made in social science–speak, if not always with the same nuance. Note, for example, Marilyn Halter's (2000:16) bald statement that "exalting a particular culture and making money while doing it are not . . . antithetical." Or Phillip Felfan Xie's (2003:6–7) unwitting syllogism:[13] because (a) "commodification does not necessarily destroy cultural products" and (b) "culture and tourism can become inseparable," (c) "the commodification of culture" is often a "positive mechanism in the pursuit of authenticity," a means in the quest for "the true self," individual and collective, "through the appropriation of pastness." Resonating closely with Xie's last phrase, Namane went on:

I have walked around in search of something genuinely mine; something I could . . . cherish as a true achievement of my forebears, something to affirm my humanity and assert my equality to all.

This restless urge, he added, is most acutely felt by persons dispossessed of their past. Observe the choice of term, of *dispossession,* with its connotations of property, propriety, prosperity, paradise lost. "What I am reclaiming

is my ethnicity, my heritage; not my 'ethnicism.'" The distinction, a striking piece of vernacular anthropology, is critical. *Ethnicity* refers here to
membership in a culturally constituted "people," one with customary
ways and means that it takes to be distinctive and to which it is affectively
attached; *ethnicism* alludes, negatively, to "tribalism," in Namane's own
words, "a propagation of apartheid." Heritage, of course, is culture named
and projected into the past, and, simultaneously, the past congealed into
culture (cf. Kirshenblatt-Gimblett 1998:149).[14] It is identity in tractable,
alienable form, identity whose found objects and objectifications may be
consumed by others and, therefore, be delivered to the market (cf. Howard 2003). Its alienation, as Namane sensed, has the curious capacity
to conjure a collective imagining and to confer upon it social, political,
and material currency—not to mention "authenticity," the specter that
haunts the commodification of culture everywhere. If they have nothing
*dis*tinctive to alienate, many rural black South Africans have come to believe, they face collective *ex*tinction; identity, from this vantage, resides
in recognition from significant others, but the kind of recognition, specifically, expressed in consumer desire. Nelson Graburn (1976:26) once
put the point in more general terms. In making artwork for outsiders,
he wrote, peoples of the "fourth world" convey a message: "We exist; we
are different; we can do something we are proud of; we have something
uniquely ours." As a Tswana elder said to us, just after the millennium:
"[I]f we have nothing of ourselves to sell, does it mean that we *have* no
culture?" He used the English term. "If this is so, then what are we?"

This calls to mind a memorable statement made in the early 1990s by
Dawid Kruiper, leader of the so-called ≠Khomani Bushmen (San), then
resident at Kagga Kamma in the Western Cape Province.[15] Referring to
himself as an "animal of nature"—an affecting description, given that
Kagga Kamma is a white-owned wild game reserve—he said, "I want the
tourists to see me and to know who I am. *The only way our tradition and
way of life can survive is to live in the memory of the people who see us*" (White
1995:17; emphasis added).[16] "Seeing" here is entirely mediated by the market: the "Bushmen," who lived where they did at the "invitation" of the
proprietors of the place, were "urged" to dress in their "traditional costumes" and to "present their crafts for sale."[17] They also performed themselves at a simulated forager camp: the men "displayed their prowess with
bow and arrow, while women threaded ostrich bead necklaces. During
the day, trackers led hikes through the veld; in the evening they danced
and told stories." Then, "when visitors retired to their 'luxury Bushman
hut' chalets," the San themselves "exchanged their loincloths for Western
rags and went home to a shanty settlement . . . hidden from the public

gaze" (White 1991).[18] At which point, all that *did* remain of their lifeways were the traces that lived on in the memory of those who had encountered them. But precisely by virtue of laying down those traces—of enacting them repeatedly for tourist-consumers—these San were *not* just shanty dwellers in Western rags, desperately immiserated though they might have been. They were seen, and reciprocally were able to see themselves, as a named *people* with a "tradition and a way of life." In other words, a culture.

To be sure, the sale of culture seems, in part, to be replacing the sale of labor in the Brave Neo South Africa[19] of Tswagare Namane, Dawid Kruiper, and their 44.8 million compatriots, a South Africa whose industrial economy, founded on racial capitalism, is presently undergoing radical reconstruction—the impact of which has included the loss of millions of jobs, an acknowledged unemployment rate of around 40 percent, the casualization of much of the remaining work force, and the privatization of previously public assets (see, e.g., Bond 2004 [2006]; Ghosh 2006). This turn from labor to culture is the subject of a great deal of public concern in the countryside. For example, a few years ago, Chief Billy Sekwati Mampuru of the Mamone Pedi, a remote chiefdom in Sekhukhuneland in the far northerly Limpopo Province, established a Commission on the Tribal Constitution. One of its charges was to ask his subjects, many of whom had once earned a living as migrant workers, to give voice to their most urgent concerns. High on the list was "how we generate income from tourists with our tradition" (Oomen 2005:231).

There was plenty of precedent across southern Africa for this impulse. From the late 1980s onward, a substantial number of "cultural villages" had sprung up as means of marketing vernacular lifeways, the more exotic the better (cf. Schutte 2003; Tassiopoulos and Nuntsu 2005; see plates 3, 4, 5a–5d)[20]—the prototype, perhaps, being Shakaland, an elaborate ethno-theme park and resort established on the site of a *faux* Zulu settlement, itself erected as the set for a popular TV series (Hamilton 1998) based on the life of the great early nineteenth-century African monarch.[21] In fact, KwaZulu, the ethno-nation *itself*, seems to be mutating slowly into a culture park, a tourist destination, the *ur*-space of tradition in the country at large. In late 2006, there appeared a floodlit billboard attached to a seven-story building on the corner of Canterbury and Roeland Streets in Cape Town, less than two hundred meters downhill from the old Roeland Street Prison, now a national archive, less than 400 meters uphill from the Houses of Parliament, just across the road from SAHRA, the South African Heritage Resources Agency (see plate 6).[22] No doubt it is to be found in other places across the country as well. Very striking, it is dominated by an enormous photograph of a comely Zulu maiden, wreathed in a mass of colorful beads. Her sparkling-white teeth shine against the sunlight, mouth wide open in a seductively knowing smile. At once global fashion model and nubile native, this icon of African femininity evokes something entirely familiar in her otherness: the interpolation of the erotic into the exotic. In the barely discernible background are the hills of her native land; as far as one can tell, they are the heights above *eMakhosini,* the Valley of the Kings, birthplace of Shaka, site of the death of a number of his successors, and sometime capital of southern Africa's most celebrated indigenous monarchy. Above the woman's head, across a deep blue sky, is written the ad line, "The Zulu Kingdom Awaits You." Beneath the blanket at her breast, a beaded badge bears the sign of a warrior's shield and, in red and black on white, "Zulu Kingdom." The tableau is undergirded by a URL: "www.zulu.org.za" The Web site turns out to be that of the KwaZulu-Natal Tourism Authority, an organ of the *provincial* government. Its headline reads "Welcome to the Zulu Kingdom, KwaZulu-Natal," as if one of the nine provinces of the new South Africa has become an extension of, indeed complicit in, the commodification of Zulu ethnicity.[23] Nor is this fanciful. Not only has "Zulu Kingdom" become a trademark, advertising—in, among other places, airline magazines[24]—a wide variety of leisure destinations in the region. Among the proposed projects of the Authority is also the creation of a "'Zulu Heritage and Cultural Trail' . . . 'meandering' throughout the whole province, thereby linking together the diversity and variety of heritage and cultural tourism sites of interest. This . . . will truly underpin the *branding* of the Kingdom of the Zulu"[25]—whose sovereign, not coincidentally, was, according to the draft provincial constitution, also "Monarch for the Province of KwaZulu-Natal."[26] The arena to be built for the 2010 World Cup in Durban, its largest city, will be called King Senzangakhona Stadium, after the father of Shaka. And a new airport planned for the conurbation is to be King Shaka International.[27] We shall return to the more general matter of branding in just a moment.

As all this suggests, ethnic incorporation rides on a process of homogenization and abstraction: *the* Zulu (or *the* Tswana or *the* San), for all their internal divisions, become one; their "lifeways," withdrawn from time or history, congeal into object-form, all the better to conceive, communicate, and consume. But the process may also, often does, open up a politics of dissent, especially when investment capital from the outside plays into inequalities within local populations: in its most brute form, when ethnic elites, by one or another means, exploit new opportunities to enrich themselves to the disadvantage of their less well-positioned kin,

neighbors, and compatriots. This may not undermine ethnic identification among the latter; to the contrary, it may underline its importance
as an object of *both* possibility and political struggle. Take another case
from within KwaZulu-Natal. In 2001, the Mabaso Tribal Authority created a company, Funjwa Holdings, to invest in a game park and ecotour-
ism along Lake Sibaya. Its stated goal was to "reap the sweets and cakes of
free enterprise."[28] Based on a belief that the "Mabaso people" might "tap
into . . . thousands of national and international visitors each . . . year,"
the plan was to offer such "authentic" African activities as bow hunting—
which, being Zulu, the Mabaso probably never did. But they *did* receive
a large measure of financial support from Nedbank, a major South African financial house, and the Wildlands Trust; animals were donated by
Ezemvelo KZN Wildlife. Many of those who actually lived on the land
were against the project from the first; accusations have repeatedly been
made to the effect that it benefits elites to the exclusion of the poor.[29] In
the upshot, discord has threatened to derail the venture more than once
(Venter 2000:5–6). But the Wildlands Trust has declared it a "shining success" (Venter 2003:13), and the Mabaso Tribal Authority has subsequently
gone on to sign a "development agreement" with a private company, Uthungulu Resorts and Leisure. One of its rural schools, in Khula village,
has become part of Unilever's Sacred Forest initiative, an extension of the
global Living Lakes project (ibid.). The story is not over. One thing is clear,
though. Notwithstanding internal differences, or maybe because of them,
their entry into the world of business has made *the* Mabaso—richer and
poorer alike—more keenly aware than ever before of their attachment to
an ethnic identity. Most of them, it seems, retain the hope that, by virtue
of this identity, they too will one day "reap the sweets and cakes of free
enterprise."

This story has a direct, now well-known parallel further north, where
the Makuleke, a Shangaan-speaking community, had 24,000 hectares of
its territory along the Luvuvhu River restored to it in 1998; the land had
been expropriated in 1969 by the apartheid regime and incorporated into
the Kruger National Park (Harries 1987; Bunn 2001). Having won it back,
its owners had a decision to make. They could either resettle and farm it
or allow it to remain part of Kruger—designated as the Makuleke Con-
cession or Makuleke Contract Park—thence to derive income from tourism and trophy hunting. The issue was deeply divisive, especially early
on. But in the end, the majority came down in favor of the second solution, to be pursued through partnerships between commercial tour operators, South African National Parks (SANParks), which was concerned to
conserve the biodiversity of the terrain, and the Makuleke, who formed a

community property association (CPA) for the purpose. Two such partnerships have been established.[30] Under their terms, the private companies enjoy the right—for thirty and forty-nine years, respectively—to "build-operate" up-market game lodges and camps in a manner consistent with the management policies of SANParks. In return, they pay 8 percent of their turnover to the CPA and use another 2 percent for the "empowerment" of their local staff. The Makuleke envisage the gradual transfer of the tourist industry into their own hands, albeit by means unspecified; more immediately, they speak of building the Makuleke Development Trust, which husbands their financial assets, into an effective instrument of corporate ethno-business.[31]

Of the two resorts, the Outpost is the more salubrious.[32] A high-design palace in concrete, steel, and wood set deep in the tropical bush, it makes no mention in its marketing materials of having anything to do with an indigenous population. The other, Pafuri Camp,[33] a riverine wood-and-thatch fantasy, is run by Wilderness Safaris, for whom it is "a showpiece of what can happen when communities, . . . conservation authorities and ethical private sector partners work together for the benefit of all stakeholders" (Robins and van der Waal n.d.:11). Unlike the Outpost, it advertises its concern with Makuleke culture and economic betterment. Its brochures tell guests that they may stay in nearby Ntlhaveni at Makuleke Cultural Village (plate 7), there to familiarize themselves with vernacular lifeways, to "experience atavism or ancestor worship," to "have a private session with a diviner," and to witness an "informative and entertaining . . . performance which portrays the Makuleke eviction from the Kruger Park, their struggle and the eventual restoration of their land."[34] Pafuri also has a craft shop for which its management is encouraging people in the vicinity to produce. In addition, Wilderness Safaris has initiated a farm program by means of a loan to Makuleke cultivators with a view to having them provision the camp.

Both Wilderness Safaris and the Outpost believe that their presence is welcomed, partly because they create jobs—sixty-three in Pafuri—in an environment in which work is hard to find, partly because the share of their turnover paid to the CPA has been usefully spent on such things as school building, electrification, and roads. Those Makuleke whom we asked in March 2007 concurred. Inevitably, though, there *is* lingering dissatisfaction among some of them. For example, their chief, whose legitimacy is disputed by the neighboring Mhinga ruler (Robins and van der Waal n.d.), is said to have misappropriated concessionary income. His critics point to a large house, recently built, and costly cars, recently bought; thus, again, do new sources of profit exacerbate "traditional" privilege. Other plaints run to the fact that locals are largely involved in the enterprise as cheap labor (Tapela and Omara-Ojungu 1999:154), to the paucity of women in decision making, to the discontent of Pafuri guides, who earn less than their SANPark counterparts,[35] and to the regret felt by the older generation over the severance of their ties to the land. But few Makuleke seem still to think that they would be better off using that land for agriculture than putting it out for "rent"; they understand the "partnerships" less as joint ventures than as simple rentier capitalism. And, generally speaking, as beneficial to them. Like among the Mabaso, the entry of this population into the business world has heightened its awareness of being "the" Makuleke. According to one prominent man, all the talk about tourism, even when it has been a cause of conflict, has "served to bind us together [into] a community."[36] NGOs, land activists, investors, and development agencies have all reinforced this—and, by extension, the image of the Makuleke as a cohesive "people." So, too, has a swelling tribal treasury, the ethno-wealth of an economy inseparably moral and material.

No wonder, then, that—despite its sometimes steep downsides (cf. Van Wyk 2003), despite its capacity to drive the wedge of inequality deeper into local populations—the Mamone Pedi should have petitioned their chief to pursue ways of "generat[ing] income from tourists with our tradition" (above, p. 11). No wonder, too, that a new breed of small private consultancy firms, like African Equations in Cape Town, has arisen to advise "tribal groups" how best to merchandise themselves and their cultural products.[37] There is growing demand for their services; also for those of large concerns, such as Enterprise IG, which advertises, among its client companies, "Royal Bafokeng,"[38] the platinum-rich kingdom of which we spoke above and to which we shall return in extenso. Most of the ethno-businesses opening across the country speak of achieving "empowerment" through commerce: "the Mabaso community game reserve," said the CEO of Uthungulu Resorts and Leisure, the company in partnership with their Tribal Authority, has demonstrated "that black empowerment is a tangible reality" (see fn. 29). Mark this term: empowerment. In the postcolony, it connotes privileged access to markets, money, and material enrichment. In the case of ethnic groups, it is frankly associated with finding something essentially their own and theirs alone, something of their essence, to sell. In other words, a brand.

The resort to things ethnic as a means of "empowerment" is, patently, not confined to South Africa, or Africa, or that part of the World formerly known as Third. The entire planet "rejoices in . . . the cult of heritage," declares David Lowenthal (1998:1); by any measure, the "cultural economy" has become a massive global enterprise (Sigala and Leslie 2005:xii; Boniface and Fowler 1993). In the USA, Marilyn Halter (2000) shows, there is a large "industry [to remind] hyphenated Americans of how valuable heritage is *no matter how remote or forgotten it may be*" (emphasis added). According to www.brandchannel.com, a Web site devoted to the topic, this has "spawned an array of ethnic marketing experts."[39] The commerce to which such culture-conjurers devote themselves—referred to explicitly, with no apologies to Adorno, as the "ethnicity industry"—yielded about $2 billion per annum during the early years of the twenty-first century; its largest profits derive from food, fashion, music, and cultural artifacts. Nor is this market directed only at middle-class, mass-custom America. US corporations, like their counterparts in other parts of the world, appear to be turning to what the *Economic Times* of Bangalore refers to as "the ethno-chic feel" in designing interiors to reflect their morally responsible, multiculturally sensitive identities.[40]

The obverse, the creation of target markets for consumer goods along ethnic lines, is also flourishing these days in the USA. Firms like List Service Direct, Inc., offer "highly effective marketing segmentation technique[s]" to those who would exploit identity in purveying their products; among its odd mélange of clients are Paine Webber, the Salvation Army, J.C. Penney, K-Mart, the Christian Coalition, Amnesty International, the NAACP, Hadassah, the Holocaust Museum, and AT&T.[41] As Arlene Dávila (2001: 2–11 and passim) has demonstrated, the creation in North America of the ethnic category "Latino" or "Hispanic," a relatively recent phenomenon, is owed largely to the advertising and merchandising industries: *Latinos, Inc.* has become the object of a great deal of investment on the part of the business world. The "marketing and making" of an identity, she goes on to say, may be closely entailed in each other: "commercial representations may shape people's cultural identities as well as affect notions of belonging and cultural citizenship in public life" (2). Her choice of the term "affect" here is apt, pointing at once to cause and to sentiment. Thus it is, for example, that a chain of "Hispanic-focused" pizza restaurants in Texas, Arizona, Nevada, California, and Colorado—they are called *Pizza Patrón*—accepts pesos, saturates its establishments with Latino music, wallpapers them in Mexican saltillo tiles, and has adopted the rather obvious logo of a mustachioed man in a fedora; all of this to create "a new context for pizza. One that sort of *feels* . . . Hispanic." The stress, quite blatantly, is on conjuring affect, itself ever more a commodity, by aesthetic means.[42]

As in America, so increasingly in the United Kingdom, if not yet on the same scale. With the decomposition of *Great* Britain, a national imag-

ining eroded by assertions of cultural particularity and political autonomy, the production and sale of English and Celtic heritage are expanding apace (cf. e.g., Hewison 1987).[43] It is thus that Scotland the Brave has
become *Scotland the Brand* (McCrone, Morris, and Kiely 1995; p. 4 above);
thus that Wales advertises itself incessantly, notably to captive audiences
on British Airways flights, as a unique business environment, unique because of the nature of the place, its history, its human capital, and the
cultural disposition of its people. Inside its own borders, England, known
historically for its indifference to difference—although it now seems simultaneously more *and* less tolerant—is also witnessing a rapid growth
in the ethnic industry. Here, too, ethno-marketing is imploding. Firms are
popping up with names like Namaste-UK Ltd. (purveyors of "traditional
ethnic screenprints"), Punjab Kitchen Ltd. ("authentic halal and ethnic
Asian meals"), Ethnic Interiors Ltd. ("hand made artefacts . . . from Kenya
and beyond"), Ethnic Britain (a national directory to put the business
community and ethnic minorities in better touch with each other), To-
tally Jewish Property ("providing professional service for buying and selling real estate in London"), Ethnic Food Action Group Ltd. ("grow[ing]
the Ethnic Food companies" of Yorkshire and Humberside), EthniCity
("bring[ing] you beautiful, Ethnic goods from many cultures all over the
world"), and the on-line www.Jewish.co.uk (publisher of a directory of
business services).[44] Yet more striking, ethnic populations have become a
target of the franchising industry: www.whichfranchise.com, an affiliate
of the British Franchise Association, is currently urging "Asians," whom
it sees as *innately* entrepreneurial, to open their own ethno-businesses,
thereby to take advantage of the "fact" that "franchising [cultural goods
and services] for ethnic minorities is . . . a natural fit."

Obviously, not all ethno-businesses in England deal in specifically cultural goods or services. A quick look through the Asian Business Directory for Greater London (or, equally, for the Midlands) makes it clear that,
while many do, others do not.[45] What is more, the extent to which communities are taking on a corporate identity varies widely. Nor does the
marketing of ethno-products and practices always derive from conventional sources. In 1998, for example, the respectable *Independent on Sunday*
carried a story—written in a tone of ironic detachment—about Heather
Campbell, a.k.a. Moon Owl, a shamanic guidance consultant. Campbell acquired her occult skills through a seven-year apprenticeship with
Chief Harley Swiftdeer of the Deer Tribe Medicine Society in California. In
point of fact, the Deer are *not . . .* Deer. Chief Harley is half-Cherokee, half-
Irish; his "tribe" is based in Los Angeles. Nonetheless, according to the
Independent, Moon Owl has been hired by such gray-suited corporations

as Shell Oil, Hasbro Bank, and Gossard Lingerie to counsel their executives, "putting them in touch with their inner goddess by replacing their boardroom rituals with her own." She takes them on medicine walks, using ethno-knowledge gained as a Gateway Roadwoman and Sacred Pipe Carrier among the Deer. We are not told whether Campbell sells her services on her own account or on behalf of the self-styled ethnic group into which she gained entry, a question that always intrudes upon the alienation of "indigenous knowledge." But her sale of Deer cultural property, an ethno-brand that does not come cheap, appears to be drawing a decent customer base.[46]

––––––

The bringing together of branding, marketing, culture, and identity—the kind of thing aspired to by Tswagare Namane and Dawid Kruiper, the Shipibo and the Scots, MEGA and the Mabaso, Catalonia and KwaZulu—finds echoes in recent scholarly discourses. Martin Chanock (2000:24–26), writing of the postcolonial world, suggests that, in an age in which "fantasies work where reality fails," contemporary advertising techniques, those neoliberal weapons of mass instruction, are replicated in the production and alienation of culture;[47] culture, that is, not in the anthropological sense of the term, but in the guise claimed by those who would assert a collective subjectivity by objectifying it for the market. In particular, he says, the process of branding—of creating an affective attachment to a named product, to both its *object*-form and to the *idea* of an association with it—is "full of clues to the understanding of how allegiances to cultures are made." Pay attention to the term "allegiance(s) to culture(s)." It may be translated, without significant slippage, into ethnic, even in some cases national, identity. But here is the heart of the matter. To survive, concludes Chanock, "[c]ultures, like brands, must essentialise . . . successful and sustainable cultures are those which brand best." This is uncannily reminiscent of what was said, if in more plainspoken terms, by the Tswana elder cited earlier, the one who asked, "If we have nothing of ourselves to sell, does it mean that we have no culture?"

The competitive edge enjoyed by those cultures "which brand best" is illustrated by a noteworthy case of the commodification of tradition among the Pedi; it is one of their chiefdoms, the Mamone, recall, whose population petitioned their ruler to pursue the tourist route to financial well-being. This case concerns the *koma,* their initiation school. Initiation rites are commonly held, by most indigenous peoples of southern Africa, to pass on the very essence of "deep knowledge." It is in this sacral context, culminating in circumcision, that the core secrets of vernacular lifeways are narrated and reproduced; also, that youths are inducted into adulthood by the proper cultural means, taught discipline, and enjoined to respect authority (J. Comaroff 1985:85–118). Such schools exist across the country and are widely attended. They are also the subject of public controversy, owed largely to the disturbing number of deaths, and serious genital injuries, suffered by participants in recent years.[48] For Pedi, writes Barbara Oomen (2005:161–62), "the *koma* [has become] a lucrative business." This is not just because "people pay between R200–R1,500 [$33–$250]" for their participation. It is also because many *non*-local youths also enroll, despite the fact that "the prices . . . are much higher [for them] than for local children" (162, n.129)—and higher than the cost of the alternatives. Pedi-brand *koma* has become a niche product in a regional culture market, edging aside other local versions of the same thing, among them, a renowned, fee-for-service female initiation among the Venda (McNeill 2007:115).[49] In this desperately poor economy, the alienation of indigenous practices, even of the deepest knowledge, *is,* as Namane predicted, simultaneously a means of self-construction and a source of material sustenance. Cultural survival, with due respect to the organization of the same name, has given way, in many places, to survival through culture. As Xie (2003:14) puts it of the Li population of Hainan Island, China, the commodification of their customary ways and means, often in reinvented form, "is vital for [their] survival and sustainability"; even for "cultural regeneration," adds Hillman (2003:183), speaking of northwest Yunnan.

Much the same thing has been said for, among many others, Maori in New Zealand (Shannon 1995), Cajuns in Louisiana (e.g., Esman 1984), and Native Americans in the southeastern United States (e.g., Paredes 1995). It is also the case in Bali, where, remarkably, funerary cremations are very popular among overseas visitors; where versions of ritual dances performed for paying guests are now so much preferred by local people that they are "staged in the holy temple," displacing the "older, sacred" ones; and where, as in Yunnan, tourism has become a "vital element in the survival and revival of cultural forms" (Sanger 1988:99–100). But there is a twist here. Or, rather, a twist-and-turn. On the face of it—this is the twist—the more successful any ethnic population is in commodifying its difference, the faster it will debase whatever made it different to begin with. And any value that might accrue to it on that account. Classical economics and critical theory, antitheses in every other way, would agree on this: the former, because of its laws of supply, demand, and diminishing marginal returns; the latter, because it presumes that, once a cultural product becomes available for mass consumption, it will lose its aura—for good or ill.[50] The same paradox is often said to inhere in the quest of those who purchase the exotic-as-commodity in order to find redemptive meaning in their lives: the more they pursue their alienated selves in the numinous *Geist* of others, the quicker that *Geist* will succumb to the corrosive effects of the market (cf. Povinelli 2001). This is why "ethnic tourism" is frequently said to "destroy . . . that which it seeks," creating, in place of [the appearance of] "authenticity," a feeling of "'cultural flatness' whereby all sense of meaning and belonging" is eroded, rendered superficial (Hillman 2003:182, after Britton 1991; cf. Boniface and Fowler 1993:2).

Here, though, is the u-turn. The process of cultural commodification, and the incorporation of identity in which it is imbricated, is less linear, less teleological, more capricious than either classical economics or critical theory might suggest. Neither for consumers nor for producers does the aura of ethno-commodities simply disappear with their entry into the market; sometimes, as we have seen, it may be rediscovered, reanimated, regained (cf. Myers 2002:316). As this implies, the ethno-commodity is a very strange thing indeed. Flying in the face of many conventional assumptions about price and value, its very appeal lies in the fact that it seems to *resist* ordinary economic rationality. In part, this is because the quality of difference it vends may be reproduced and traded without appearing to lose its original value (Alexander 2004:119). Why? Because its "raw material" is not depleted by mass circulation. To the contrary, mass circulation reaffirms ethnicity—in general and in all its particularity—and, with it, the status of the embodied ethnic subject as a source and means of identity. Greater supply, in other words, entails greater demand. The implication? That aura may reside as much in the duplication of these objects as in their uniqueness (Steiner 1999), in their becoming what Bruner (1999) calls "authentic reproductions." And authentic reproductions, like "genuine fakes," tend to underscore the uniqueness of the original (Comaroff and Comaroff 2006:13–14). Not always, of course. Cultural products and practices *do* sometimes succumb to the logic of supply and demand (see below). But the "drama of the aura and its decay,"[51] when it comes to ethno-commodification, often acts itself out in unpredictable ways, raising, as we shall see shortly, some very general theoretical questions about triangulation of culture, identity, and the market.

What conclusions may be drawn from all this? Could it be that we are seeing unfold before us a metamorphosis in the production of identity and subjectivity, in the politics and economics of culture and, concomitantly, in the ontology of ethnic consciousness? Or are we merely witness to the intensification of something that has been around for a long time, something immanent hiding in the half-light of the convoluted, often unexpected history of capitalism, something now being forced fully into view? Are *both* things possible? If so, how do we account for them? And where is this all leading? Note that, in posing the problem thus, we treat ethnicity, culture, and identity *not* as analytic constructs but as concrete abstractions variously deployed by human beings in their quotidian efforts to inhabit sustainable worlds. We will argue that the emergence of Ethnicity, Inc.—if not everywhere in the same way, to the same extent, with equal passion, or in equal proportion—involves a double process; a dialectic, albeit not in the overdetermined, totalizing sense from which so much postmodern theory takes almost hysterical flight. One element of that process lies in the incorporation of identity, the rendering of ethnicized populations into corporations of one kind or another; the second, in the creeping commodification of their cultural products and practices. How these two sides of the dialectic relate to one another, thus to shape the future of ethnicity, will become clear in due course. So, too, will other unresolved questions, some of which we have hinted at: What, precisely, is the part played by rise of neoliberal capitalism, broadly conceived, in the incorporation of identity? Who, if we may be so unsubtle, are its primary beneficiaries? Who suffer it, and in what measure? What are the implications of Ethnicity, Inc. for everyday ethno-politics, not least those conducted by violent means? And for the affect so long held to be an integral element of ethnic consciousness? Are any parts of the new global order likely to escape the processes described here?

But we are running ahead of ourselves.

One thing *is* already clear: that the interrogation of Ethnicity, Inc., has some nontrivial consequences for theorizing the age in which we live, whether we know it or not, understand it or not, like it or not.

THREE

Questions of Theory

Let us pause, at this juncture, to offer three sets of theoretical observations, each of them critical to the exploration of Ethnicity, Inc. One has to do with the nature of culture, so to speak, with its conception, its possession, its circulation, its commodification. We treat it first because, archetypically, it is held to lie at the existential core of ethnic consciousness: ethnicity = *cultural* + identity, adjective and noun locked in indissoluble embrace. The second set of observations has to do with ethnicity itself, with its ontology and the manner of its treatment in the social sciences; the third, with identity, subjectivity, and selfhood, especially as these tropes have come to lodge themselves in the twenty-first century nation-state and its increasingly uneasy, polymorphous self-imaginings.

i. On the Commodification of Culture

Ethno-Commodities, Culture, and the Market: Critical Theory as Caricature, Adorno as Farce

It will already be evident that there is more at stake in the incorporation of ethnicity than either the march of the market or the global growth of an ethic of enterprise. While it *is* ever more blatantly merchandised across the world, the conceit persists that cultural identity is inalienable; that, insofar as it inheres in human essence, it defies commodification. Scholars have been strangely slow to dispel this fantasy. Not only have they shied away from exploring the economic dimensions of identity formation (Halter 2000:12). They have also tended to take for granted that culture is the bona fide expression of collective *Geist.* Notwithstanding the fact that, already by the 1970s, anthropologists were documenting its sale "by the pound" and had begun to describe ethno-tourism as "cultural commoditization" (Greenwood 1977). Its aura was still held to remain inimical to commerce. Cultural being, Clifford Geertz (1963:108–111) and others told us (cf. Chabal and Daloz 2006: 113–4), exists in ineluctable tension with the rationalizing thrust of modernity. All of which resonated closely with critical theory (pp. 19–20 above); not least with Adorno's insistence (2006:236) that, when mass media take possession of the cultural "homelands," even those they celebrate, they reduce their "unique character . . . [to] interchangeable sameness." Palpable, here, is an old modernist angst, "the specter of difference vanishing" (Bayart 2005:7). But the "ethnicity industry" replays critical theory as caricature, Adorno as farce,[1] banking its future on precisely the kind of mass marketing deemed fatal to the unique, auratic value of cultural products. Is this an instance of Rancière's (1999:113) thesis, according to which prevailing global conditions ensure that we relive the dark secrets of modernity—in this instance, the complicity between culture and commerce—shamelessly, in plain sight?

The vision of modernity as a relentless advance marked by commodification and rationalization, by the dissolution of concrete particulars into abstract universals, has long been questioned: on one hand, by invoking the ineradicable distinctness and the defiance of the "local" (cf. Graeber 2002); on the other, by calling into doubt the totalizing telos of both Hegelian and Marxian dialectics (Comaroff and Comaroff 1997:410; Mazzarella 2003). It is the second species of critique that concerns us here. Like Mazzarella (2003 41–43), we take issue with historical imaginings that presume a "one-way process of abstraction," a process that, in the postmodern era, is often said to be eradicating all vestiges of unalienated existence, any "outside" from which global consumerism can effectively be countered: capitalism, however ethereal it might appear to have become, remains a *grounded* social formation, one that is given manifest shape by the practices of living beings, one whose history is not overdetermined from the first (cf. Postone 1993). Neither its determinations nor its abstractions are *ever* absolute. They are always exceeded by the messy intractability of the concrete, the contingent. Shades, here, of Marx's insistence that the fetishism of commodities never conceals fully the conditions of their production. Even images that enter into the reproduction of capital, Mazzarella (2003) adds, have a material exuberance, an excess, irreducible to the "abstracting requirements of exchange value"; note, in this respect, how Balinese dances designed for the tourist dollar so captured the imagination of the "natives" that they ended up replacing the sacred, auratic originals previously performed only in the temple (p. 19).

The tension between the abstract and the concrete, the universal and the particular, has been endlessly replayed throughout the history of modernity. And continues to be. The identity industry is a prime case in point. Those who seek to brand their otherness, to profit from what makes them different, find themselves having to do so in the universally recognizable terms in which difference is represented, merchandised, rendered negotiable by means of the abstract instruments of the market: money, the commodity, commensuration, the calculus of supply and demand, price, branding. And advertising. Ethnicity, Inc. is also shaped by the centrality of mass mediation to the age of planetary consumerism, the effect of which is that the counterpoint between the singular and the generic is now enacted, a la Rancière, "in full public view." Hence the Zulu maiden captured on that huge billboard in Cape Town, whose seductive visage cannot but leave undecided whether it is Zulu femininity or the global erotic, ethno-chic or world fashion, that she conjures up. Or whether there is a whether at all: whether her commodity-image simply exceeds any effort to make it stand for any one thing in particular.

Indeed, the identity industry is an especially apt instance of this multiply mediated tension between the universal and the particular. Ethno-commerce feeds an ever more ubiquitous mode of production and reproduction, one born of a time in which, as we have noted, the sale of culture has replaced the sale of labor in many places. This raises two immediate questions. What, in the realm of the identity economy, counts as capital, what as labor? And who controls the conditions under which culture is represented and alienated? The quick answer to both is that there is enormous empirical variation. In many instances, outside entrepreneurs exploit marginal peoples in the name of cultural tourism, giving birth to new ethnic dependencies (cf. Cohen 1983).[2] Among insiders, to the degree that neat boundaries may be drawn at all, the division of labor and dispositions of profit often follow endogenous lines of inequality (pp. 14–15 above). But not always. Ethno-commerce may open up unprecedented opportunities for creating value of various kinds, and not only for the previously well-positioned. Chambers (2000:102f), among others, shows that any number of minority populations, north and south, have enhanced their autonomy, their political presence, and their material circumstances by adroitly managing their tourist potential—and all that it has come to connote (cf. Swain 1990; Maurer and Zeigler 1988; see also below).

As this implies, vendors of ethnic authenticity, however bound they may be to the market, are *not* an alienated proletariat, in thrall to the fetish of their own estranged essence. Nor have they simply become fetishes themselves. Save, perhaps, *in extremis,* they have more than mere "exhibition value" (Benjamin 2002:106) that withers with exposure to the public gaze. Take, again, Tswagare Namane, who made it plain that there is at work here a process "of simultaneous self-distancing and self-recognition" (McLuhan 1994:57).[3] Namane's quest for identity was rooted in the hope that, by finding something viable to market, he might reclaim a collective heritage to cherish, something to affirm his self-worth. And his humanity. To be human these days, he suggests, one must "have culture." These feelings have parallels elsewhere. Geismar (2005:453) points out that the reproduction and sale of North Ambrym carvings in Vanuatu "shows how an indigenous social and moral order" and a sense of "indigenous agency" may be "extended through the commoditization of *kastom . . .*" Recall, also, Xie's syllogism linking commerce to cultural authenticity and affect: tourism in Hainan, he wrote (2003:6), has turned a "commodified dance performance into an "authentic" aboriginal cultural expression," heightening the desire for identity and offering an affective vehicle for finding "a true self." Exactly the obverse, this, of alienation-by-abstraction, corrosion-by-commodification.

To wit, many of the subjects we have encountered thus far have been passionate, questioning, often ironic observers of the unforeseen possibilities engendered by the marketing of their identities, their essence, their cultural products and practices. Nor only them. Xavante traditional dancers from the Amazon, performing for urban Brazilian audiences, are said to do so in pursuit of "'existential recognition' . . . from outsiders, which they consider to be essential to their ultimate goal of perpetuating 'cultural continuity'" (Graham 2005: 625). Their audiences may interpret the performances as "second order indexicals" (637, after Silverstein 1996), conveying little more than "Xavanteness" or "indigeneity." But, for the performers, this effort to "broadcast their unique Xavante identity and culture outward—horizontally—into national and global public arenas," (636) evokes an enriched web of emotions, desires, passions, and interests.

The distinction here between production and reception, performer and consumer, brings us to a further complexity. Remember Dawid Kruiper's remark that the tradition and lifeways of the ǂKhomani San would endure "in the memory" of the tourists who interact with them. For those tourists, those consumers, the native "other" in this drama might serve as a fetish, albeit here in the Freudian, rather than the Marxian, version: a stand-in for their own lack of cultural authenticity and fullness of being, their own exile from the untainted affect of natural life-in-the-world. Such unalienated savagery is, in Žižek's (n.d.) phrase, a "necessary supplement" to the myth of civilized modernity. Not that the encounter can ever fully allay that sense of lack. The search for a "true self" by such means, Lacan might well have reminded us, is more likely to *heighten* its felt absence, to reproduce the unrequited desire, at the core of identity. To San, the exchange has a somewhat different valence, a different configuration of identity, loss, and the regeneration of selfhood. At one level, it *is* tragic evidence of the plight of people whose survival depends on running with the romance of their own primitivism—and on the fitful recognition of fee-paying strangers.[4] Or worse. To return once more to Benjamin (1968:216): the aura of historical objects, he argued, may be compared to that of "natural" ones, to a mountain range on the horizon or a branch and its shadow. In both instances, the aura is a "unique phenomenon of distance, however close it may be." This is the distance of elusiveness, in time as well as space. It is shattered by the modern impulse to render all qualities equivalent, to "bring things closer," to get hold of them by consuming their likeness in mechanically reproduced forms. These forms offer accessibility at the cost of authentic presence. They "liquidate . . . the traditional value of . . . cultural heritage." Benjamin might have predicted, then, that, by making themselves and their artifacts available to tourists, the Bushmen run the risk of annihilating their mystique,"[5] of being reduced to the token of a type, another "second order indexical."

It is the case that the intensive marketing of ethnic identity may well involve a Faustian bargain of sorts, leading to self-parody and devaluation. But, if we believe the likes of Kruiper or the Xavante dancers or the Hainan islanders, it also appears to (re)fashion identity, to (re)animate cultural subjectivity, to (re)charge collective self-awareness, to forge new patterns of sociality, all within the marketplace. And it often does so—herein lies the complexity, the codicil to Benjamin—by *ambiguating* the distinction between producer and consumer, performer and audience. How so? Because the producers of culture are *also* its consumers, seeing and sensing and listening to themselves enact their identity—and, in the process, objectifying their own subjectivity, thus to (re)cognize its existence, to grasp it, to domesticate it, to act on and with it; Namane, Kruiper, et al., were all fairly explicit about this. Conversely, consumers also become producers, complicit in that enactment: it is by lodging itself in the consciousness of the tourist-other, according to the San, that their tradition persists. Marjorie Esman (1984:465) makes a similar point about Louisiana Cajuns. They are "tourists within their own culture," she says, their customary lifeways being as exotic to them as to outsiders. Even more, the version that is commodified and enacted for, and with, the *"required . . . assistance"* of visitors *becomes* the "authentic," the "original"; as Xie (2003:6) suggests, authenticity "is not a fixed property of an object or a situation but is a negotiated attribute." In the course of their negotiation, those exotic lifeways are domesticated, giving manifest form to contemporary Cajun identity.

Does this not suggest that those who seek authenticity and meaning by commodifying their identity remain, in the end, dupes of the market and its mystifications (cf. MacCannell 1989)? At first glance, it would certainly seem so: ethno-commodities and the value they accrue remain subject in many ways to the whims of capital and to the predations of those who profit from its circulation. But this is much too simple. Those who would (re)claim their ethnic "nature" by means of grounded ethno-preneurialism appear to do so, more or less often, with a good measure of critical and tactical consciousness. Like the Xavante who, by means of their dance performances, sought to enrich their conditions of existence within the Brazilian Amazon by impressing on outsiders their status as "indigenous peoples"—with the entitlements that now entails (cf. Graham 2005:632). Or the Catalonians, who are deploying the identity economy—in pursuit, they say, of a renewed sense of collective sentiment—by recuperating past modes of production as "an alternative to globalization." Or Tswagare Namane, who made that subtle distinction between "ethnicity," identity-as-self-possession, and "ethnicism," an identity forced upon his people by the political economy of a racial state. Admittedly, all of these things occurred *within* the culture of the market. But, in each instance, complex differences were drawn between past and present, between what is and what might be, between vernacular agency and the forces of the world beyond. And in each of them a desire was evinced to act upon that world, to make its abstractions concrete. In short, to the extent that the commodification of culture is refiguring identity, it is doing so less as a matter of brute loss, or of abstraction, than of intensified fusions of intimacy and distance, production and consumption, subject and object. Even if the transaction of cultural products and practices *were* entirely reducible to cash, it does not necessarily mean that they would be denuded of all auratic, affective, or social worth: the very fungibility of money lends itself to transformations of value that may reinforce difference—and add substance to identity (cf. Cattelino 2008).

The point we seek to make here is this: against the telos of both classical and critical theory, the rise of ethno-commerce in the age of mass consumerism is having counterintuitive effects on human subjects, cultural objects, and the connection between them. While the commodification of identity is frequently taken as prima facie evidence of the cheapening of its substance, the matter has never been quite so straightforward. It has become yet further complicated of late, with the ever more active investment of capital in diversity.[6] The widely noted shift in the production of value from the material to the immaterial—to the sale of knowledges and intellectual property, of experience, affect, and modes of self-production—signals the entry into the market of domains of existence that once eluded it. It also underlines the fact that commerce, *sui generis,* now far exceeds the mere sale of goods and services. To a greater extent than ever in the past, perhaps, it involves the fulsome cultivation of highly charged attachments, at once emotional and cognitive, to chosen lifestyles.[7] And, as significantly, to the means of accomplishing them. We have noted that this process, which is intimately connected to the construction of identity-though-consumption, lies at the heart of commodity branding; also, that it closely parallels the manner in which cultural affiliations congeal into affectively rich ethnic consciousness. Which is why it is possible to create a "new context for pizza. One that sort of *feels* . . . Hispanic" (above, p. 16).

We stress, then, that it is not just that culture is being cumulatively commodified. Or that vernacular ways and means ("tradition") are made and remade, visibly, in the course of their transaction (cf. Handler and Linnekin 1984). It is that commodity exchange and the stuff of difference are inflecting each other, with growing intensity: just as culture is being commodified, so the commodity is being rendered explicitly cultural— and, consequently, is increasingly apprehended as the generic source of sociality. As Brian Massumi puts it, both the realm of production and the realm of consumption deal ever more in "intangible . . . cultural products or products of experience that inevitably have a collective dimension to them."[8] The upshot is that "the difference between marketing and consuming, and between living and buying is becoming smaller and smaller." Also that those "cultural products," duly fetishized, become an overtly acknowledged force of world making. Which is why the discourse of ethno-preneurialism frames identity as a mode of finding selfhood through vernacular objects; why the line between production and consumption in the identity economy is often blurred; why cultural exchanges, not least in the context of tourism, are said to yield "magic moments," small epiphanies in which sellers and buyers, brought together in fleeting encounters across lines of difference, alike feel "touched by the real" (Daniel 1996:783; cf. Bruner 1999). Herein lies the open-ended dialectic in which, under the impress of the market, human subjects and cultural objects produce, reproduce, and refashion each other.

Culture-as-Property: The Geist of Culture Past, Present, Future

"Throughout history," Phillips and Steiner (1999:3) point out, "the physical presence of the object has been central to the telling of cross-cultural encounters with distant worlds . . ." Nor only the telling. Modern colonial missions almost everywhere sought to make diverse others into ethnic subjects through objects (Comaroff and Comaroff 1991). With the turn of the twenty-first century, however, we seem to have entered a phase in which otherness is not transacted only as trophy, talisman, souvenir, or subjection. Identity is increasingly claimed as *property* by its living heirs, who proceed to manage it by palpably corporate means: to brand it and sell it, even to anthropologists, in self-consciously consumable forms. It may well be, as some have asserted (Postone 1993), that the particular idea of difference on which this rides—in which vernacular use-values are defined in relation to universal standards of value—*required* the rise of the commodity form. After all, the "priceless" authenticity often said to put cultural aura beyond the reach of commerce depends on a prior conception of price. And on the presumption of a sharp line between what can be reduced to cash equivalence and what cannot. To be sure, modern colonialism fudged that line by opening up markets for "traditional" ethnic arts and crafts. Precisely by virtue of its *not* being Culture, upper case, the culture transacted in those markets was integral to—and signified, materially—the contrast between the enlightened and the primitive, the refined and the naive, the universal and parochial, on which the modernist sense of Western civilization and Euro-nationalism was erected (Clifford 1988:204f; Said 1993; Pratt 1992).[9]

The colonial trade in ethnic objects, George Pierre Castile (1996:743) has argued, is evidence of the way in which the images and identities of others were extracted as raw material, refashioned, and transacted by Western elites "entirely free" of native control. Broadly speaking, he is correct. But it is not so evident that exchange value triumphed over all in this process, that the tangible trace of those natives did not spook their representations as they circulated abroad; a latter-day variation, this, on *hau*, the human essence of the giver, that once infused Maori gifts as they proceeded along circuits of exchange in Oceania (Mauss 1966). Either way, the consolidation of nineteenth-century states and their colonies gave rise to much tighter regulation of the commerce in alien cultures (Castile 1996:744). Having substituted universal citizenship for ethnic identities at home—in theory at least—these worldly regimes appointed themselves custodians of "tribal" peoples overseas, peoples whose lifeways, aesthetics, and material possessions were deemed all of a piece with their lowly status on the evolutionary scale of human types.

And so it remained throughout the age of empire, during which the rise of anthropological "science," and the sociology of knowledge on which it was founded, served further to reify and value cultural otherness. In fact, the discipline's arguments for relativism had limited impact on the hegemonic, high-modern Eurocentrism that undergirded the epoch. If anything, its assertions of the resilience of distinctive, self-reproducing "traditional systems" were taken to justify colonial overrule under the sign of difference (Asad 1973; cf. Wilder 2005). But, as decolonization gathered momentum, as stigmatizing "ethnicisms" gave way to claims for sovereignty and civic rights, the legitimacy of external custodians of culture came into question (Banaji 1970; Magubane 1971; Mafeje 1998; cf. Comaroff and Comaroff 2003). This was intensified with the eclipse of the old international order; in particular, with the emergence of a global regime of nongovernmental organizations that, though diverse in scope, ideology, and motivation, bore with them the mantras of late liberalism: structural adjustment, privatization, human rights, intellectual property. Under these conditions, marks of otherness morphed from devalued tokens of difference into scarce, desirable commodities, exacerbated by the growing heterogeneity of nation-states everywhere and by an implosion in the politics of identity across the planet (below, pp. 46, 53). It was merely a matter of time before bitter, legally inflected arguments would arise over "who owns native culture."

Those arguments, as Michael Brown (1998, 2003) lays them out, pivot between two positions. One, pithily caught in the bumper sticker slogan "Give the Natives Their Culture Back," is more soberly represented by, among other advocates, the Total Heritage Protection Movement and the Society for Applied Anthropology (Greaves 1994).[10] Like indigenous peoples' movements, both essay the absolute and exclusive rights of those "natives" to their history, knowledge, and creative works; rights already recognized, in variably explicit degree and to various ends, by the United Nations and several of its specialized agencies, notably the Convention on Biological Diversity, the Commission on Human Rights, the International Labor Organization, the World Intellectual Property Organization, and UNESCO, which adopted the *Convention for the Safeguarding of Intangible Cultural Heritage* in 2003.[11] The other position maintains that culture is inherently public, organic, unbounded, and therefore, irreducible to private property, individual or collective. Concomitantly, any effort to reduce it to the commodity form would not merely be exclusionary and inequitable, alienating it from those—anyone, potentially—who might enjoy it, enrich it, inhabit it. It would make it something else entirely: Culture, not culture. This is why, according to the Bellagio Declaration of 1993,[12] a sophisticated exercise in applied legal reason, vernacular knowledge and practices are inimical to the existing global intellectual property regime (cf. Reddy 2006). The former is vested in a "commons from which all people . . . are free to draw"; the latter, in a modernist episteme that takes as axiomatic, and celebrates, authorial signature on all "creative" work (cf. Coombe 1998).

The argument between these positions takes many forms—and, often, a local flavor. In Canada, for example, it has centered on the alleged appropriation of "cultures other than one's own," on such things as the removal of artifacts to museums and the piracy of plant knowledge. But it has focused most of all on prose fiction and nonfiction writing, giving rise to arguments over "whose voice is it anyway?"[13] And it has polarized, on "familiar liberal terrain," into what Rosemary Coombe (1993: 250) describes as a "Romantic" defense of the unfettered, individual imagination against "Orientalist" invocations of native authenticity. Michael Brown (ibid.) has suggested a way out of this sort of impasse by advocating an "enlightened pragmatism" that explores the usefulness of notions like "group privacy," thereby to break the brute opposition between individual rights and unqualified publicness (Alexander 2004:113). He also seeks to avoid the single-minded application of a priori legal and ethical formulae to settle differences over vernacular property. Instead, he puts his faith in informal norms—like respect for "cultural integrity"—that permit negotiated compromise on a case-by-case basis. Brown provides a wealth of trouble cases in order to make plain the need to ground coexistence in the particularities of circumstance. His approach to solving the problems inherent in native entitlement to things indigenous has been read as an appeal to "imaginative realism" in the face of "identity politics" and "political correctness" and has been commended as such (Shweder 2003; Starn 2004; Neascu 2004). But it has also elicited reservations. For one thing, it has been said to overdraw the contrast between Western and non-Western notions of intellectual property (Geismar 2005:439–450). For another, it presumes an equality of bargaining power among interested parties and a level playing field on which struggles over intellectual property actually occur; neither are likely, especially when powerful corporate players are involved. Which is why Alexander (2004:123), for one, argues that even imperfect international legal protections might better serve the weak.

The commodification of identity makes an end run around all of these ethical arguments, however. And around the idea of polite, norm-driven negotiation or case-by-case compromise. The marketing of heritage-as-possession, sometimes with anthropological assistance, has clearly been spurred on by the worldwide recognition of cultural entitlement, of the "inherent" right of indigenous peoples to profit from the fruits of their vernacular ways and means; there even exists a scholarly serial whose name, *International Journal of Cultural Property* (b.1993), bears tacit testimony to the fact. Furthermore, the Bellagio Declaration and UNESCO *Convention* notwithstanding, that right *is* being asserted via international legal protections, imperfect though they may be (cf. Coombe 1993:285). In the process—in the commodification of identity—elements of *both* liberal paradigms of possession, Romantic and Orientalist, are brought into play.[14] Where they run up against each other, where more complicated questions of ownership *do* arise, as we intimated in speaking of Heather "Moon Owl" Campbell, are in intraethnic struggles: struggles over the lines to be drawn between public and personal knowledge, between the ordinary and the expert, between things communal and individual (cf. Reddy 2006 on India). This, ultimately, is the trouble zone in which the homogeneity assumed by cultural branding—of *the* Tswana or *the* Catalans or *the* Deer or *the* Shipibo—is often torn asunder by conflicts among antithetical kinds of interest. We shall return to it.

More immediately, the "who owns native culture?" debate may not grasp fully the real world complexities of ethno-commodification. But the very fact that it has drawn such lively interest itself marks a tectonic shift in the way in which its terms of reference (*culture, native, ownership*) are now conceptualized. And contested (cf. Brown 1998:194). One of the corollaries of that shift, for example, is the queering of Bourdieu's (1977) classic distinction between cultural and economic capital. Being founded from the first on a misleading antinomy between the symbolic and the substantive, the immaterial and the material, it can no longer be sustained when the two species of capital merge so overtly: when culture is objectified by those who inhabit it, thence to be deployed as a brute economic asset, a commodity with the intrinsic capacity to compound wealth of its own accord. Which, again, underscores the singularity of ethno-commodities: (i) their capacity for infinite replication without necessarily losing their essential, auratic character (Alexander 2004:119, above, p. 20); and (ii) their entailment in an open-ended dialectic in which, on one hand, cultural property constitutes the distinctive identity of those who possess it, while, on the other, it is this very identity that makes the property "cultural" to begin with. To put it in concrete terms:

it is their "traditional" art objects that separate the Shipibo from those who live around them, giving manifest form to their difference; but the value of those art objects, which appear to maintain their mystique despite duplication or reinvention, follows from the fact that they embody Shipibo-ness. The dialectic that binds subject to object, object to subject, underlies the fusion of cultural and economic capital; also, the enduring auratic quality of many cultural products and practices in the face of their mass marketing. But most of all, it is the mechanism by which ethnic consciousness is materialized. This, in turn, poses a problem: given the very strange things that ethno-commodities are, in what measure are they illuminated by Euro-modernist terms like intellectual property, copyright, and patent?

Patent Truths: Culture, Copyright, and Intellectual Property

Copyright—the legally protected entitlement of individuals or groups to control and to profit from the circulation, duplication, and sale of their creative work—looms large in discussions of the commodification of identity. Predictably so. The neoliberal age has seen a marked expansion in the domain of intellectual property (IP): in the laws that govern its possession, in the benefits accruing to it, in the spheres of human knowledge, activity, and existence over which it extends. This, in turn, has led to a growing recognition of "inherent rights" to "intangible cultural heritage." And to the tendency, typified by the Bellagio Declaration,[15] to draw a sharp contrast between international IP regulations and principles of property holding among indigenous peoples across the world. That distinction has been questioned, however. Haidy Geismar (2005) argues that, on Vanuatu, an island in the Southwest Pacific, high-ranking men have successfully merged vernacular notions of copyright with those embodied in recent national legislation; ni-Vanuatu use *koporaet* to refer to both. As it happens, there were close parallels here, ab initio, between global and local conceptions of cultural property (441–42). Traditional practices, artifacts, and designs were *owned*. Rights in them were bought and sold and their reproduction had to be remunerated, an arrangement that buttressed internal lines of social distinction, most elaborately inscribed in a ceremonial complex of "graded societies." By forging a strategic analogy between endogenous rules of possession and the new national law—with explicit reference to *koporaet*—men of status, who dominate local ritual hierarchies and the exchange of everything from pigs and yams to cash, have managed to extend a gerontocratic political economy. Drawing lawmakers, cultural activists, and others into their concern with copyright, they have also gained control over "the cultural politics of the market-place" (451), thus to constrain the enterprises of expatriate dealers in exotic carvings. None of this is a simple consequence of the import of Western possessive individualism to the South Pacific: it is neither a case of the appropriation of the Vanuatu vernacular by the global IP regime nor the opposite. What has been opened up, rather, is a complicated back and forth between legal rationalization and refractory local specifics, where one regime of legitimate monopoly has been used to bolster another.

Intellectual property law, Geismar insists (439), is not the restricted code that it is frequently made out to be. IP is intrinsically evanescent. By their very nature, its production and negotiation demand the constant reconsideration of relations between the material and the immaterial, creativity and entitlement, author and object. As a result, the moving frontier of what may legitimately be owned in the field of ideas and aesthetics is an ongoing site of fierce struggle, one with broad metaphysical overtones (cf. Coleman 2005). Hence the claims of the Brazilian government to be spearheading a "revolution" against copyright on everything from music and internet file sharing through genetically modified crops to HIV drugs.[16] Its minister of culture, the legendary musician Gilberto Gil, has attacked "the fundamentalists of absolute property control," corporations and states alike. He accuses them of thwarting the democratic promise of digital technology in order to defy the "semantic abundance" of the world.[17] Derrida (1988:30f) famously cast radical doubt on the very possibility of "putting a signature" on expressive acts, of limiting their form and iteration: copyright is as much phantasmatic as it is legal, he asserted, its conventions being transient norms on ever shifting terrain. Perhaps. But IP rights are alluring to those "fundamentalists of absolute property control" precisely because they promise to seize and freeze the amorphous qualities of creativity. And to permit the monopolization of the value that accumulates around them. Therein lies their significance, too, in the process of ethno-commodification. Like the senior men of Vanuatu, anyone who wishes to claim title in perpetuity to their "authentic" culture, and to its proceeds, is compelled to ply the points of convergence between *koporaet* and copyright. Tellingly, the term has become common usage throughout the Pacific islands (Geismar 2005:454, n.7).

If copyright is a semiotic switch-point between Western and non-Western cultural property regimes, what of patent? We take this term to refer to the sole legal right, granted for a fixed period of time, over an original invention, concept, or design; specifically, over its application, production, replication, dissemination, use, and sale as an object or a procedure. Marilyn Strathern (2001) reminds us that patents acquired their current meaning during the Industrial Revolution in England. Their object was to stimulate technical innovation by conferring temporary monopolies—which, simultaneously, encouraged privatization in pursuit of profit *and* public circulation in the interests of cumulative knowledge. Patents pertain to invention, copyrights to authorship; but they may overlap, as they often do in the domain of industrial design.[18] Strathern compares the sort of title vested in patents to that vested in Malanggan, mortuary sculptures in New Ireland that serve as the "body" for the life force of a person in transition to the spirit world. Carved to be recognizably ancestral by the clan of the deceased, a Malanggan is disposed of at the end of its brief ritual career, often to European traders. This act releases the multiple dimensions of the corpse's identity into the world. It also disperses the identity of the person who made—and hence "owns"—the object, which is fashioned according to a unique configuration of designs to which he is entitled by descent (5). The motifs themselves are alienable after a Malanggan has been decommissioned: rights to reproduce one in a new composition may be bought and sold (6).

It has been argued that these New Ireland sculptures are regulated by an indigenous version of copyright (Gunn 1987). Much like Vanuatu carvings. Together, in fact, the two point to a fascinating possibility: a vernacular instrument for franchising cultural patrimony that refuses the dichotomy between privatization and public circulation—and, with it, the equation of sale and purchase with a loss of original, auratic value. To be sure, they demonstrate, in an ethnographic key, the theoretical point we sought to make earlier. But Strathern disagrees with the copyright analogy. A Malanggan is more like a patent, she says: it congeals the technical expertise that went into its making, rewards its first use, and disperses it again for a limited time to new owners. *More like,* yet still too different to take even this parallel very far. Quite simply, for her, there is an incommensurable gulf between Euro-American practice and local ideology in the Pacific. The former treats "invention" as an individually driven act of discovery and is concerned to protect profits accruing to it; the latter accentuates "acquisition" as a socially indexed process and hinges on the right to reproduce what others have done before. Social science may have come to terms with the invention of culture. But, it appears, cultural invention remains somewhat beyond the conceptual fringe.

This categorical distinction between innovation and reproduction evokes old anthropological antinomies between hot (Western) and cold (non-Western) cultures, open and closed systems, and the like; in the here and now, it makes the idea of copyrighting or patenting "tradition" seem like an oxymoron. Pragmatically speaking, however, the recognition of an "inherent," legally enforceable entitlement to "intangible heritage" on the part of indigenous peoples—the kind of thing essayed by the various agencies of the United Nations—amounts to a form of "natural copyright" (see below). Similarly, patent may or may not have a literal equivalent in the Pacific. But cultural knowledge has become vulnerable to the kind of monopolization that it grants to capitalist enterprise, especially from the outside. The agribusiness firm, RiceTec, for example, was recently granted far-reaching rights by the US Patent and Trademark Office over *basmati* rice. It claimed to have "invented" the "product" and intended to charge *Indian* farmers for the privilege of growing it.[19] This was only reversed, and then not completely, once the Indian state had been goaded into action by public interest litigation and by a worldwide NGO campaign (Randeria 2007:11). In like vein, an American concern, Battle Creek Food Company, registered itself a few years back as owner of the trademark to *Rooibos,* a South African herbal tea associated with the Khoisan peoples of the Western Cape Province. The term itself is Afrikaans for "red bush." It refers to *Aspalathus linearis,* which grows only in the Cedarberg area. This case also led to a legal wrangle in the US Patent Office, in which Virginia Burke Watkins, owner of Battle Creek Foods, argued that she had spent "tremendous amounts" of time and money developing the beverage for the market. It may not have helped her cause that she first sold it as "Kaffir Tea"; the K-word to black Africans has approximately the same connotation as the N-word has to black Americans, except that the former *never* use it of or among themselves. Eventually, but not without a lengthy struggle, the South African complainants won.[20]

Within ethnic communities, too, there are increasing signs of conflict over individual rights to indigenous expertise and cultural creativity. For some it is anathema, for others a panacea. "I am an innovator, adding to my ancestral knowledge," says Shipibo healer Mateo Arevalo; this in the context of an expanding market in shamanic rites for foreigners (above, p. 3).[21] Arevalo's claim is echoed by many others like him. The *geist* of ethno-commodification that they embody resonates with the spirit of modern patent law. The impulse to treat "tradition" as intellectual property, subject to innovative action, goes along with the idea that privatizing the products of human inventiveness helps put them into public circulation; that this is a "socially beneficial bargain" (Coombe 1998:340 n.59), yielding returns alike for producers, consumers, and humanity at large. If, nowadays, it is "almost a civic duty to have an ethnicity as well as to appreciate that of others" (Wood 1998:230; Halter 2000:9), the same ethic of appreciation fuels the identity industry. Not only is it said to offer a lifeline to those facing economic and social extinction. The cultural diversity it promotes is espoused, like biodiversity, as a self-evident good.

But the uneasiness that surrounds the privatization of patrimony alerts us to something else. Patents, ostensibly, are outside of nature. Their *raison d'être* is to foster *human* ingenuity, initiative, expertise. Which is why the organic, the wild, the uncultivated fall beyond their purview. The corollary, it has been said (Strathern 2001:9f), is that patenting, as a process, has the unintended effect of reinventing, over and over again, the ineluctable opposition between things natural and things cultural. Arguably, however, ethno-commodification troubles that opposition. Efforts to render identity and its products into private property keep running into a slippage between—and the inseparability of—essence and artifact, genetic endowment and personal creativity. For it is difficult to establish the grounds on which to make a claim for adding value to nature; vide disputes over patenting human genes and plant varieties (Knoppers 1999; Andrews and Nelkin 2001:chap. 3).[22] What is more, ethnicity *itself* is ever more vested in both naturalization and commodification. We shall elaborate on this in due course. For now, one illustration, a particularly vivid one as it happens, will suffice: Dawid Kruiper's desire that paying tourists gaze upon him, an adult male "Bushman," as "an animal of nature." Ethnic identity, by contrast to race, may manifest itself primarily in expressive culture, in collective practices and products; in, say, San hunting, tracking, bead threading. But it also betokens a unique, innate substance, a substance that inhabits individuals and communities alike, a substance that congeals in "traditional" objects and activities and expertise—which, by extension, are the *naturally* copyrighted property of the people who embody them. As this suggests once more, difference, these days, takes shape at the intersection of culture, biology, the market, and intellectual property law.

Here, at that intersection, lies the point of conjuncture between the three things with which we have been concerned: between (1) the way in which the incorporation of identity, far from producing ethno-commodities bereft of aura, makes plain how culture and the commodity form inflect each other ever more tightly, providing novel means for animating social connection; (2) the way in which, under the impact of incorporation, the principles governing ownership of "native" cultural products and practices become the object of contention, both uniting people(s) in relation to the world beyond *and* dividing them internally; and (3) the way in which the reduction of those products and practices to "naturally" copyrighted intellectual property has engendered new lines of tension between private and public possession, collective *Geist* and individual innovation. These three things, taken together, compose one half of Ethnicity, Inc.: the half by which *culture*—in the equation *ethnicity = cultural + identity*—interpolates itself into the domain of capital, thus to constitute the *Inc*. The other half, of course, is ethnicity itself.

ii. On Ethnicity, in the Ongoing Present

Ethnicity—like "identity," with which it is often twinned—has become a taken-for-granted usage in the argot of everyday life across the planet. Its status as a sociological concept has always been equivocal, however. Chabal and Daloz (2006:203–4), for instance, assert that the phenomena described by it are so diverse as to make it "unrealistic to suppose that there could be a 'single' theory of ethnicity" (cf. Cohen 1985:107; Banks 1996:10).[23] This reiterates a point made way back by Max Weber (1968:395). "If we define our terms exactly," he said, the "ethnic group . . . is unsuitable for rigorous analysis." For our own part (e.g., Comaroff and Comaroff 1992:49–67), we have long argued that ethnicity is neither a monolithic "thing" nor, in and of itself, an analytic construct: that "it" is best understood as a loose, labile repertoire of signs by means of which relations are constructed and communicated; through which a collective consciousness of cultural likeness is rendered sensible; with reference to which shared sentiment is made substantial. Its visible content is *always* the product of specific historical conditions which, in variable measure, impinge themselves on human perception and, in so doing, frame the motivation, meaning, and materiality of social practice. What concerns us here is the history of the present. Or, more precisely, its effects: how it is altering the manner in which ethnicity is experienced, apprehended, enacted, represented. Some fifty years ago, as he contemplated the surge of separatist sentiments welling up in a string of "new" nations, Clifford Geertz (1963:155) was moved to remark that the "comparative sociology . . . of ethnic change remains to be written." Since then the politics of difference—and its transformations across both time and space—has become the raw material of a veritable industry in the human sciences. And yet the unfolding history of "ethnic change" is still to be fully plumbed.

In order to open up that history to further scrutiny, let us make two general sets of observations about cultural identity. One is ontological; the other, orientational.

First, Ontology: From Genesis to Genetics

Max Weber (1968:385–98, 926–38) might have harbored doubts about "ethnic groups" as an object of analysis. But his writings placed them securely on the agenda of modern sociology.[24] In contradistinction to affiliations founded on kinship and class, he suggested, ethnicity is vested in subjective beliefs and identities: it gives rise to "status groups" and facilitates the formation of associations whose means and ends lie elsewhere. Nonetheless, for reasons that need not detain us, the term came to be taken by the positivist social sciences to describe a concrete, objectively measurable phenomenon. And to be treated as an independent variable with the capacity to shape choices, life chances, and social processes.[25] Within this tradition, the oldest, most foundational question of all about ethnicity—ethnicity as disposition, ethnicity as a sociological category, ethnicity as a principle of collective being-in-the-world, ethnicity as a sentiment deep enough to die for—is existential. Does it arise from primordial affect, affinity, affiliation, aggregation? Or is it a historically conditioned, instrumentally motivated construction? *Primordialism* takes it to be inscribed in the irreducible facts of shared biology, ancestral origins, and innate disposition (Cohen 1974:xii). Geertz (1963:109) again: "These congruities of blood, speech, custom, and so on are seen to have an ineffable, and at times overpowering, coerciveness in and of themselves." The *instrumentalist* position, by contrast, views ethnicity as a reaction against threats to the integrity, interests, and self-determination of persons who, for one or another historical reason, come to imagine themselves as sharing a culturally rooted destiny (Wallerstein 1972)—even where their "traditions" are invented (Hobsbawm and Ranger 1983). Hence the question: Which of the two offers a better answer?

Happily, that question, once the subject of heated debate, has receded in significance. Few anthropologists, sociologists, or political scientists would argue any longer for primordialism, pure and simple, although ethno-nationalists around the world continue to kill for it. Fewer still would defend the evolutionary telos that associates the primordial with the antimodern, although some organic intellectuals persist in protecting "ancestral custom" from historical deconstruction.[26] More to the general point, for many social scientists, bromides about ethnicity really being *both,* being part primordial and part social construction, offer a banal compromise: a way of distancing a problem that, phrased in Manichean terms, *is* intractable. Thus Bankston and Henry (2000:282) argue that ethnic consciousness arises "from the solidarity created by a common socioeconomic position among people who . . . see themselves as sharing ancestry and historical experience."[27] But, they add, the "emotive, primordial character of ethnicity"—which they take as axiomatic—remains a "useful basis for political organization." A "useful basis," also, for the pursuit of material interests, sometimes by violent means. Self-evidently, this sort of synthetic compromise, to quote a phrase from Allahar (1994), reduces cultural identity to the "social construction of primordial attachment," largely for utilitarian ends.

In fact, the synthesis is incoherent, less a fusion of complementary opposites than a confusion of incommensurables. Primordial attachment and the social construction of identity describe inimical ontologies of being, inimical determinations of collective consciousness. As such, they cannot dissolve into each other, neither logically nor sociologically. Unless the primordial is understood purely as a vernacular trope, a semiotic vehicle for speaking subjectively about affect and affiliation. In that case it is not an *explanation* for ethnic consciousness at all. It is a phenomenological *representation* of how that consciousness, once constructed, is experienced (Comaroff and Comaroff 1992:49–67; J. L. Comaroff 1996). But—and this is our point—socio/logical incoherence and theoretical con/fusions notwithstanding, the effort to find ontological grounding for ethnicity in a synthesis of primordialism and instrumentalism itself mimics a social fact we have already encountered. In its *lived* manifestations, cultural identity appears ever more as two antithetical things at once: on the one hand, as a precipitate of inalienable natural essence, of genetics and biology, and, on the other, as a function of voluntary self-fashioning, often through serial acts of consumption. It is, in other words, *both* ascriptive and instrumental. *Both* innate and constructed. *Both* blood and choice.[28]

For reasons that will become clear, this doubling is endemic to cultural identity in the neoliberal age.[29] Thus, for instance, Jewishness is currently being reconfigured in such a way as to show that it always-already inhered in a fusion of choice and genes. According to a New York University School of Medicine study, notes Nadia Abu El-Haj (n.d.), "[r]ecent work from *genetic* labs has validated the Biblical record of a Semitic people who *chose* a *Jewish way of life* several thousand years ago."[30] Abu El-Haj goes on to point out the complexities lurking in this reconstruction. It asserts that acts of volition expressed in culture—in marriage, kinship, religious rites, oral traditions—yielded a genetic endowment that, in turn, has reproduced a specifically Jewish identity and its characteristic practices over millennia. Tautological? Probably. More significant for our purposes, though, is the fact that, like the Trobriand myth making that detained Malinowski many years ago, the NYU study rewrites the past in the image of the present. The simultaneity of biology and self-construction attributed retrospectively to biblical Hebrews belongs securely to the twenty-first century, to the manner in which cultural identity is *now* experienced and negotiated; to the politics, that is, of the contemporary moment.[31] It is a narrative that, at a stroke, closes the distance between Genesis and Genetics, between the old and the newest of the testaments.

But perhaps the most remarkable living example of the doubling inherent in cultural identity lies elsewhere: in "recreational genomics," which is taking root—literally, see http://www.rootsforreal.com—at the interstices of science, enterprise, and ethno-sociology. The term itself is owed to DNA Print Genomics, a US corporation that styles itself "the world leader" in "the measurement of population structure for disease genetics, personalized medicine, recreational genomics and forensic profiling." In 2002, it marketed a test (ANCESTRYbyDNA 2.0) that, for $150, undertook to "prove within a few percentage points" a person's "racial mix." While the bulk of its business is in therapeutic applications, one of its early "successes" was "to enable a Utah man to prove he qualified for a venture exclusive to Native Americans."[32] Much the same services are sold by, among others, GeneTree, GenBase Systems, DNA Solutions (UK), DNA Tribes, and Ethnoancestry, the last two names being especially telling. For a modest price ($99 and $250), they "promise to satisfy the human hunger to learn about one's origins—and sometimes much more."[33] GeneTree, in particular, echoes Abu El-Haj's point about the juxtaposition, in the new Jewish genetics, of culture, choice, and biology: "Not only will you discover the birthplace of your ancestors" by genomic means, "but the path they [elected to take] and their unique discoveries . . . which set them aside from others as they traveled from continent to continent over the course of human history. It's your unique anthropological identity."[34]

In short, if an informed consumer so chooses—*our* choice of words here is obviously pointed—she or he can seek out their identity by means of genomic oracle. Not unexpectedly, this commerce has received its share of criticism from scientists. Kim TallBear (n.d.) notes, of the Native American case, that genetic genealogists have voiced deep doubts about the manner in which a company like AncestrybyDNA tests for biogeographical ancestry (BGA)—which it does by utilizing a select panel of ancestry informative markers (AIMS), genetic loci showing alleles with "large frequency differences between populations." But the vast majority of markers do *not* show such radical distinctions in frequencies between human groups. By focusing on the "very few" that do, AncestrybyDNA calls into question what it is that they actually measure. Concerns also surround the precision and rigor of the procedures themselves—and the manner in which those who administer them interpret and cite scholarly sources in order to legitimize their "science" (TallBear and Bolnick 2004). Thus, for example, while the Genographic Project, initiated by National Geographic and IBM, purports to look for Native American markers, those which it uses are not unique to Native Americans; other populations have them too, if in smaller proportions. Neither can such tests, despite intimations to the contrary, provide information on tribal affiliation (TallBear 2007:420).

Still, none of these technical doubts about genetic testing, the US media report, have "stopped many [people]" from turning to genetic testing in pursuit of self-definition. Or from "adopting new DNA-based ethnicities," especially for the instrumental purpose of winning minority entitlements—including shares in the profits of ethno-enterprises. "Americans of every shade," like the Utah man served by DNAPrint, "are staking a DNA claim to Indian scholarships, health services, and casino money." There have also been more imaginative, less pecuniary applications. Like that of a "Christian" who used recreational genomics to prove his "Jewish genetic ancestry" in order to acquire Israeli citizenship.[35] And those of celebrities, notably Oprah Winfrey and Whoopi Goldberg, who have "discovered" their African roots, the former in "the rainforests of Liberia," the latter in a "forgotten corner" of Guinea-Bissau.[36] If all this gathers momentum, and there are signs aplenty that it is doing so, willful efforts to construct or recreate social identities may come to depend increasingly on the purchase of "scientific" certification. This is likely to reinforce the discursive connection between cultural being and biology. And it also makes the *production* of identity contingent on the *consumption* of mass-marketed means of its "proof."

Clearly, there is a great deal more to the ontological founding of ethnicity—or, more precisely, to the forms of subjectivity denoted by that term—than the positivist social sciences have even begun to glimpse. The counterintuitive conjuncture of choice and essence is just where it begins. Ethnicity, Inc. is where it ends. Between beginning and end lie, among other things, the (re)discovery of genealogy, broadly defined, as an especially compelling basis of human connection, of connection more "true," less deceptive, than other bases of common being, common interest, common destiny. Which, in turn, points us in the direction of the politics of identity.

Second, Orientation: From the Politics of Identity to the Political-Economy of World Making

Across the social sciences, treatments of cultural identity—where they extend beyond its semiosis and phenomenology—orient overwhelmingly toward its political dimensions. Perhaps this is a corollary of the fact that constructivist perspectives, now in the ascendance, tend to take the assertion of *any* kind of collective consciousness to be, by nature, a political act; indeed, the quintessential political act (cf. Hall 1996:442f). Which is why *politics* and *identity* are so often coupled, discursively, as if each completes the other. And why, by extension, the economics, ethics, and aesthetics of ethnicity are almost invariably reduced to a politics: to the pursuit of more-or-less shared social and material interests, rights, and entitlements (cf. Jung 2001; Chabal and Daloz 2006:115); to redress for injury, violence, and victimhood, real or imagined (cf. Brown 1995); to the quest for protection against the state or from it against others—or, more affirmatively, for a share in its beneficence; to struggles, in the face of homogenizing hegemonies and demographic heterodoxy, for the right to engage in "different" bodily and domestic practices, music, poetics, moral conventions. Thus it is that a recent multidisciplinary volume on ethnicity and democracy in Africa (Berman, Eyoh, and Kymlicka 2004:2) begins with the claim that "everywhere the politics of identity and ethnicity appears resurgent." Its motivating question is, "Why is ethnicity a *political* problem?" Parallel work on the Caribbean (Premdas 2000) and Latin America (Maybury-Lewis 2002) echoes both the claim and the question; so does a special edition of *African Issues* published by the African Studies Association in 2001.[37] All of which is interesting in light of Courtney Jung's (2001:13 and passim) finding that, while ethnicity remains socially significant in post-apartheid South Africa, only two parties, with just 13 percent of the total vote in the 1994 elections, actually build a power base upon it; cultural identity would seem to have limited purchase in the realm of *formal* politics in this part of the global south. To prioritize the political is not necessarily to end with it, of course. For Berman, Eyoh, and Kymlicka (2004:3), who take a decidedly Weberian view, ethnicity comprises "complex and protean expressions of the often distinctive African experiences of modernity, grounded in the changing material realities of state and market, and the confrontations of class, gender and generation." Still, those experiences and realities remain situated within "the internal and external dimensions of communal *politics.*" In like manner, while Castells (2004:56, 69) speaks of the importance of cultural affinities in the "networking and trust-based transactions" characteristic of the "new business world," he eschews the notion that ethnicity might objectify itself *fur sich*. Fundamental though it is, it is more likely "to be processed by religion, nation, and locality, whose specificity it tends to reinforce." For Castells the key to understanding identity in the Information Age, the age of the network, lies in *Power*.[38]

Patently, the political dimensions of ethnicity *are* critical. All the more so because neoliberal capitalism has a well-recognized tendency to short-circuit deliberative and distributive politics—contestation, that is, over ideological principle and the public good, over social values and ethics, over the means and ends of governance—in the name of economic efficiency, capital growth, the workings of the "free" market, the imperatives of bio/science and technology, and the sovereignty of the law (Comaroff and Comaroff 2001). At the same time, this stress on the *politics* of ethnicity above all else has a number of critical costs: it depends on an underspecified, almost metaphorical conception of the political, the primary referent of which is the pursuit of interest; it reduces cultural identity to a utility function, the measure of which is power, again underspecified; and it confuses the deployment of ethnicity as a *tactical* claim to entitlement, and as a means of mobilization for instrumental ends, with the *substantive* content of ethnic consciousness.

With respect to this last point, it is arguable that ethnicity–as–*political identity* and ethnicity–as–*cultural identity* are quite different phenomena, despite being conditions of each other's possibility. The former, ethnicity-as–political identity, usually presents its cultural bases not as a "thick" ensemble of lived signs and practices (i.e., of ethnicity-as-culture in its anthropological sense), but in rather "thin" terms that, purged of nuance and density, evoke very general values (cf. Jung 2001:22–24). Like *ubuntu* in South Africa, a vernacular Nguni word—a version of it exists in all the major indigenous languages—that denotes "personhood" but connotes African "human(e)-ness." Usually taken to refer to a communalist, socially oriented sensibility, the ethos to which it speaks "permeate[s] [both] the Constitution" of the postcolony and its public discourses.[39] This is in spite of the fact that it has intermittently come under debate and, allegedly, is rapidly being rendered "a commodity [rather] than a philosophy" by "big business."[40] Ironically, a "how to" volume was published in South Africa in 2005, without any trace of irony, under the title *Ubuntu Management Philosophy* (Broodryk 2005); the word, translated as "unity," has even become the slogan of a US professional basketball team, the Boston Celtics. *Ubuntu* is explicitly contrasted to Western liberal individualism, itself embodied in such equally thin ethno-national tropes as "Britishness," which, according to the current prime minister, Gordon Brown, consists in such qualities as good neighborliness, mutuality, fairness, tolerance, responsibility, and above all, a respect for liberty.[41] Former populations colonized by Britain have been known to voice a rather more cynical view of its content. So have some public intellectuals[42] and anthropologists, one of whom refers to the concept as "meaningless" (Fox 2004:21). But that is another story.

Most of all, the stress on the political, in the narrow sense of the term, misses precisely what set us off on our excursion into the history of the present: ethno-futures. Recall the president of Contralesa, who said that it was time for those entrusted with protecting cultural identity in South Africa to turn their attention away from the struggle for rights toward the world of venture capital; recall the Mabaso "people," who sought empowerment in the "new" South Africa by establishing a company through which to tap into the tourist industry; recall "the Kingdom of the Zulu" and its efforts to assert itself through its brand; recall, too, the ruler of the Bafokeng, "traditional" sovereign-become-CEO. None of them lacked a politics. What they recognized, instead, is that the terrain of the political is changing. The notion that culture, politics, and economy might subsist in distinct institutional and ideational domains, a founding principle of liberal theology, is a thing of the past, eroded by the imperatives of laissez-faire. Ours, to invoke Rancière (1999:113; below, p. 117) once again, is an epoch in which political-economy, hyphenated afresh, is ever more overtly the site of world making, an epoch in which politics inheres unashamedly in the effective management of capital. The political and the economic (or rather the economic and political, given the priorities of the moment) are indissoluble as never before, anchored alike in the market and in the law, in their materialities and moralities and signifying practices. Thus Halter's (2000:12–13) observation that identity—now commonly seen, from within, to be produced by purchase—has more and more to do with the manifest realities of mass consumption (cf. also Bankston and Henry 2000:381–85); that, conversely, it has less and less to do with the political, beyond the pursuit of recognition and interest. This appears so even in contemporary China, says Arif Dirlik (2000:129), where "ethnic groups . . . which were defined earlier through political classification, are increasingly beginning to perceive themselves also as 'natural' economic groups"; by one account,[43] the term for such groups, transliterated as *zuqun*, also refers to a group of stockholders, not least those who hold corporate shares in common. Pay attention also to the stress here on *natural* economic groups. It will have further echoes as we proceed.

––––––––

These two general observations—(i) the *ontological* one, that contemporary cultural identity is experienced as the product, at once, of shared essence and self-fashioning, and (ii) the *orientational* one, that its reduction to a politics misses the complexity of its reembedding in neoliberal political-economy—are closely connected with what we said earlier about incorporation and the ethno-commodity. The latter, we argued, has a "strange" capacity to conjure an open-ended dialectic in which ethnic subjects and cultural objects, genetic endowment and elective practice, constantly configure each other; to render those cultural products and practices into "naturally" copyrighted intellectual property, owned by dint of indigenous knowledge or innovative elaboration; and to retain its auratic value even under conditions of mass-mediated replication. These properties of the ethno-commodity fuse biology and self-construction, the genetic and the generative; just as the incorporation of identity entails, indivisibly, a political claim to sovereignty and an economic claim to ownership.

The conclusion? That, in the unfolding history of the present, there is a palpable consonance between the nature of ethno-commodities, the incorporation of identity, and the existential grounding of ethnicity. But the two observations also lead to another question. If both are true, should it not follow that the *context* in which cultural identity is situated is itself under reconstruction? That context is typically taken to be the nation-state—the point of reference, after all, for the *trans*national, the *supra*national, and the *sub*national as well—and, ever more nowadays, the global order of which it is part. Let us interrogate further the varieties of political subjectivity and selfhood taking shape within and across its borders.

iii. On Political Subjectivity, Identity, and the State of Nationhood

Modern European polities, according to Benedictine history—Benedictine, that is, as in Benedict Anderson (1983)—were built on a sense of "horizontal fraternity," itself imaginatively embedded in the fiction of cultural homogeneity.[44] Much has been said about this imagining: that Euro-nationhood has always been more aspiration than achievement, always more diverse than its historiography has allowed, always tenuously hyphenated to the state in which its governance is vested, always a work-in-progress. And always compromised by the presence of "others" within, others whose primordial identities have been taken to threaten civic unity—and have had, therefore, to be confined to the "private" interiors of home, congregation, association, community. Still, the idyll of a citizenry founded on sameness has been willfully sustained, at times by violent means. The world is changing, however. Nation-states everywhere are having to come to terms with heterogeneity as never before.[45]

Three things have made this especially visible. *First* is the fact that previously colonized populations have reversed the colonial flow from center to periphery with increased intensity, asserting their alterity, diversifying the metropole, and forcing the "problem" of difference into the public sphere. *Second,* and related, is the so-called global indigenous people's movement that, abetted by nongovernmental organizations the world over, has interpolated itself into the planetary politics of identity, entitlement, recognition, and rights. This movement, which began primarily in the Americas and in Canada, gained momentum from the establishment in 1982 of the UN Working Group on Indigenous Populations and its Draft Declaration on the Rights of Indigenous Peoples (Sanders 1989; cf. Niezen 2003; Stamatopoulou 1994); also from the adoption in 1989 by the International Labour Organization of an Indigenous and Tribal Peoples Convention that acknowledged the right of fourth-world populations to control their own development, from the UN International Year of World's Indigenous Peoples in 1993, and from the UNESCO Convention on cultural heritage of 2003 (above, p. 30; cf. Cameron 2004:139; Igoe 2006:403–12). Its objectives have been variously articulated, but they have typically focused on territorial, political, linguistic, and cultural claims (cf. Wilson 1997)—conducing to what has been dubbed, perhaps too strongly, "globalized aboriginality," expressed in "the embryonic creation of a worldwide indigenous macro-community" (Sylvain 2005:357, after Forte 1998). *Third,* and maybe the most fundamental, is the transformative impact of neoliberalism, broadly defined, on the moral and material sovereignty of polities, especially since 1989. Their heterogeneity has been compounded by the heightened mobility of capital, of sites of production, and of labor: vide the long-distance migration of ever more people in pursuit of income; the inability of many European nations to reproduce themselves demographically or to sustain their social infrastructure, without the uncomfortable presence of "alien" workers; the transnational, mass-mediated flow of signs, styles, commodities, and information, itself accelerated by the rise of an electronic commons. All of which are corollaries, direct or indirect, of the hegemony of the market—a hegemony simultaneously semiotic and economic—whose effect is *both* to breach and buttress sovereign borders, *both* to extend and to constrain the regulatory ambit of states, *both* to valorize the local and to cast it into force fields well beyond itself.

These gathering historical circumstances have pushed nation-states, often apprehensively, toward more heterodox self-imaginings (J. L. Comaroff 1996:177).[46] Hence the accretion recently of literatures—scholarly and vernacular, philosophical and sociological alike—on citizenship, sovereignty, multiculturalism, minority rights, and the limits of liberalism. Hence, too, the reactive xenophobia that haunts heterodoxy almost everywhere. Hetero-nationhood seeks, usually out of practical necessity rather than ethical principle, to encompass cultural and religious diversity within a civic order of "universal" citizens, all ostensibly equal before the law. It embraces difference, in other words, in the capacious language of pluralism while subsuming it within a single, overarching juridico-political regime, constituting itself, so to speak, by recourse to constitutionalism;[47] since 1989, over a hundred new national constitutions have been promulgated, most of them much more affirmative toward heterogeneity than their predecessors, most of them couched in the language of rights. Notoriously, however, attempts to contain polymorphous populations within liberal modernist political communities have run into difficulties (Comaroff and Comaroff 2003a), difficulties mediated by different cultures of difference. Compare French and British attempts to grapple with the Islamic head scarf. Where France has banned it from public institutions under the sign of *laïcité*, Britain has learned to live with it, if neither willingly nor without a fight.[48] Since 2001, female law enforcement officers in London have been permitted to don a *hijab*, albeit fringed with the motif of the Metropolitan Police;[49] Sikh males have been allowed to wear turbans instead of helmets for many years now. In the Netherlands, to triangulate the contrast, the tolerance of *any* Muslim presence, indeed of multiculturalism, has run up against a wall, especially since the globally infamous murder in November 2004 of controversial filmmaker Theo van Gogh by Mohamed Bouyeri, a dual Dutch-Moroccan citizen; this in outraged response to his provocatively critical portrayals of Islam.[50] Or compare Botswana, whose alleged efforts to erase a distinctive San way of life have become the subject of international controversy, to South Africa, which has tried hard, if not successfully or without argument, to find ways of accommodating high levels of cultural and linguistic diversity. Difficulties, dissent, desire to embrace it or no, heterodoxy—with all the problems it poses for reimagining nationhood—is an inescapable feature of the history of the future.

Heterodoxy, Subjectivity, ID-ology: From the Trading Pits of Relativism to Policulturalism

What does this mean for the ways in which Homo sapiens construct and recognize themselves as social beings and political subjects, singular and plural? In a world in which almost everything is framed in the idiom of the market, freedom presents itself as a capacity for self-determination; crudely, for the exercise of choice. And self-determination, in turn, entails a counterpoint between "authentic" self-recognition and social acknowledgment (Taylor 1994; cf. Geertz 1963:118). As other bases of aggregation—most notably, in a post-Marxian, post-Weberian world, class—are undermined, as they dissolve into empty metaphors, as the social itself seems ever less "real" (cf. Kapferer 2005), as the nation is compromised by heterogeneity and relativism, individual and collective attachments come to inhere in what appear to be the unmediated, elemental bases of human life itself: race, religion, gender, sexuality, generation, ethnicity. Which is why there has been a radical intensification of claims, since the last decades of the twentieth century, made in the name of all of these things, and sometimes in constellations of them; claims that frequently transcend and transect national frontiers. Mark the move here from metaphor to metonym: from the body politic to the politicized body as the *fons et origo* of concrete social connectedness.

Among these putatively elemental bases of human life, ethnicity— which has the potential to found populations of variable scale, from a handful to millions of people—has proven particularly compelling as a principle of similitude, recognition, attachment, consociation, and mobilization; the active components, that is, which together congeal into identity. Like the nation, it is rooted, presumptively, in shared blood, culture, and corporate interest, a conjuncture that seems all the more real as civic nationhood is less able to pass itself off as fictive kinship, to hold difference in check, to subsume it within a political community imagined-as-one, or to confine it to the realm of the private. To the degree that ethnic consciousness has become the sociosemiotic vehicle of cultural diversity, situating it in both the *existential* (in biology) and the *elective* (in self-determination), it has emerged as a common language of transaction "in the trading pits of pluralist relativism" (Vanderbilt 1997:140) that characterize hetero-nationhood. What is more, from the vantage of an organic, "folk" functionalism, the most obviously effective way to demand moral and material preferment in a putatively postideological age is to assert a *natural,* heartfelt ("inherent") right to it: a right that grows out of genetic substance, out of "bare life" itself. This, in large part, is *why* culture is taken to be a quintessential site of self-construction; *why* ideology is giving way to ID-ology, the ontology of identity, as the grounding of political engagement (Comaroff and Comaroff 2003a); *why* those politics center less on the pursuit of the good than on the pursuit of goods, less on older forms of material production than on contemporary modes of consumption; *why*, also, culture is sedimenting into genealogically endowed, passionately held, naturally copyrighted intellectual property—and, as such, into a species of monopoly capital.

While most people continue to live as citizens *in* nation-states, then, they tend more and more only to be conditionally citizens *of* nation-states. Thus, to return to South Africa, which seems fairly typical in this respect,[51] a recent study shows that less than 25 percent of the population regard themselves primarily as South Africans. The "vast majority . . . principally think of themselves" as members of "an ethnic, cultural, language, religious, or some other group," to which they "attach their personal fate." At the same time, most of them do *not* "reject their national identity" (Gibson 2004:chap. 2).[52] Therein lies the complexity. The conditionality of citizenship, the fact that it is overlaid and undercut by a politics of difference, does not necessarily entail the negation of the national subject, merely its uneasy alignment with other priorities. Mostly, the priorities of otherness.

To the degree that identity has come to rest, at once, on ascription and choice, conviction and ambiguity, ineffability and self-management, it has embedded itself in a human subject increasingly seen, and experienced from within, as entrepreneurial. Not least, in enacting her or his otherness.

The rise of the entrepreneurial subject has hardly gone unnoticed. In the lecture "The birth of bio-politics" at the Collège de France in 1979, Foucault addressed the topic by distinguishing *neo*liberalism from its historical precursor. Along the way, he stressed two major transformations (Lemke 2001:200).[53] The first concerned the relationship between state and economy: whereas, before, the state directed and monitored the workings of the economy, the neoliberal turn makes "the market itself the organizing and regulative principle underlying the state." The second involved rational government and *homo economicus*: classic liberalism took the "natural" freedom of the individual as a precondition of rational governance, believing that any undue constraint on "human nature" endangered government itself—the task of which, by implication, was to nurture that freedom. By contrast, neoliberalism, which reduces social life to economic cost-benefit calculation, limits government to the "artificially-arranged" protection of the "entrepreneurial and competitive behaviour of economic-rational individuals."[54] Accordingly, the moral autonomy of those individuals is gauged in terms of their capacity, as Wendy Brown (2003:6) puts it, for "'self-care'—that is, the ability to provide for their own needs [and] service their own ambitions." For its part, the state devolves to them responsibility for all social risks and for the consequences of their actions, whatever structural or ecological conditions may intervene; "the" population, concomitantly, is regarded as an assemblage of calculating entrepreneurs and consumers rather than rule-abiding citizens (7).

And production is construed as a process in which each worker optimizes their relations to and of themselves, and with others, as "human capital"; this at a time when, says Brian Massumi, our entire existence "becomes a capitalist tool."[55] Rather than being employees, then, laborers are "autonomous entrepreneurs" endeavoring to accumulate surplus value. They are, from this perspective, "entrepreneurs of themselves" (Foucault 2004; see Lemke 2000:199).

This phrase also evokes a mode of being and self-imagining at the core of a new global initiative, an initiative intended as a panacea for the problem of world poverty: the microfinance movement, whose object is to lend—note, *not* give; it is meant as a purely business transaction, not a "handout"—small amounts of capital at low interest to large numbers of very poor people; this to encourage them to cultivate their "natural entrepreneurial instincts" by starting, then expanding, their own enterprises. Already recognized in the award of a highly publicized Nobel Prize, this initiative has enjoyed a flurry of media coverage and is garnering a great deal of attention in government, nongovernmental, and philanthropic circles.[56] In South Africa, the Productivity Movement, orchestrated by the National Productivity Institute, a private sector operation, is rooted in the same ideology. It implores all South Africans to see themselves as "assets." Take "accountability for your actions," it continues, "be innovative." Then "your productivity, my productivity" will "grow into a prosperous company called," in bold script, "South Africa (Pty) Ltd."[57]

As this implies, too, there is a close parallel between the rise of the entrepreneurial subject and the rise of ethno-preneurialism. The latter interdigitates, at a collective level, with the former: it is, so to speak, me-as-we, individuality-become-identity. Ethno-preneurialism, we have stressed, entails the management and marketing of cultural products and practices, *qua* intellectual property, as sources of value—indeed, as monopoly capital—inseparable from the being-and-bodies of their owner-producers; as we noted before, it has displaced the sale of labor power, conventionally conceived, in yielding the means of material life. In this respect, the neoliberal ethos of entrepreneurialism would seem to invert Marx's conception of labor as *alien* to the laborer, as being *unfree,* as being *estranged* from his existence to the extent that "he is at home when he is not working, and when he is working he is not at home" (Marx 1988:74). But critics of contemporary neoliberalism have observed, correctly, that the "theory of human capital," in celebrating the entrepreneurial subject and discounting the structural dimensions of economic processes, legitimates a new mode of domination and (self-)regulation. As Wendy Brown (2003:8), Thomas Lemke (2001:203) and others have said, this mode of domination does more than just reproduce existing regulatory mechanisms and forms of exploitation; it provides enhanced techniques of control through freedom itself. Which, it turns out, is less a radical departure than an intensification of the modernist myth of "free labor" under industrial capitalism against which Marx railed so passionately.

But is there not something different, something emancipatory, about ethnic enterprise? Have we not shown that the identity economy has permitted long-marginalized, impoverished populations to turn the means of their exclusion into sources of profit *without* alienation, estrangement, or a loss of "true" selfhood? This is a complex question, one that yields deeply ambiguous answers: On one hand, ethno-preneurialism *does* open up fresh opportunities for producing, controlling, and redistributing value. But, to reiterate a point already made, the commodification of culture may also entrench old lines of inequality, conduce to new forms of exclusion, increase incentives for the concentration of power, and create as much poverty as wealth. Sometimes demonstrably more. This is the underside of struggles over authenticity, membership, and belonging, like those between "real" and "fake" Bushmen; over the distribution of ethno-capital, as among the Mabaso or the Makuleke; over the growth of global tourism and its brazenly neocolonial modes of extraction, as in parts of Kenya; or over the perennial issue of whether the fruits of ethnic marketing ought accrue to individuals or to communities, especially when, as with Shipibo crafts and shamanic practices, they involve innovations that might be patented, signed, or made subject to *koporaet*. The promises and prospects of ethno-preneurialism are, to say the very least, equivocal. We shall return to them at the end of our narrative.

More to the present point, the fact that ethno-preneurialism has spawned these kinds of conflict emphasizes, yet again, that the identity economy is not confined to economics; that it is, simultaneously and indivisibly, about politics as well. Corporate ethnicity, under conditions of hetero-nationhood, often expresses itself as a demand for sovereign self-determination (Comaroff and Comaroff 2003a), for the right of ethno-nations to rule themselves according to their own vernacular means and ends. This is *not* just a plea for recognition, the kind of thing typically subsumed under the sign of "multiculturalism"—the kind of thing sufficed by a polite appreciation on the part of the majority of the population for the "colorful" customs, costumes, and cuisine of one or another compliant minority in its midst. Where ethnic assertion plays, at once, on primordial connectedness, natural right, corporate interest, and a will to sovereignty, it is better grasped by the concept of *poli*culturalism. The prefix, "poli-," marks a fusion of two things: plurality and its politicization. It is a *strong* statement, an argument grounded in cultural ontology, about the very nature of the pluri-nation and citizenship within it: about its constitution and the spirit of its laws; about its governance and its hyphenation; about self-rule and the means of its conduct. It also challenges the nation-state with the limits of its tolerance of heterodoxy; "We as a Zulu nation will not be told what to do about our culture," said the Zulu king, Goodwill Zwelithini, in September 2007. "There is no [government] department that we'll ask permission from to uphold our culture and tradition."[58] Notwithstanding the faith of some humanist philosophers in multiculturalism—whose origins lies in an optimistic, liberal vision of the late modern world—the room allowed to difference in most contemporary polities falls well short of acknowledging radical alterity (cf. Povinelli 1998). Few of them countenance claims in its name to more than the barest modicum of political or legal sovereignty. As a result, policulturalism— as in Bosnia, Cyprus, India—may spawn explosive civil violence. In South Africa, led by Contralesa, it takes the form of an ongoing, low-level confrontation between Euro-modern liberalism and variously expressed, variously formulated notions of "traditional authority." Elsewhere in Africa, "ethnicity . . . [is] a principle of exclusion and even death," although it is also "the vehicle of a new moral economy of the *polis*" (Bayart 2005:40). In the USA, it manifests itself in the long-simmering animosity, and in intermittent courtroom battles, between Native Americans and the federal government over the question of self-determination for First Peoples. Everywhere, however, it feeds, more or less directly, into Ethnicity, Inc.— in particular, into struggles over the dollar worth of difference. Violence, lawfare, business: the three dimensions in which, singly or in combination, the zero-sum logic of identity plays itself out.

Incorporation and the Language of Legality: From the Judicialization of Politics to Lawfare

Observe how, in speaking of the incorporation of identity, of the commodification of culture, even of policulturalism, we keep returning to the language of legality: to copyright, ownership, patent, title, intellectual property, litigation, sovereignty. It bespeaks another characteristic of our times: the fetishism of the law.[59]

The modernist polity, as Montesquieu (1748 [1989]) reminds us, has always rested on jural foundations. In theory at least, its citizens have from the first been *right*-bearing individuals (Taylor 1989:11f). But the rise of neoliberalism—itself erected on a highly voluntarist, utilitarian conception of moral, material, and social relations—has intensified greatly the reliance on legal ways and means. The symptoms are unmistakable: among them, the subjection of ever more embracing, ever more intimate domains of human life to litigation; the remarkable spread of human rights advocacy; the proliferation of law-oriented NGOs all over the planet; the development of a global jurisprudence far more comprehensive than its internationalist predecessors; the rash of new national constitutions written since 1989 (above, p. 48); the frequency with which states are being sued by their own subjects; the growing recourse to tort proceedings as a weapon with which to reverse wrongs, real or imagined; and, as we have seen, the elaboration, across the world, of intellectual property regimes. People almost everywhere, even in the most remote of places, are finding reason to behave as *homo juralis*. So are communities of diverse kinds, which, increasingly, act as, or mimic, bodies corporate. The incorporation of identity, as this implies, is itself part of a planetary culture of legality.

An anthropological irony lurks here, one to which we have already alluded in passing. In the Great Age of Structural-Functionalism, the founding fathers of the discipline likened African kin groups to corporations (Fortes 1953); "the corporate lineage," definite article, became a theoretical term of their trade, a fetish in its own right, since it reduced flesh-and-blood human relations to a legal abstraction—to which was attributed the capacity to explain social behavior. This made many of their students, ourselves included, uneasy. Apart from all else, we were never sure whether they were speaking analytically or analogically (cf. Kuper 1982). As it turns out, it was the latter. Nowadays the appeal to the corporate by groups that define themselves with reference to descent and consanguinity is anything *but* analogical. It is founded on the materialization of genealogical relations into *real* corporations rooted in blood, culture, and the law. Thus it is that a fetish of the anthropological past has returned *not* as an abstraction but as a palpable fact. Parenthetically, "real" corporations have long been likened to ethnic (or "tribal") groups, replete with their hierarchical authority structures, their communal rituals, their ceremonial gatherings, even their "divine" chiefs. But that is another matter.[60]

One corollary of the fetishism of the law is a gradual shift of the political—specifically, of the negotiation of collective rights, recognition, and interests, of sovereign self-determination, civic values, and the public good—into the domain of the legal, this being part of the more general mutation of politics under contemporary historical conditions (above, p. 44). As Chanock (2000:34) explains:

In place of a politics in which rights of substance were supposed to be delivered through the political process, now rights jurisprudence is . . . [the site of] important allocatory decisions. No longer part of the constant bargaining and struggle of the political arena, decisions about who is entitled to what are . . . conceived of as de-politicised and rendered according to a set of legal principles.

More and more are differences of *all* kinds being dealt with by means of law, whether they involve private freedoms or public resources, access to medical treatment or title to territory, cultural knowledge or civic author-ity, the physical and fiscal entitlements of rulers or the property, liberty, and well-being of their subjects, religious tolerance or ethnic aspiration. Also, *in extremis,* life, death, and states of exception. What once happened primarily in parliaments, street protests, and other political theaters now finds a new—or, to be precise, a parallel, expanding—terrain of contesta-tion. Politics may or may not be about class any longer. But it certainly *is* about class actions. Which, in turn, is transforming the modernist con-ception of the political *tout court.*

Nor is it only the politics of the present that are being fought out in the courts. So is the past, thereby to be repossessed—sometimes, explic-itly, as cultural property. For example, there have been a rash of suits initi-ated against the British government by formerly colonized peoples, each demanding cognizance of, and compensation for, an old wrong: by the Nandi, in Kenya, over the killing of their legendary leader Koitalel arap Samoei in 1905, and by the Bunyoro-Kitara, in Uganda, over the trans-fer of some of their ancestral territory to Buganda in 1900, to name just two.[61] Cases of this kind have also come to postcolonial judiciaries. Thus the Maasai Civil Society Forum recently petitioned the High Court in Nai-robi to order the return of land leased to settlers from the United King-dom in 1884 (Igoe 2006:405). They lost. Bushmen in Botswana have been more successful. In December 2006, after a protracted struggle, their gov-ernment was ordered by its own judicial authorities to readmit onto their "traditional" terrain those who had been evicted from the Central Kala-hari Game Reserve. Having been "unlawful[ly] and unconstitutional[ly]" expelled, they were to be allowed to resume hunting and foraging, fol-lowing their time-honored techniques—though, as we shall see, this did not put an end to the conflict.[62] Halfway across the world, in New Zea-land, six Maori groups laid a complaint in 1991 to the Waitangi Tribunal, a quasi-judicial body, insisting on recognition of, and proprietorial rights to, their vernacular lifeways (Watson and Solomon 2001). The Treaty of Waitangi of 1840, they argued, guaranteed them "self-determination (*tino rangatiratanga*)," ownership of their ecological resources, and protection for their cultural "treasures," all of which had repeatedly been "breach[ed] by the Crown." Their action, known as WAI 262, sought also to preserve their "intellectual heritage rights in relation to indigenous flora and fauna and their *Matauranga,* or traditional knowledge, customs and practices related to that flora and fauna."[63] By mid-2006, for complicated reasons, the tribunal had not yet arrived at a final judgment. Tellingly, in light of what we had to say earlier about culture, nature, and patents, a plea made in the course of the dispute was that "genetic tampering with the DNA structures of native flora and fauna" in New Zealand constituted an offence against the Maori. Why? Because they have, since time immemorial, had "a particular *whakapapa* or genealogical relationship" with the natural environment that was "not . . . respected or understood by science, and scientists." Their endeavor to reclaim their cultural and ecological heritage, concluded Watson and Solomon, has had the dual effect of hastening "the incorporation of Maori *tikanga* (custom)" and of "judicializing [that] process." The struggle for cultural identity, past and present, seems to be morphing in many places—if unevenly, often uneasily—into lawfare.[64]

Lawfare, the use of legal means for political and economic ends (J. L. Comaroff 2001; Comaroff and Comaroff 2006:30f),[65] is endemic to the technology of modern governance. Democratic and authoritarian states alike have always relied on constitutions and statutes, on charters, mandates, and warrants, on emergency and exception—on the violence inherent in the law (Benjamin 1978; Derrida 2002)—to discipline their citizenry. Its deployment by "little peoples" against others more powerful also has historical precursors: intermittently throughout the nineteenth and twentieth centuries, colonized populations appealed to courts to protect them against settler predation, state oppression, and the excesses of capital. But lawfare as a so-called "Lilliputian strategy" appears to have found its historical moment in the late twentieth century, gaining ground in parallel with human rights advocacy; rights, critically, that have come to include sovereign ownership of cultural knowledge. In times past, where ethnic groups *did* assert themselves, it was more usually by conventional political means. Even those who were acutely sensitive to the availability of legal remedies often chose not to use them: the Seminole of Florida, for instance, went as far as to hire lobbyists and lawyers to *avoid* litigation over tribal business (Cattelino 2008).

No longer. Ethno-activists and ethno-preneurs tend now to believe strongly in the insurgent potential of lawfare. They seem ever more ready to put intellectual property regimes to work in the effort to secure the value vested in difference—and, in so doing, to render cultural identity into the language of copyright, sovereignty, and patent; also to "forum shop" (cf. Benda Beckmann 1981) for the most advantageous jurisdictions and legal institutions both within and beyond the nation-state in which to pursue their collective interests.[66] Some, like the Bafokeng and Makuleke in South Africa (see below), have become seasoned law-mongers; adept at eliciting the aid of "trusted legal advisors," they are quick to challenge inconsistencies in national legislation dealing with indigenous rights (Robins and van der Waal n.d.:9).[67] Similarly in the US, where the California Indian Legal Services (CILS) regularly report their legal battles with the state in an online newspaper.[68] Given what we have said about the expanding hegemony of the market, it stands to reason, too, that tort law should be a popular weapon of choice among those who defend cultural property. A number of them, again with the assistance of NGOs, have sought to make use of such transnational instruments as the US Alien Tort Claims Act, which renders multinational corporations operating abroad subject to liability suits in American courts; this act dates to the late eighteenth century but appeals to it seem to be increasing dramatically in the twenty-first (cf. Shamir 2004). Hence the lodging of class action suits like the one brought in Louisiana against Freeport-McMoRan, Inc., by Yosefa Alomang of Irian Jaya (West Papua) in Indonesia.[69] Freeport-McMoRan were accused of "egregious human rights and environmental violations . . . against . . . Indigenous Tribal people," including "the purposeful, deliberate, contrived and planned demise of a culture . . . and a unique pristine heritage which is socially, culturally, and anthropologically irreplaceable." Ethnic groups within the USA have also made use of other statutes, like the Unfair Business Practices Act (a.k.a. California Business and Professions Code section 17200), designed to allow "any person or organization to sue a business entity for any illegal actions it has taken in the course of its . . . activities." In 2003, the Middletown Rancheria tribe, represented by the CILS, settled a suit against Snows Lake Vineyard and Lake County over the destruction of archaeological sites "known to have been hunting camps and believed to contain ancestral burial sites" and sensitive environmental areas.[70]

Insurgent lawfare does not always yield what it seems to promise. It goes without saying that, in general, litigation favors the powerful and well-resourced. In the USA, says Jeffrey Rose, "Supreme Court, Inc." is ruling "in favor of corporate defendants" as never before.[71] Elsewhere too. Suits that appear, prima facie, to have legal merit are often unsuccessful—like the one initiated by the Maasai Civil Forum in Kenya. Or the effort of the Ogoni to hold Shell Oil accountable for collusion with the Nigerian government in the alleged murder of their compatriots. At times "little people" lose even when they win: although the government of Botswana was ordered by its High Court to readmit Bushman into the Central Kalahari Game Reserve, the Mogae administration, which was *not* required by the judgment to provide "basic and essential services," has been excoriated for making it impossible for the plaintiffs actually to live on the land (see below). Not infrequently, too, indigenous populations become collateral victims of lawfare, even lawfare intended to protect "the indigenous" and the "endangered." Hollowell-Zimmer (2001) has pointed out that Alaskan Natives find themselves "enmeshed in a web of state, federal and international laws" concerning species at risk, laws that embargo their trade in polar bear fur, whale baleen, and walrus ivory. They are also aware that "global attitudes" are seriously affecting access even to their subsistence harvests—and, thereby, to the means of cultural production. "[W]e are a people," complained one craftsman, who are "stymied from practicing art traditions developed over centuries because of the . . . concern [of] others far removed from our ancestral ways." Others, in the instance, more concerned to protect nonhuman than human forms of diversity.

In sum, the growing resort to legal combat in the conduct of ethno-enterprise is attributable to a conjuncture of two things. The first is the fetishism of the law itself: the ever deeper inscription of personhood, sociality, and identity within it; the almost occult faith in its capacity, as a medium of commensuration, to enable the transaction of value across lines of difference; the reduction of the social to the contractual; the judicialization of politics. The second is the association of ethnicity with "naturally" owned property and, by extension, its sedimentation into a jural status: a right-bearing, commodifiable species of collective being-and-consciousness. Under these conditions—in an era in which power is measured in materialities, in which a global culture of human rights essays indigeneity and its endowments—the law represents itself as an instrument of empowerment. Even though it oftentimes is just the opposite.

———

To what, then, does all this add up? What are the implications of the fact that cultural subjects, in many parts of the world, tend ever more explicitly to conceive of themselves, discursively, with reference to ethnic objects and practices? Or of the fact that the commodification of those objects and practices may *not* simply banalize them, erase their aura, alienate their "owners" from their essence, or annul their capacity to realize collective selves and shared futures? What of the fact that this process of commodification has interpellated itself into an identity industry in which it is not easy to distinguish use-value from exchange-value, the particular from the universal, producers from consumers, natives from tourists?

Or of the fact that vernacular cultures increasingly embrace concepts of private ownership and innovation, copyright and patent? What of the fact, too, that difference, especially cultural difference, is casting a lengthening shadow over civic identities, universal citizenship, national belonging? Or that, while it opens up some populations to new sources of value, it also may subject them to new, more intricate forms of control, even dispossession? Or that ethnicity has come, phenomenologically, to exist in two registers: as genetic endowment *and* the object of voluntary self-construction, as essence and interest, as nature and choice? This doubling underscores the irreducibility of things ethnic either to the calculus of pure utility or to a liberal politics of recognition, important though these may be. The same may be said for the intense human passions that frequently swirl around the assertion or suppression of cultural identities. In the new age of capital, those identities represent themselves, hyphenatedly, as at once political-economic and ethico-legal. Which is why—in their semiosis, their sentiment, their praxis, their politics—they are articulated ever more volubly in the language of right, possession, property, propriety. And defended by resort to lawfare.

Project the cultural subject onto the terrains of the market and the law, add the reduction of culture to ("naturally copyrighted") intellectual property, mix it with the displacement of the politics of difference into the domain of jurisprudence, and what is the result? It is, to close the circle that we opened up at the beginning, *Ethnicity, Inc.*

FOUR

Commodifying Descent, American-style

Our ancestors sold Manhattan for trinkets. Today, with the acquisition of the Hard Rock Cafe, we're going to buy Manhattan back one hamburger at a time.
MAX OSCEOLA, VICE CHAIRMAN, SEMINOLE TRIBE, 7 DECEMBER 2006[1]

Popular archetypes of ethno-business in North America tend to focus on the burgeoning identity economy of its First Peoples. This idée fixe is reinforced, periodically, by fabulous stories of gambling-rich tribes, epitomized recently in primetime footage of patchwork-clad Seminoles announcing their $965 million purchase of the Hard Rock hotel, café, and casino chain from Rank Group PLC; also, if not as dramatically, by mass-mediated spats over such things as the franchise names of the Washington Redskins football team and of America's oldest, most renowned motorcycle, the classic "Indian." But, as we have said repeatedly, neither the incorporation of ethnic groups nor the commodification of culture is new. *Per contra,* the interpellation of identity in the market goes back a long way. Cattelino (2004:67; see above) notes that "traditional" Seminole practices have been inextricably entwined with economic "development" since the early 1900s; even more, that culture and economy here have, from the first, been mutually constitutive. Nor only here. There is abundant evidence elsewhere, too, of the early emergence of ethnically branded commodities in response to colonial enterprise: the "authentic" moose-hair embroidery of "the Huron" that evolved out of the lively circulation of styles and souvenirs among Woodlands Indians, settlers, and visitors in mid-nineteenth-century Eastern Canada (Phillips 1999); the Plains Indian dances that took on their "customary" character in Wild West shows staged across the USA and Europe at the turn of the twentieth century (Nicks 1999); the "Hopi rugs" whose ethnic provenance was fixed by traders dealing in new sorts of weaving born of the "[meeting] in the marketplace" of Pueblo, Navajo, and Spanish blankets (Kent 1976:90). Nor were these processes simply a matter of First Peoples responding to colonial economy and legality. Those peoples were often quick to seize the initiative, sometimes in straitened circumstances, thus to produce novel sources of value: the Seminole, for example, opened up the earliest of their signature casinos "before any US law on tribal gaming had been passed or any judge had issued a ruling on the matter" (Cattelino 2006:108). Of course, anthropology was not uninvolved in the genesis of cultural branding. Its own brand, after all, is *Other Cultures* (Beattie 1965), a brand that helped brand other cultures.

The explicitly *legal* incorporation of identity, *sensu stricto*, began in the USA with the Wheeler-Howard Act, also known as the Indian Reorganization Act (IRA) of 1934, two sections of which, 10 and 17, dealt specifically with the matter of corporate identity. According to section 17, the secretary of the interior might

. . . issue a *charter of incorporation* to [a] tribe: Provided, That such charter shall not become operative until ratified at a special election by a majority vote of the adult Indians living on the reservation. Such charter may convey to the *incorporated tribe* the power to purchase, take by gift, or bequest, or otherwise, own, hold, manage, operate, and dispose of property of every description, real and personal, including the power to purchase restricted Indian lands and to issue in exchange therefore interests in *corporate property,* and such further powers as may be incidental to the *conduct of corporate business,* not inconsistent with law . . . (emphasis added)[2]

The stated purpose of the act—or, rather, its conceit, coming after centuries of brute violation, predation, enslavement, expropriation, and contrapuntally, struggles for both survival and sovereignty—was to turn history back on itself by typically modernist means: in the words of its preamble, by "conserv[ing] and develop[ing] Indian lands and resources," extending to tribes, among other things, "certain rights of home rule," the "right to form businesses and other organizations," and, under the terms of Section 16, the right to promulgate an "appropriate constitution and bylaws." In short, the right to become a corporation.

Other legislation, like Indian Claims Commission Act (1946), followed (Rosenthal 1990). But the apotheosis of the process, of the animating

Geist behind the IRA, was contained in ANCSA, the Alaskan Native Claims Settlement Act, passed in 1971. Under its terms the indigenous peoples of that state were to be organized into twelve regional corporations—and into village corporations within them—each of which was (i) to "conduct business for profit," (ii) to be "vested in a board of directors" elected under its "articles of incorporation," and (iii) to issue "one hundred shares of stock to each Native . . . ,"[3] a "Native" being defined by autochthony and genealogy.[4] Or, in the precise words of the Act, by at least "one-fourth degree" native blood.[5] The settlement granted to the population covered by ANCSA, under the aegis of the corporations, approximately one-ninth of the area of Alaska and $962.5 million in cash—a bit less than the Seminole of South Florida paid for the Hard Rock empire thirty-five years later—in return for the extinction of all further territorial claims.[6] More significantly, it converted Indian country into private, alienable property; that is, real estate. In this last respect it differed from the IRA, which specifically *precluded* the sale of reservation land.[7] Initially, shares were not issued to persons born after 1971. A 1991 amendment, however, allowed bodies corporate to extend the provisions of the act in order to "make new Natives." Those that chose to do so—not all did—set about promulgating rules of devolution to transfer assets to what one local jokingly dubbed "New Kids on the Stock."[8]

ANCSA, too, was justified in the familiar terms of liberal-modernist materialism; because it would be in their own best interests, shareholders would push for corporate development and economic mainstreaming, thereby creating jobs and reducing welfare dependency. Some native enterprise *did* prosper—Sealaska, a regional corporation, is now the largest timber holder in the southeast reaches of the state—but often at the expense of less successful neighbors. Critics of the act voiced three objections to it: that it was designed above all to prevent new demands for "Indian territory," however well-founded they might be (Dombrowski 2002:1064); that privatization would encourage those who owned "native" real estate, especially those populations *in extremis,* to sell it for short-term gain; and that public resources transferred to indigenous peoples were more than likely to end up in the hands of industry, since those peoples would be put under persistent pressure to dispose of their assets (1068). To be sure, the alienation of First Peoples' territory through treaty and land transfers, a notorious species of lawfare, has a long, sorry history in the lower forty-eight states of the USA. Castile (1996:144) refers to this, slightly awkwardly, as "the free market of ethnicity": in the 1950s, he notes (citing Clifton 1977), federal "cash settlements of outstanding Indian land-loss claims" brought many "out of the ethnic closet to vote for liquidation of the assets of 'their' tribe and its (sic) redistribution."

ANCSA was a little more complicated in both intention and effect. It allowed—indeed, encouraged—native claimants to participate in the national economy, but "only through the corporate/stockholder format" (Dombrowski 2002:1064; emphasis added). In so doing, the act recast ethnic selfhood, identity, and reproduction less in the mold of historical lore than property law; not least, intellectual property law.[9] Thus indigenous corporations were granted the right to issue trademarks in respect of their cultural, aesthetic, and ritual products, a growing proportion of which were directed toward the market: since 1972, the Silver Hand logo has been used as a "guarantee of the authenticity" of vernacular arts and crafts (Hollowell-Zimmer 2001). Anyone with a sufficient blood quantum (again, one-quarter or more) may register for the right to use this branded emblem—which gives Native Alaskan ethnicity, literally, a biophysical stamp of recognition. And demonstrates unambiguously how it fuses the two senses of incorporation: one vested in the body, the other in business. Cultural performances among the indigenes of southeast Alaska now also depend on the imprimatur of ANCSA corporations: Celebration, a biannual "festival of song, dance, crafts, and the revitalization of Native languages," has, since its advent in 1982, evolved into one of the preeminent ritual events of the region; it is organized by the Sealaska Heritage Institute, which describes it as a "new tradition," there to replace vernacular ceremonies of the Tlingit, Haida, Tsimshian, and other peoples that had "founder[ed]" under the impact of a "rising cash economy."[10] Celebration has evoked diametrically opposed reactions. Some Natives decry, and seek actively to disrupt, such "new traditions" and their corporate provenance;[11] others have grown quietly attached to them. Either way, they are vehicles through which the two sides of incorporation have come together to take on a palpable—sometimes heated, sometimes humdrum— emotional loading. And, in the process, have added to the affective freight of ethnic identification.

In the lower forty-eight states, too, the formal incorporation of identity, as bespoken in the Indian Reorganization Act, predated the advent of casino capitalism, if very unevenly. According to Paredes (1995:353–54), southeastern Native American communities began to constitute themselves as nonprofit enterprises back in the 1950s, strengthening claims for federal recognition—itself an enduring historical pursuit of First Peoples—and laying the foundation for their emergence as "corporate polities." Which seems to have led, by turn, to their maturation into for-profit, "quasi-socialist businesses in which all members [were] share-holders"; in some instances, shareholders who received "periodic dividend checks" from the proceeds of the sale of culture. On the whole, concludes Paredes (354), these peoples have been "remarkably successful" in a wide range of enterprises, from manufacture through the hospitality industry to agriculture. Elsewhere in the USA, some have been much less successful—however such things are to be measured, itself a problem of major proportions—others, more so. But nowhere nearly as "successful," in gross terms, as those who own gambling operations like the Mohegan Sun in Connecticut, a billion-dollar-a-year profit machine. Or the Pequot Foxwood Resort at Mashantucket, also in Connecticut, a massive monument to ethno-marketing, to expertly commodified culture, and to the architecture of vernacular kitsch; en route to it, off Interstate 95, are found such satellite establishments as the Ethnic Concepts International Gifts and Smoke Shop and a Pequot Museum and Research Center that sells craft objects and subscriptions to the public.[12]

The term "casino capitalism" has been used to describe neoliberal economies *tout court* (e.g., Strange 1986). It points to the increasingly overt role played, in those economies, by financial speculation, a species of practice that, in its less respectable, popular forms, was long seen as the shameful underside of Mammon—and long associated with such unregulated frontiers of business as offshores, reservations, and free-trade zones, where the limits of the law open up zones of "irregular" accumulation (Comaroff and Comaroff 2001). Its history among US First Peoples is typically taken to begin with the Seminole of South Florida (see above). They were among the first to experiment in the betting industry, later deploying their sovereignty to establish high-stakes bingo halls, tax-free smoke shops, and, eventually, casinos (Paredes 1995:355f; Kersey 1992; Cattelino 2004, 2008), a process intermittently stalled by judicial and administrative fiat before and after the Indian Gaming Regulatory Act of 1988.[13] To some ethnographers of the region, it is especially ironic that the Seminole "were so pivotal in unleashing the juggernaut of Indian gaming in modern America"; this because they were "so long respected for clinging to the 'ways of their ancestors'" (Paredes 1995: 355). To us, the irony lies less in the revelation that these people saw no contradiction between culture and capitalism than in the fact that so many anthropologists once did. And still do. After all, it appears to have been their enterprise—in particular, their exploitation of the commercial benefits of their political status—that brought many Indian groups "back from the brink of cultural extinction" (357); just as, in Hainan and Yunnan, Cajun Louisiana and Maori New Zealand, Bali and Sekhukuneland, entry into the tourist market has underwritten the Return of the Native by yielding substantial Returns on Nativeness, both material and social. What is more, some contemporary Natives show themselves to be resourceful ethno-preneurs in the mainstream economy; as state lotteries and others in the betting world compete for their customers, they have diversified quite effectively. Thus the Viejas Band of Kumeyaay Indians, said to operate the largest casino in California, have opened a $35 million factory-outlet center and have become major stockholders in the Borrego Springs Bank. And the Mississippi Choctaw have ploughed their gaming profits into new businesses, among them a car dealership and an electronics plant (Darian-Smith 2002:120; cf. Cattelino 2008).[14]

As all of this makes plain, and as an unrelenting stream of media reports attest,[15] the identity economy of Native America does not reduce to a simple narrative accounting. It also yields some extraordinary ironies. Like the fact that some of the First Peoples best placed to invest their futures in casino capitalism, the Navajo notably among them, have long resisted it. Or, in another register entirely, like the fact that, as a consequence of their buyout of the Hard Rock chain, the Seminole have taken private ownership of US pop cultural relics of the sort more usually found in the Smithsonian Institution—Jimi Hendrix's Flying V guitar, for example, and a Madonna bustier—while they struggle to repossess their own, priceless heirlooms from museums across the country.[16] The unfolding history of this identity economy, its past and its continuing present, its ironies and absurdities and tragedies, fall well beyond our present purview; in any case, there are others much more qualified than are we to plumb its depths. But it *does* point to seven things anticipated in our theoretical reflection above, seven themes that will become critical as our story unfolds, seven key dimensions of Ethnicity, Inc.

Ethno-capital, American-style: Seven Dimensions of the Identity Business

The *first* concerns inclusion and exclusion. The more that ethnically defined populations move toward the model of the profit-seeking corporation, the more their terms of membership tend to become an object of concern, regulation, and contestation. And the more they do, the greater is their proclivity to privilege biology and birthright, genetics and consanguinity, over social and cultural criteria of belonging.

In the past, as Strong and Van Winkle (1996:555) note, "blood quantum," although given priority in US legislation and written into many tribal constitutions after the Indian Reorganization Act, was "never the sole marker of Indian identity." Equally significant were "genealogy, private property, and 'competence in civilization'" (after Biolsi 1995). Some First Peoples, they add, like the Lumbee, refused entirely "to designate tribal identity in terms of blood (after Blu 1980); others, like the Mashpee, stressed their "shared history, social ties, and attachment to . . . place" (after Clifford 1988; Campisi 1991). But blood is not necessarily devoid of these things. Until recently Kim TallBear (n.d.:347) observes, most Native Americans spoke of the blood quantum as a measure of the multiple ties that rooted an individual in a natal community, within a web of named kin. It was not simply a vehicle of lineal descent, the understanding reinforced by the logic of DNA. But nonbiogenetic considerations, it seems, are receding in relative significance, at least when it comes to reckoning membership. According to Eve Darian-Smith (2002:119), blood, in the biogenetic sense, has become much more prominent, "an obsession," she says, among nearly all the First Peoples of the USA.[17] There is a growing body of evidence to support the claim. Take the remarkable case—it made the international press—of the Pechanga Band, resident on the Luiseno Mission Indian Reservation in San Jacinto, California, whose casino resort has been reported to yield $184 million per annum. In 2003, its enrollment committee, faced with the problem of limiting access to their newfound wealth, expelled one hundred and thirty of the nine hundred and ninety members, more than 13 percent, on the genealogical ground that they were "non-lineal descendants."[18] Elders of the Band responded to the ensuing class action suit, filed in January 2004, by arguing—successfully, before the Fourth District Court of Appeal, and with the eventual concurrence of the Supreme Court—that, having "sovereign immunity," they could not be challenged under prevailing US law; federally recognized tribes, of which there are five hundred and sixty-one, are free to lay down formal rules of inclusion for themselves, not least the requisite "degree of Indian blood." Traces here, more or less, of Agamben (1998): in the right to exclude, and in matters of lifeblood and sociolegal death, lies their sovereignty.

Cases of this kind have become commonplace across the USA. Even before the Pechanga action, in May 2002, hundreds of persons struck from various tribal rolls congregated for a "A Day of Healing and Empowerment" in the hope of finding means to stem the rising tide of those denied ethnic identity by not "meeting the blood quantum." The Indian Gaming Regulatory Act of 1988 has been the object of gathering criticism in this respect, especially among the disenrolled: promulgated in a climate of frenzied privatization, argue its detractors, it is so ambiguous, its monitoring institutions so ill-defined, that some Native Americans and their non-Indian backers have been able to use it to make untold fortunes while large numbers are being disinherited, often by highly dubious means.[19] Hence Angela Mullis and David Kampers's (2000) terse question: *Indian Gaming: Who Wins?*

Both the obsession with blood and the conflicts to which it is giving rise are entirely predictable. The doubling that has come to haunt ethnicity—its ontological rooting in both essence *and* choice—is insupportable under conditions of legal incorporation. These, self-evidently, demand the drawing of unequivocal lines of inclusion and exclusion, of inside and out. No wonder the commerce in recreational genomics, which turns out to be more than merely recreational when the stakes are large, is growing so quickly; the likes of DNA PRINT GENOMICS, DNA Tribes, and Ethnoancestry (above, p. 41) claim to have technologies that provide "hard" scientific evidence of identity, evidence that puts the matter of membership beyond construction, debate, or question. Which they can never do, except by making a fact of the fiction that being and blood are coterminous.

The *second* dimension of the incorporation of identity seems, by contrast, counterintuitive—although, again, by now we should not be surprised by it. Frequently, it is commerce that produces an ethnic group, not the other way around.

Vide the Lytton Band of Pomo Indians—Pomo in name, postmodern by predicament—that, in the early 1960s, lost its land in Sonoma County after the US government "terminated" many small Indian communities under the California Rancheria Act (1958). In return for their dissolution as legal entities, their members were given individual title and the (unkept) promise of electricity, water, sewerage, roads, and other "infrastructure";[20] under pressure of extreme poverty and dire social conditions, they sold off all their plots within two years. The Pomo, once a large congeries of seventy or so groupings, have a truly tragic history of murderous despoliation at the hands, *in seriatim,* of eighteenth-century Russian fur traders and of nineteenth- and twentieth-century American adventurers, militias, treaty mongers, bureaucrats, and others; a history, also, of struggle to repatriate their territory by political means and by purchase, to recover their spiritual, social, and cultural integrity, to resist being scattered across the Californian landscape, to escape their enduring immiseration. The Lytton Band was no exception. After its "termination," its diminishing membership, increasingly afflicted by alcohol, substance abuse, and indigence, dispersed all over the San Francisco Bay Area. By the account of its leader, Tribal Chairwoman Margie Mejia (see n.20), it "lost . . . its identity"; its very existence was deeply in question, notwithstanding the fact that a proportion of those who still identified as Pomo maintained relations with one another. Eventually, however, what remained of the grouping, a somewhat spectral population, joined in a class-action suit that, in the late 1970s, challenged the implementation of the California Rancheria Act; at the time, dispossessed First Peoples, encouraged by the nonprofit California Indian Legal Services, were discovering the possibilities of insurgent lawfare. As a result, the sovereign tribal status of the Lytton Band was restored in 1991. But it came with a condition. Gaming would *not* be permitted on their patrimonial terrain in the Alexander Valley; Sonoma Country is home to wealthy wineries, which do not want Indian enterprise on their doorstep. This meant, effectively, that return was unfeasible. By their own account, the *only* potential source of income for these Pomo, the only way "to rebuild [their] tribal community," was via the gambling economy, now open to them by virtue of their legal standing.

What followed is a long, involved story. It ended with the Lytton Band being permitted, under a somewhat misbegotten federal law,[21] to purchase a 9.53-acre property with a small gaming house on it—it has been called a "cardroom"—as an "official reservation"; this in the City of San Pablo, not far from downtown San Francisco and the Golden Gate Bridge. Here, abetted by private investors, a matter to which we shall return in a moment, it opened a casino. Note that this "reservation" was never intended as a place to live. It is purely a commercial holding, a sovereign space for the grossing of profit, with no previous connections to Indian culture or society; not unexpectedly, it drew loud criticism on this count from those opposed to First Peoples being allowed to open gambling establishments on sites with which they have no historical ties.[22] Nor was this the only issue that the venture was to raise. It also became a source of conflict with the State of California when, a couple of years later, the Lytton Band and its backers sought to expand their business into a mega-gaming facility, larger than the MGM complex in Las Vegas; the conflict, which went as far as a Senate Committee hearing,[23] was finally resolved in May 2007 with an agreement that the Indians would maintain a more limited operation in return for their permanent corporate presence in San Pablo. Which is where the matter rests. Suffice it to say, though, that the entry of these Pomo into the world of casino capitalism has been lucrative. Their company, under CEO Margie Mejia, the tribal chairwoman, employs some five hundred and twenty persons. It contributes significant sums of money to both the city and the state; San Pablo received $22.6 million in 2003. And its two hundred and fifty-two shareholders, the members of the Lytton Band, receive annual per capita distributions, housing assistance, subsidized health care, and support for the education of their children. What is more, a portion of the income has been dedicated to the purchase of fifty acres in Windsor, Sonoma County, thus to "build a reservation"—a *residential* reservation, that is—wherein the Band can finally realize its sovereign ethnic existence as, well, Pomo.

This case, we stress, is anything but exceptional. A rather more extreme one involves the Augustine Band of Cahuilla Mission Indians. In 1986 or 1987—sources differ slightly on the details—this grouping suffered the death of its last remaining member, Roberta Ann Augustine. Here, too, a protracted history of epidemics and ethnocidal killings had reduced the tribe to a shadow of its earlier self; by 1951, it had a mere eleven members. As *Indian Country Today* tells the story,[24] some years after Ms. Augustine's death, her granddaughter, Maryann Martin, who had been raised African-American in Los Angeles and had "no knowledge whatever of her heritage while growing up," became aware of her Indian roots. By what means this occurred is not entirely clear. But, in the 1990s, she moved back onto the abandoned reservation at Coachella, in Riverside County, southern California. With her she took her own three children and the four children of her two brothers, both of whom had been killed by gang gunfire some time earlier. It is this extended family of eight persons, only one of them an adult, that "currently comprises the entire tribe." Its five hundred acres had become an "illegal dumping ground for household garbage, trash, appliances, animal carcasses, commercial waste, car batteries, and thousands of tires";[25] in 1994, with the assistance of state and county agencies, a cleanup began. Soon after, under California Proposition 1A, Martin, as tribal chairperson, signed a compact with the state governor to build a casino. Developed in partnership with Paragon Gaming LLC of Las Vegas, it opened its doors on 18 July 2002,[26] with the enthusiastic support of the California Nations Indian Gaming Association. Neighboring bands seemed especially approving of the fact that a "people" reduced to just one adult should have succeeded in finding a means of survival. As a result, said a local Native American leader, "we will not see another tribe disappear." Quite the opposite: the establishment of the gaming house was, quite explicitly, a rite of rebirth, a rite celebrating the mutually constitutive power of finance capital, cultural capital, and human capital to produce a future. In the process, Ms. Martin and her dependent children have come to constitute a certified ethnic group. Hers is one of many, in California, composed of "small, extended family groups" living on so-called "rancherias" of a few acres.[27]

But perhaps the most dramatic case of an ethnic group raised from the dead by the occult power of capital to manufacture identity is that of the

Me-Wuk Indians of Buena Vista Rancheria in Amador County, northern California. Like the Lytton Band of Pomo, they had been "terminated" under the California Rancheria Act, had joined the class action against its implementation in the late 1970s, and, in consequence, had had their sovereign status restored in February 1985, when they were listed in the Federal Register. And, like the Augustine Band, they, too, had become "a nation without people." Until the turn of the new century, that is, when two women went to law over which of them was its one remaining member—and sole heir to an unprepossessing sixty-seven acre plot, replete with a trailer and a cemetery, thirty-five miles southeast of Sacramento.[28] Donna Marie Potts, who inhabits the trailer, claims to have been adopted into the tribe by Louie and Annie Oliver, the last Me-Wuk who had lived on the land.[29] Ms. Potts also described herself as a "niece by marriage" of the lone surviving lineal descendant of the Olivers, their daughter, Lucille Oliver Lucero, for whom she cared in old age and with whom she "formed a tribal government"; when Lucero eventually died in 1995, she left the sixty-seven acres to Potts, who then won recognition from the Department of the Interior as "tribal leader." On this basis, she went ahead and signed a contract with the Louisiana-based Cascade Entertainment LLC to develop a $150 million casino on the site. Unprepossessing or not, Buena Vista was set to become one of the biggest gaming complexes in the region, linked by Highway 88 to Sacramento and the Bay Area. The millennium promised a great deal, literally, to Donna Marie Potts and her "people."

But the venture was stopped in its tracks. In December 2001, Rhonda L. Morningstar Pope, who until then had been working as a bookkeeper in Sacramento, was granted an injunction by the Bureau of Indian Affairs against Potts and her plans. Claiming to be the great-granddaughter of Louie Oliver, she argued that her father—Jesse Flying Cloud Pope, Louie's grandson—who had died of a gunshot wound when she was four years old, was buried on the tribal land. Pope expressed outrage at the prospect of a casino on the site. Her nation had been stolen from her, its patrimony despoiled: "We are reminded every day of what our ancestors sacrificed for us." When the BIA ruled in her favor, she declared: "What we do now, as a Tribe and as a family, will be in recognition of our heritage."[30] In short order, a newly designed Web site reported that "the Tribe" had "hosted its first annual Memorial Day Event, which had not been held in nearly 30 years." Pope, it said, was rebuilding the tribal government and reviving cultural traditions. She had also launched a "restoration and beautification project on the Reservation," which included the reconstruction of "historical structures." But there was one addition to those structures. A casino. Barely had her rival been defeated than Rhonda Morningstar Pope secured a gaming deal of her own, this one with a New York developer of regional malls.[31] That is how it goes with casino capitalism. Fortunes may be reversed with a turn of the wheel. Or a new spin on genealogical facts. In the upshot, the home page of the Buena Vista Rancheria—mouthpiece, it appears, of Pope herself—announced that, in their "efforts to provide economic viability and security for future generations," the Me-Wuk Indians had decided to *develop, construct and operate* a class III gaming and resort facility [the "Flying Cloud"] on its reservation land" (emphasis added). Actually, on seventeen acres of it. The rest were to be designated "Tribal Archeological" and "Biological Resource" Protection Areas.[32] Thus it is that, in some circumstances, ethnicity is born directly of enterprise, cultural identity of commerce, imagined community of incorporation. Thus are forgotten ancestors re-membered. Thus, once again, is the dialectic of capitalism and culture set in motion. And not only in small Californian rancherias.

The phrase *"develop, construct and operate"* here raises, and obscures, critical questions of agency—of *who* it is, precisely, that initiates the processes of commodification and incorporation at the heart of the identity business. In so doing, it introduces the *third* dimension of the US cases. And of Ethnicity, Inc., *sui generis*. In many instances, most perhaps, the establishment of a corporate ethno-economy has been set in motion by venture capital from outside. Difference, patently, may produce profit in a wide variety of ways. But those who embody its essence are often too marginalized by it to be able to control its potential market value. On the other hand, the odds for "foreign" investors are often extremely favorable, recalling the unrestrained privateering of colonial enterprise. Not to mention its moral murkiness. Thus, in its "Special Report on Indian Casinos," *Time* noted that the celebrated fortunes reaped by some native entrepreneurs pale by comparison with the bounty that has accrued to non-Indian backers who bankroll betting palaces from "behind-the-scenes." It also estimated that, in 2001, the overall takings of the "industry" nationwide would, if they were the turnover of a single firm, place them among *Fortune* magazine's twenty most profitable US corporations, ahead of J. P. Morgan or Merrill Lynch.[33] Some Indian gaming officials reacted with outrage to these disclosures, accusing the *Time* reporters of misunderstanding the sovereignty of First Peoples. They insisted, too, that "few lenders would touch anything in Indian country in the first place."[34] This was certainly true in the past: banks and other creditors were reluctant "to invest on reservation land" (Cattelino 2005:188). In general, they may still be. But gambling is another thing entirely. Hence the likes of Paragon

Gaming LLC, the "partners" who introduced the Augustine Band of Cahuilla Mission Indians to casino capitalism and who style themselves as
a virtuous concern that specializes in joining "with Native American and
Canadian First Nation aboriginal groups" to develop and operate "gaming
based properties."[35] Or Cascade Entertainment LLC, the company that
began to build the Me-Wuk complex before the intervention of Rhonda
Morningstar Pope. Or many others. Given the prevailing ethos of privatization in the US, the growing acceptance of difference as a right to corporate self-determination, and a common perception that on-reservation
operations enjoy "very little [regulatory] oversight,"[36] there is every reason for capital to find its way to Indian country.

Which is where, and how, the proverbial moneylenders come in.

Venture capitalists in the Native American identity economy are often
global players, already experienced in exploiting pariah industries on de-
regulated, ethnicized frontiers. Some of them also benefit, as "others,"
from radically reduced tax obligations in the US. A few are foreign "financial godfathers." One of them, the Chinese-Malaysian businessman Lim
Goh Tong,[37] who made untold millions operating the only casino in his
predominantly Muslim homeland, is widely believed to be the biggest
winner to date in Indian gaming. He underwrote Foxwoods, the largest
gambling venue in the USA, and, allegedly, has secured 10 percent of its
net income until 2018.[38] Another, Sol Kerzner, is notorious in South Africa
for having profited from extravagant casinos built in the starved ethnic
dumping grounds, a.k.a. "homelands," of the apartheid era; these, at the
time, were the only legal sites of gambling, cross-racial sex, and soft porn
in a sea of Calvinist piety. Kerzner's dubious dealings necessitated that
he move his base of operations abroad once the apartheid bubble burst.
But he continued to reap rich rewards in places like Morocco and the Ba-
hamas—and was well poised to take advantage of the Native American
gaming bonanza fanned by Reaganomics. When the Bureau of Indian
Affairs recognized the Mohegans as a federally listed tribe in 1994, he
and several partners struck a fabled deal with their representatives and
the National Indian Gaming Commission: they would develop and manage a large, flamboyant casino, the Mohegan Sun, on a strategically situated "ancestral site" in Connecticut. Their fee? In the first instance, a
mind-boggling 40 percent of net revenues. The rest is history. Or, in the
opinion of many critics of the US gambling business, usury.

Some of the biggest backers of Native American casino operations are
also home-grown. Like Lyle Berman, one-time dealer in leather goods,
gambler extraordinaire, and member of the Poker Hall of Fame, whose
Grand Casinos Company merged with the Hilton Group some time back

to form the largest gaming business in the world; he is said to have secured returns as enormous as those of Lim and Kerzner from well-located Indian casinos in the Midwest and California.[39] Even more notable, perhaps, is Samuel P. Katz, a sports financier and three-time Republican candidate for mayor of Philadelphia, who took up the cause of the Lytton Band when they sought to open their casino in California. According to various accounts,[40] it was Sam Katz—or, rather, his Sonoma Entertainment Partners, L.P., backed by twenty investors and a "casino tribal lobbyist"— who actually found the site in San Pablo, bought it from Ladbroke USA (a Pennsylvania-based arm of the Hilton Group), helped exert the political pressure necessary to have the gaming reservation officially recognized, and played an active role in fighting off legal challenges to the undertaking. His own financial investment—or, if you prefer, his stake in a highly speculative gamble—has been put at $88 million. Katz has been described as the "guardian angel" of the Lytton Band. At times he has certainly played God with their destiny. He claims to have paid for the very means of their existence: for all the administrative expenses incurred in the process of acquiring their real estate, for the requisite environmental, archaeological, historical, and traffic surveys, for their leases on property and equipment, for their "public affairs activities" and legal costs, for "tribal government staff," and for their "lobbyists, consultants and advisers," of whom there seem to have been quite a few. One story even has it that he had bought the real estate for the "residential reservation" in Sonoma County, thus paving the road to the Pomo Promised Land. Neither the provenance nor the probity of this Mosaic myth, however, is clear.[41]

For non-Indian investors, lobbyists, consultants, and advisers, real or virtual Native American tribes are, in prospect, franchises licensed to make a killing; the manner in which some of them wheel and deal was brought into stark focus by the 2006 trial, before a federal court in Washington, D.C., of Jack Abramoff, a notorious figure in this stygian world.[42] To be sure, the odd mix of deregulation and dependency produced by granting tribal sovereignty to historically disadvantaged peoples—in an age in which welfare and "development" are entrusted to the market— create conditions especially conducive to ethno-capital;[43] conditions, that is, in which capital and ethnic identity coproduce each other, yielding new sorts and sources of value. There is a rider here, though: venture capital may thrive by hitching itself to business done in the zone of ethnic difference. But ethnic business, to retain its bona fides, has to keep its distance, and its distinctiveness, from mainstream venture capitalism. Why? Because Indian enterprise that succeeds in the competitive fray of global markets and does so *unmarked* by otherness, is open to the charge that it does not require, nor does it warrant, sovereign exclusion, protection, or preference (cf. Spilde 1999; Darian-Smith 2002:125). This is why, as Eve Darian-Smith (2002:124) has observed, many Native Americans—though not all[44]—work hard to sustain the impression that they inhabit "localized jurisdictions" founded on "laws that cannot operate outside . . . culturally specific tribal reservations"; or, more simply put, that their universe, and the commerce that goes on within it, *does* depend on their sovereign difference. This is also why there has been so much discomfort with, and controversy over, the likes of the Lytton Band, which still has no proper home of its own, no historically recognizable terrain, merely the restless, profit-hungry sovereignty of the downtown slot machine.

As this suggests, *fourth,* ethno-enterprise is always mandated by cultural difference. But it may not originate in, nor have much to do with, the *content* of that difference. Among the sovereign First Peoples we have discussed thus far, several had retained little connection to the world of signs and practices that once marked the fact and the fabric of their nativeness; recall that Maryann Martin, the last human trace of the Augustine Band of Cahuilla Mission Indians, was raised African American and had no knowledge of her Indian-ness before her return "home." Once on the road to incorporation, however, these ethnic groups typically began to assert—if necessary, to rediscover—their "traditions"; after all, from within, as Deloria (1979:27) has intimated, sovereignty itself may come to be defined "in the final instance, as a matter of . . . cultural integrity." Thus the Me-Wuk of Buena Vista have created annual ceremonies in order to dedicate themselves anew to the ways of their ancestors, ways lost to them by the exigencies of their recent history; these include a Land Blessing, a Memorial Day, and a Fall Festival, the substance of which is being fashioned largely de novo.[45] Sometimes, as we saw in the case of the Alaskan Native Celebration, the recuperation of cultural life actually occurs under direct corporate supervision. It was at the behest of Sealaska that the rites of the Tlingit, Haida, and Tsimshian were "replaced" by the freshly minted biannual festival. And under the branded logo of the Silver Hand that, after ANCSA, indigenous objects came to be manufactured and marketed.

There is considerable variation in the degree to which those who author such processes of cultural production build on the ("traditional") practices that they presume to be recuperating; on the content, that is, of the difference they assert in justification of their sovereignty. Some entertain a clear sense that they are revivifying a well-known, if dormant, repertoire of ways and means . . . celebration, for one, is explicitly said to combine familiar elements derived from the cultures that it displaced. Others

ENTERPRISE

Bafokeng-Amplats

Kgosi Lebone Molotlegi II
CEO of Bafokeng Inc.

Supplement to ENTERPRISE SEPTEMBER 1999

Amplats. A proud partner of the Bafokeng Nation.

AMPLATS
WORLD LEADER IN PLATINUM

1 "Kgosi Lebone II: CEO of Bafokeng Inc," *Enterprise* (Mining Magazine), 1999.

2 "Platinum Prince: Meet the New 'CEO' of Bafokeng Inc.," Creamer Media's Mining Weekly, 2000.

3 "Lesedi: Cradle of African Living Culture," near Hartebeespoort, North West Province, South Africa.

4 Chiyema Curio Market, Gundu. Chief Mukuni Village, near Livingstone, Zambia.

5a Mafunya Cultural Village, Limpopo, South Africa: (i) enacting "culture": children of Mafunya and American tourists watching a group trained to perform "traditional" dances.

5b Mafunya Cultural Village, Limpopo, South Africa: (ii) enacting "culture": children of Mafunya and American tourists watching a young dancer in *faux* traditional costume.

5c Mafunya Cultural Village, Limpopo, South Africa: (iii) learning the dance: American tourists performing their otherness.

5d Mafunya Cultural Village, Limpopo, South Africa: (iv) "traditional" healer, in translation, performs a divination for African-American tourists, September 2007.

6 "The Zulu Kingdom Awaits You: www.Zulu.org.za." Roeland and Canterbury Streets, Cape Town, November 2006.

7 Makuleke Cultural Village, Limpopo, South Africa. Photograph by Marie-Jean Bulter.

8 "Welcome to Cultural Heartland: Mpumalanga Tourism." Mpumalanga Province, South Africa.

9 "More Space, Real African." Central Namibia, 2007.

10 Selma Helao and Herero Dolls. Khomasdal, Windhoek, Namibia. Photograph by Jutta Dobler.

11a "Wellcome to Graft Market." Blaauwkrans, Damaraland, Namibia.

11b "Wellcome Grafts." Blaauwkrans, Damaraland, Namibia.

find themselves compelled to be highly inventive, having precious little vernacular material to work with; yet others draw from neighboring, cognate peoples to make patchworks for the present out of spatially dispersed things of the past; a few go in active pursuit of what they believe themselves to have lost to history. Thus the Augustine Band, Maryann Martin's extended family, is reported to have built a museum in Palm Springs specifically to house the heritage that it is seeking to buy back (Darian-Smith 2002:119). Similarly, if on much grander scale, the state-of-the-art Mashantucket Pequot Museum and Research Center in Connecticut has assembled a rich array of exhibits and houses a capacious library, complete with archives, special collections, and linguistic materials. The largest American Indian resource of its kind in the world, it now hosts an ambitious educational program, a program whose pedagogy treats "culture" as a domain set apart from mundane life—and, simultaneously, as a resource to be salvaged, systematized, disseminated (cf. Cattelino 2008). This is "culture" fully recognizable to the modernist sensibility, culture validated by accrediting institutions like the National Science Foundation (NSF), culture also commercially accessible to Natives and outsiders alike. While the center is maintained by the Foxwoods Resort, it is supported, as well, by the NSF. Its Web site advertises special holiday programs, conferences, and books—like *Narrative of the Life and Adventures of Paul Cuffee, A Pequot Indian*—for sale at *The Trading Post*. And "gourmet black-tie affairs," catered in "native style" on a terrace near "a recreated 16th century Indian village . . ."[46]

The recuperation of "tradition" under the impact of Ethnicity, Inc. may have the effect of reifying "culture" as a thing in and of itself. And, in the upshot, its products and practices, rendered as intellectual property, may be more or less directed at the market. But, invariably, the process also has an impact on everyday conduct: on those less-objectified, unremarked upon ways of doing things—even things instrumental, bureaucratic, and commercial—that embed themselves, "thickly" or "thinly," in local conventions, styles, and values. Like Indian "rez car" culture (Cattelino 2008),[47] which merges the pragmatics of poverty, the ecology of movement, and parodic self-fashioning into an assertively material semiosis. Or the thirty ways of "BEING NDN" listed online in the *Meswaki Nation Times* of 9 March 2007,[48] which include such ordinary items as: "loving frybread and soup"; being "broke all year long because you try to make every Pow Wow, gathering, and ceremony"; knowing "how to barter or trade for things you need and things you don't"; singing "49 songs using a garbage can for a drum"; celebrating "the buffalo hunt, or the ripening of the corn, Indian days or the time of year"; being "asked constantly if you still live in tee-pees or ride horses"; always "losing your job when the grant ends" and going to conferences "because you [might get to] work for a new grant program"; feeding "anyone and everyone who comes to your door hungry, with whatever you have"; reading about "your ancestors and relations in an anthropologist's paper"; and, noteworthy in light of our narrative, "hoping to make friends with a dividend Indian," someone like a Pomo of the Lytton Band who receives an annual per capita payout, "from California." If the penultimate clause reduces an older generation of anthropology to the object of ironic detachment, this last nugget of quotidian culture—culture, that is, fashioned under the impact of incorporation—closes our own hermeneutic circle. It also highlights the fact that a good number of Indian tribes have *not* benefited from the identity economy. Of those who have sought to enter the world of casino capitalism, many, for one or another reason, have failed.

The *fifth* dimension of Ethnicity, Inc. involves the dialectics of self-determination. Not only have Native Americans sought energetically to have their sovereignty officially recognized but, once it has been, they have tended to assert it *against* the state. This is hardly unprecedented: the claim of sovereign autonomy by indigenous tribes as a rhetoric of refusal in their dealings with the US government runs deep into the archaeology of modern American racial politics. And up against the liberal ideal of an American nationhood founded, constitutionally, on equal, horizontal citizenship under one law (cf. Aleinikoff 2002; cf. Smith 1997). But these days the claim takes on new resonances, mediated by the exigencies of the market—which complicate relationships between the economic, political, and legal dimensions of the status of Indians (cf. Kamper 2000; Cattelino 2005:196). For them, corporate identity does not merely derive from, nor is it just an expression of, their "special" entitlements as First Peoples. Or from a polite politics of multicultural recognition.[49] It is the very substance of their sovereignty, their *positive* right of exclusion, exemption, self-determination, in its material aspect. Thus, when Navajo Agricultural Products Industries undertook to sell its branded foodstuffs to Cuba—they included Navajo Pride corn, "the foundation of Navajo culture" that, interestingly, is grown from genetic hybrid seeds supplied by Monsanto and other companies—it was agreed that the deal be done as a "binational trade agreement," under the signature of the "sovereign Navajo Nation." Soon after the announcement, its President, Joe Shirley, described the pact as "a step forward for Navajo sovereignty."[50] Historically, it has been hard for Native Americans to realize that sovereignty; the Lumbee, ninth-largest tribe in the country, *still* lack full recognition, despite a century of strenuous effort (Sider 2003).[51] True, federal accreditation *does* appear to have become steadily easier to acquire since the 1960s (Castile 1996:745–46)—hence the passage of the Indian Self-Determination Act in 1975—but this has not laid all problems to rest. *Who,* precisely, ought to be officially "listed" as sovereign, and what the precise limits are of that sovereignty, have been continually contested, notwithstanding a Code of Federal Regulations (1992) meant to resolve such questions. Furthermore, as Cattelino (2008) and others have shown (cf. Coffey and Tsosie 2001), Native Americans have actively remade the meaning of their ("semi-autonomous") legal status in their own ("sovereign") image: in *poli*cultural terms that often challenge the jurisdiction of the federal state, its means of governance, and its statutes concerning "Indian affairs." Also, in ways that, in some places, have led to deeper lines of social differentiation and inequality within (see e.g., Sider 2003).

In the circumstances, it seems overdetermined that, as the stakes of indigenous rights are inflated by casino capitalism, the politics of "government to government" relations—stoked by lobbying, litigation, patronage, pork barreling—would become ever more fraught. All the more so because, for many cash-strapped states, Indian gaming presents itself as a potential panacea. But it is not a straightforward one, since the profits of sovereign tribes cannot be directly taxed; therein lies their immunity. As a result, governors of the likes of New York, Connecticut, and California, who have long "cast a covetous eye" on this "gushing revenue stream," have negotiated so-called compacts—recall the one involving the Lytton Band—with hard-driving Native leaders, their financiers, and their lawyers. In return for a share of the takings, the more the better, state legislatures expedite land transactions and write the necessary codes, conditions, and contracts under which the casinos may operate.[52]

It is against this background that recent, corporate-driven assertions of Indian sovereign autonomy against government have occurred. A few years ago, for example, the Mohawks of the St. Regis reservation came into conflict with the State of New York when its governor insisted that Native American cigarette wholesalers be licensed by his administration. Indigenous leaders refused, citing their sovereign exclusion. The Mohawk, like other tribes on the East Coast—the Shinnecock, among them, for whom "selling tax free cigarettes [is] the economic engine" of their community, and whose activities have also come under state scrutiny[53]—make their own tobacco products. Evincing the new spirit of ethno-preneurship, they were determined to protect their market. In this instance, as in others of similar sort, a compromise was reached, in part, significantly, because the dispute had become an obstacle to the settlement of a land claim, pursuant to the establishment of a casino in the Catskills.[54]

Much more conflict-laden, much less conciliatory, however, has been the intrusion of Native sovereignty into the market for political influence. The trial of Jack Abramoff, to which we alluded earlier, also revealed that Indian groups have become major investors in Congressional lobbyists and, by way of campaign contributions, in federal legislators. But it is at the state level that their efforts to gain leverage by financial means have been most openly asserted and most visibly fought. Although Native Americans are subject to rules that limit individual offerings, sovereign tribes can give without constraint. And give they certainly do: First Peoples are now said to be the largest "special issue" donors in the political field.[55] They have also refused consistently to report their donations, claiming to be exempt from the law in this respect.[56] Here is the rub: this claim, playing as it does into nationwide anxieties about the hawking of political influence, has provoked strong reactions. In 2006, the Senate Indian Affairs Committee, under the chairmanship of John McCain, held hearings on the legal status of contributions by Native American tribes under the Federal Election Campaign Act;[57] this with a view to introducing new regulations. Even before then, in 2002, the Fair Political Practices Commission (FPPC) in California had taken action against the Agua Caliente Band of Cahuilla Indians, citing them for their failure to report handouts in excess of $8 million over the previous four years.[58] When the commission offered to work out a settlement, the Agua Caliente refused to negotiate, proclaiming their exemption from all campaign-finance laws. The commission responded by filing suit.[59] It sought an injunction against, and civil penalties for, the tribe's alleged violation of the Political Reform Act; this measure, which governs the conduct of local and state elections, required them to give notice of their substantial payments to political campaigns and to declare other lobbying interests.[60]

Permit us to go into some detail about the legal process that ensued. While it involves some tedious juridico-technical minutiae, it throws into sharp focus the dialectics of sovereignty at the heart of ethno-incorporation. Faced with the FPPC action, the Agua Caliente filed a motion to quash the serving of a summons upon them. Predictably, they argued that, as an officially recognized First People, the doctrine of sovereign immunity protected them from suit. But the trial court denied their motion. It said that a grant of immunity in this case would, first, intrude on the state's authority under the Tenth Amendment of the federal constitution to regulate its own electoral and judicial processes and, second, interfere with the republican form of government backed by that constitution, especially in its "guarantee clause."[61] The tribe then did the only thing that remained to it to put a stop to the FPPC case. It petitioned the Court of Appeal to issue a writ vacating the previous ruling. Again, it was denied. But, crucially, its petition for review was granted on one key issue: the matter of sovereign immunity.

In the hearing that followed, the Agua Caliente contended that, where Congress has *not* specifically authorized a species of suit against Indian peoples—which, in limited circumstances, it has done in the past—their historical immunity against legal action remains intact. By extension, they repudiated the authority of a state to sue a tribe in order to collect taxes or to regulate it in any way unless the tribe itself had waived its sovereign exception or Congress had explicitly curtailed it. In reply, the FPPC asserted that sovereign immunity was enjoyed under a federal common-law doctrine that did *not* give those to whom it applied the right to interfere in a state's authority over the conduct of elections—and, by implication therefore, the right to contravene its rules governing campaign contributions. In December 2006, the Court of Appeal found in favor of the FPPC, permitting it to file its original action. The interest of preserving "the very essence of the political process" from corruption, it ruled, outweighed the Native American claim to exemption from legal accountability. "Immunity from suit," the judgment added, is "not synonymous" with sovereignty, not for "domestic dependant nations."[62]

The appellate bench might have noted, but did not, that sovereign nations across the world, not only "domestic dependent" ones, are being successfully sued ever more these days—sometimes, in fact, by ethno-nations within them (Comaroff and Comaroff 2006). Pace Agamben, sovereignty, *sui generis,* does *not* necessarily entail unaccountability to the law; although sovereigns often *do* evince aspirations to make it so, not least by deploying space-time vacuums in existing jurisprudential geographies in order to create temporary terrains of immunity for themselves (J. A. Comaroff 2007:385). In this respect, it—sovereignty, that is—may be a *claim* to unconstrained exception. But it is always incomplete, always ambiguous, always relative, always vulnerable to the existence of a commensurate or superior power beyond, beside, or inside itself. It is because of this, not in spite of it, that the language of sovereign autonomy is so commonly mobilized by ethno-corporations against the state. The very act of bespeaking it opens up a sociolegal *lebensraum,* under the alibi of exemption and self-determination, in which to assert foundational rights and endemic interests. This is itself a corollary of something we noted, and sought to explain, above: that, in the political-economy of identity, as in many other realms of contemporary social and material life, the law has become *the* prime space of contestation. It is also the ground on which the state, at all levels, seeks to constrain the expansive capacities of Ethnicity, Inc.

Mention of the spatial, here, leads directly to the *sixth* dimension of Ethnicity, Inc. It has to do with property, self-possession, and once again, the politics of sovereignty.

The process of becoming an ethnic corporation generally involves, and often begins with, a land claim of one kind or another. This is true of virtually all the cases we have mentioned, from the Mohegan in Connecticut through the various Californian bands to the Mohawk and Shinnecock in the State of New York. Such claims differ in substance and scale. They may (i) seek formal recognition of existing real estate as a tribal reservation, (ii) demand the return of terrain partly or wholly expropriated in times past, (iii) attempt to take possession of contested holdings, or (iv) pursue the acquisition of property ab initio. But they all grow out of the same axiom: that land, jointly owned in perpetuity, a.k.a. *territory,* is a founding principle of modern sovereign existence. To the extent that the concept of sovereignty in the contemporary world order (still) presumes the nation-state as its normative model, a physical space with delineated borders is the *sine qua non* of its accomplishment. This "imagined [sovereign] geography," Biolsi (2005:239–41, 53–54) suggests of Native Americans, is intrinsic to the essentialism at the core of their identity. It is also brought profoundly down to earth, in both senses of that term, by a brute reality: that, in the absence of land, US federal accreditation is unattainable. What is more, as Muwekma and Pomo Indians told a business reporter from San Francisco in 2001, tribes *sans* territory are routinely excluded from state benefits, be it college funding, health care, housing. Or casino licenses. Without a place to call home, they asked rhetorically, "How do you prove you're Indian?"[63] Without a home/land, to be sure, it *is* difficult to exercise the self-possession necessary here to substantialize a corporate ethnic identity. Nor just a home/land. Also a home page. Grounded sovereignty and cybersovereignty increasingly shadow one another, all the more so as the virtual displaces the concrete in anchoring the real. Adds Biolsi, most "recognized tribes"—like nation-states—now have Web sites; one, the Rosebud Sioux, has even "enacted legislation to protect its airspace" (254). Many "use the nsn.us or nsn.gov . . . domain designations." Nsn stands for "native sovereign nation."

Native Americans are not alone in seeking to ground their sovereignty in soil. Indigenous movements across the world act in parallel, and sometimes abet each other, in the effort to make territory the basis of their claims for recognition and self-determination. As Moringe Parkipuny has put it, "cultural identity and the land . . . constitute the very foundation of existence" (Igoe 2006:403); Parkipuny is Maasai. Nor is this land mere real estate, although it may start out that way. It is invested with ethnic essence, self-possession, passion. Often marked, in fact or in fancy, by the death and interment of ancestors, patrimonial ground provides the material basis of consubstantiality, polity, and economy. Even where some, most, or even all of a people do not actually live on it, it has the capacity to serve as a politico-legal alibi, as a sheet-anchor for ethno-capital, and as a space from which to speak, to assert subjectivity, to claim exception. The Lytton Band of Pomo Indians are not the only First People who have built their ethno-regenesis on a "shopping reservation," little more than a gaming hall and a parking lot, thence to aspire to a "residential" home. In the future, elsewhere.

The fact that a territory may be recently acquired, or recuperated after a long interruption, does not necessarily imply an absence of affective ties to it. Land, symbolically saturated, intensifies ethnic identification, whether it be by condensing historical memory or by animating the sorts of emotionally laden attachment that come from "taking place." Hence the spirited building of museums, the revivification of local crafts, the ritual celebrations of the soil that so often follow upon sovereign recognition. Hence the anxious desire to perform "traditional" ceremonies on that soil, often for a witnessing tourist public; shades here of similar impulses, recounted earlier, in Africa and Asia. Hence, too, the avid reclamation of archeological sites and the repatriation of ancestral remains— iconic residues, these, in which to ground corporate identity by fusing past and future, physical substance and human agency, blood and enterprise (cf. McLaughlin 2002: 211).[64] The concrete emplacement of those remains serves as collateral for a people-in-place, for their title to property in perpetuity and, with it, their eternal sovereignty. It may also mandate *multiple* assertions of the right to territory. For the Wyandotte Nation, to cite just one instance, the traces of a peripatetic history over two centuries permitted them to petition for reservation land in two states, Oklahoma and Kansas.[65] Territorial claims turn history into geography, sedimenting restless pasts into the stable fixities demanded for framing-and-claiming an ethnic identity. And all the possibilities that it opens up. These possibilities, we have seen, ride on an impossibility. For corporate ethnicity to sustain its legitimacy, it must remain, conceptually and substantively, "on the reservation." Yet, to realize itself fully, it has to move beyond, playing on the ambiguous, labile frontiers between the margin and the mainstream, the exotic and the ordinary, sovereignty and dependency. Such are the contradictions of the identity economy.

———

Let us pause, for mnemonic purposes, to reprise these six dimensions in summary form. As we said, they will greatly illuminate the remainder of our account. We phrase each in the indicative, then as proposition:

- The first had to do with *belonging:* processes of incorporation are typically accompanied by a growing stress on blood and biology, rather than merely on social or cultural connection, in determining inclusion and exclusion;
- the second, with *ethno-genesis:* it is frequently commerce that produces and/or congeals an ethnic group, not the other way around;
- the third, with *capital:* the establishment of corporate ethno-economies are, more often than not, set in motion by venture capital from outside;
- the fourth, with *culture:* while ethno-enterprise is always mandated by cultural difference it may not originate in, or have much to do with, the *content* of that difference;
- the fifth, with *sovereign existence:* once ethnically defined populations have their sovereignty officially recognized—itself the object of a great deal of political and economic exertion on their part—they tend to assert it *against* the state; and
- the sixth, with *territory:* the process of becoming an ethnic corporation generally involves, and often begins with, a land claim of one kind or another, this being a corollary of the close interconnection between property, self-possession, and the politics of sovereignty.

Which leaves the seventh dimension. We have kept it for last because it stands orthogonally to the others. And because it complicates our New World narrative.

We reiterate that the Native American archetypes of Ethnicity, Inc., those born of casino capitalism, presumed a cultural identity at their core; without one, claims for sovereign recognition would have had no ground. Literally. But—as the fourth, the cultural, dimension made clear—the substance of that identity was often largely incidental to the process of incorporation itself. The latter depended, in the first instance, on a legal status; cultural content could be, has been, invented, added, thickened after the fact. However, and here is the *seventh* dimension, there are cases that invert this: First Peoples whose corporate history began not with casino capitalism but with the commodification of their cultural products and practices; specifically, with the rendition of those products and practices into intellectual property. Take the Indians of Zia Pueblo who, in the 1990s, demanded financial compensation from New Mexico for the unauthorized use of their "ancient" sun design on state flags and auto license plates (Brown 1998:197). The figure, with its elaborate symbolism and distinctive spiritual powers, they argued, has always been their wholly, and holy, owned cultural property; the Zia—the name, incidentally, means "sun"—did not actually use the term "natural copyright," but they might as well have. Not only was the appropriation of their sacred emblem blatantly illegal, went the claim. It was both an affront to their dignity and a blasphemy that could unleash misfortune upon them. In 1999, they approached the US Patent and Trade Office to seek protection for the image; the State, meanwhile, acknowledged publicly that it did indeed "belong to the Pueblo of Zia" and had been "appropriated . . . without proper permission or authority." No compensation was offered, however, and none was legally enjoined. To add fuel to the controversy, the figure is also used as a logo by any number of corporations. According to a CNN report, "it even appears on portable toilets." Said a Zia elder at the time, if companies are going to use it, "we want royalties."[66] Perhaps in an act of preemption, the business sector has begun to pay. In 2005, according to the Tribal Administrator, Peter Pino, some twenty corporations, including Southwest Airlines, had decided that "the pueblo should be compensated, [and] had begun donating money to a trust fund in exchange for using the Zia sign."[67]

Incorporation by means of the commodification of culture, *qua* intellectual property, may equally derive from material practices. Thus, again in New Mexico, the Indians of Sandoval County—where the Zia Pueblo happens to be located—are famed for cultivating a ritually valued variety of dark corn that is at once highly nutritious and drought-resistant. As Pinel and Evans (1994:45) tell the story, this variety, which was developed over centuries, became the basis of a gourmet health food fad in the 1980s. Consequently, in 1984, a company, Five Sandoval Indian Pueblos, Inc. (FSIP), was established to manage the interests that accrued from it. Finding the seed hard to patent—it is too easy to hybridize commercially—FSIP moved into the production and packaging of trademarked agrigoods, most notably *Hopi Blue*. Here, in other words, an ethno-corporation arose from distilling local knowledge into a brand that, in turn, sedimented sociologically into an ethnic federation; just the thing Chanock pointed to in his observation that " . . . sustainable cultures are those which brand best" (above, p. 18).

There are many other instances that could as easily be cited in illustration of the general point. We have already noted the remarkable one of the Navajo, who long refused casino capitalism but whose commercial agrigoods, among them Navajo Pride, are now touted as "the foundation of [their] culture"—and, by virtue of their sale to Cuba, are said to be productive not merely of ethno-nationhood and its economy but of sovereignty itself. In a similar vein, in the American Midwest, wild rice "is now widely recognized by the federal courts as . . . cultural property." It is being branded by a few First Peoples, who appear by this means to be charting their own pathways to incorporation;[68] although, now that this foodstuff is being subjected to genetic modification, some Indians in Wisconsin may end up in the same situation as the South Asian farmers who were told that they had to buy back—from RiceTec, under a US patent—the right to grow the *basmati* that their ancestors had harvested for generations (above, p. 36). In the circumstances, it seems prescient that, in the 1990s, an Inter-Apache Summit on Repatriation (1995:4; see Brown 1998:202) gave notice of its sovereign title to all "symbols, beliefs, customs, ideas, and other physical and spiritual objects and concepts" associated with their lifeways. Therein lies the route to Ethnicity, Inc. via the *koporaet* of culture. We use the Melanesian vernacular here. Remember it? Phonemically, it seems to elide "copyright" with "corporate"—an elision that reminds us how localized the global regime of intellectual property has become, how capaciously it serves to redefine parochial knowledge as capital.

What this seventh dimension makes evident is that there is, at the core of our account, an unresolved dialectic. It is the dialectic between, on one hand, the incorporation of identity and, on the other, the commodification of culture. These two things, it will be patent by now, are not the same. Ethnicity, Inc. may have its genesis in either of them. Hence the contrast between (i) those First Peoples that became ethno-corporations by virtue of being shareholders in commercial enterprise enabled by their sovereign legal status, and (ii) those that began their corporate life by virtue of the rendering into intellectual property of their vernacular signs, knowledges, or practices. As it turns out, the contrapuntal relationship between these two tendencies, the proclivity of each to seek to complete itself in the other, holds the key to the resolution of our unfolding narrative. Herein lies the point of our excursion into Native America; an excursion, we repeat, *not* intended as an accomplished analysis of its identity economies—given our lack of specialist expertise, that would be pure hubris—but as means of arriving at a clearer understanding of the phenomena that, together, constitute Ethnicity, Inc. And of the problems at once conceptual and empirical, ethical and analytic, political and philosophical that they pose.

Which brings us to a Tale of Two Ethnicities, a tale that explores the two sides of the dialectic—and the manner of their often incomplete, rarely unambiguous, invariably convoluted, sometimes troubling resolution. It is a tale that returns us to where we began: southern Africa.

FIVE

A Tale of Two Ethnicities

The First: Into the Land of the Rising San

The first of the two stories takes us to the edges of the Kalahari Desert, to the Land of the San, known more commonly,
and pejoratively, as Bushmen. It involves the *Hoodia gordonii*
cactus, which San call *xhoba*. By all accounts, they have im-
bibed cuttings of this plant since time immemorial. In the
past, they relied on it to stay their appetites as they tracked
game across the inhospitable reaches of the desert. These
days, it seems, it is used more to stave off the effects of poverty. Long before the colonial epoch, San suffered subjuga-
tion and servitude at the hands of the neighboring Tswana
and other peoples. But their predicament has worsened
steadily over the past two hundred or so years, continuing,
with some exceptions (Hitchcock et al. 2006:1–3), into the
postcolonial period: severely stigmatized, victims of various
forms of violence, driven off ancestral lands by governments
and settlers, prey to illness and alcohol, their numbers had
diminished greatly by the end of the twentieth century. In
South Africa, most San communities had disintegrated, their
surviving members having dispersed into the immiserated
"coloured" population of the Northern Cape Province. In
Botswana, the Bushmen—they prefer this term to Basarwa,
their official designation (see chapter 3, n. 62)—have long
complained of unremittingly harsh, often brutal treatment
at the hands of the state. The forced removal of the Gana and
the Gwi from the Central Kalahari Game Reserve in 2002,
a policy that has been explained in a wide variety of ways,[1]
provoked a torrent of criticism from outside. It also called

forth material and moral support for the hunter-gatherers from Cultural Survival, Amnesty International, and the International Land Fund.[2] And from the Navajo of Arizona, with whom, as a fellow ethno-nation, they have had formal exchanges.[3] It was this expulsion that led to the high court case we mentioned earlier; the case that ended in pyrrhic victory for the Bushmen when, in 2006, they won the right to return to the land, only to have the authorities refuse to provide essential services on it, thereby making it extremely inhospitable.[4] While the Botswana government has consistently justified its actions in positive terms—claiming, apart from all else, that the resettlement of the Basarwa would enable the extension of health care, education, water, and the like—its critics read things rather differently. So antagonistic is the state toward these people, says Nigel Crawhall (in Evans 2003:13), that it appears "embarrassed" by their very existence (cf. Taylor 2007:3); indeed, would prefer them not to exist at all. In Namibia, where there are six San groupings, some have fared a little better, although there, too, a good number are in imminent danger of being dispossessed, yet again in the name of land reform; so-called Western Bushmanland, it is said, is being coveted by their more powerful white neighbors.[5]

The hoodia saga was to have—is having, will yet have—a palpable impact on the plight of these San populations. Essentially, it is an alchemic tale, a tale of primitive poverty–turned–modern prosperity by means of intellectual property, a tale riddled with twists and turns, ambiguities and ambivalence, promise and problems, a tale still far from complete. All because a rather plain plant has the capacity to suppress human hunger. And because San hunter-gatherers, well known for their ecological intelligence, learned this a long time ago. Not surprisingly, in an era in which mass mediation plies the spaces between fantasy and reality—like "nature," media hate a vacuum—the story, once it became known, unleashed a global reportorial frenzy (Evans 2003:12–16). In the USA, CBS's *60 Minutes* attested to the efficacy of hoodia, speaking in awe of its potential for the fat-fighting industry.[6] In Britain, the BBC told how it had sent one of its correspondents "far out into the desert," home of "one of the world's oldest and most primitive tribes," to sample the "extremely ugly cactus" that "kills the appetite, attacks obesity . . . [and] has no known side effects";[7] this, apparently, by acting on the hypothalamus and elevating blood sugar levels at ten thousand times the rate of glucose, thereby creating the sensation of fullness without food intake. Fascinated by these facts, celebrity slimmers like Oprah Winfrey announced, portentously, that the "secret of weight loss," might lie "deep in the . . . Kalahari."[8] E-mail inboxes and internet Web pages throbbed with money-back offers for the miraculous "diet pill breakthrough," soon followed by messages warning of cut-price fakes. Enthusiasts even conjured images of "Hoodia cafés in London and New York" that would serve cactus salads and "mak[e] Kalahari bushmen millionaires."[9]

By most accounts, the story began in 1963, when the Council for Scientific and Industrial Research (CSIR)—a leading research-and-development organ of the South African government, committed "to improv[ing] national competitiveness in the global economy[10]—became interested in the medicinal properties of *Hoodia gordonii;* it is here that the state, primary "shareholder" in the CSIR, enters into our analytic frame. As it happens, a Dutch ethno-biologist had done some early research on the plant, which he published in 1937. But the attention of the CSIR seems only to have been drawn fully to it in the early 1960s; this as a result of repeated reports of its use by San trackers in the South African Defence Force. These men, who had been conscripted by the SADF in its counter-insurgency campaigns against liberation armies deployed across Namibia and Angola, were said to be capable of almost miraculous feats of endurance, moving over huge distances for long periods without the provisions required by ordinary soldiers. CSIR scientists tested the appetite-suppressant capacities of the cactus, corroborated them, and identified their bioactive component. In 1996, the council took out a patent on that component under the label P57.

P57 was then licensed to Phytopharm, a small British pharmaceutical company, whose double-blind trials confirmed the CSIR's claims—and whose share price rose palpably in the expectation that hoodia could well revolutionize the £6 billion market in slimming aids.[11] Phytopharm swiftly sold the rights to develop the drug to Pfizer for $21 million; ironic perhaps, since *xhoba* is said by San to have aphrodisiac properties similar to those of the company's other sensational product, Viagra.[12] In fact, Phytopharm initially dubbed the cactus "the next Viagra."[13] It is at this point that the story becomes especially interesting. Not, we hasten to add, because of its sexual subplot. That died away quickly; the pharmas seem to have decided to bank their investment on female vanity, not male potency. It becomes interesting here because this where Ethnicity, Inc. makes its appearance.

The San first heard about the patent when Phytofarm announced P57 to the media. Or, more precisely, it was Roger Chennells,[14] a savvy human rights lawyer from South Africa, who was alerted to the matter by a journalist from the *Observer* in Britain. He told Chennells that the head of Phytofarm, Richard Dixey, had claimed that the San, the peoples from whom knowledge of the effects of hoodia had derived, were extinct. At the time, Chennells was representing those peoples, including Dawid Kruiper and the ‡Khomani then living at Kagga Kamma, in a land dispute (Robins 2003:12–14; Isaacson 2002; see chapter 2, n.15). The ‡Khomani sought, and in 1999 were awarded, some 65,000 acres on the fringes of the Kgalagadi Transfrontier Park, a large game reserve along the borderland between South Africa and Botswana.[15] In the course of this litigation there emerged an NGO, the South African San Institute (SASI), itself mandated by the Working Group of Indigenous Minorities in Southern Africa (WIMSA), which had been formed in 1996 to coordinate efforts to pursue San rights and recognition in five southern African countries; efforts stimulated by the heady climate of policulturalism that flourished in the region after 1994.[16] The array of institutions, associations, and organizations that grew up around San identity at this time, exacerbated by various territorial and other conflicts, is quite bewildering.[17]

Suffice it to say that Chennells, who also served as a consultant to WIMSA, concluded quickly that "the Bushmen" were victims of biopiracy at the hands of Phytofarm. He was aware that the eventual commercial return on the patent, in royalty income, could run into many millions, even billions, of dollars; its value in the US market alone was estimated, some five years ago, to be $3 billion per annum (Evans 2003:16). The effort to assert their intellectual property rights, though, required that "the" San assert a collective social and legal identity, for which purposes a San Council was established in 2001 under the tutelage of WIMSA. Its objective was to set up national representative bodies in each country of the subcontinent—but to do so in a manner that recognized and accommodated the distinctive hunter-gatherer legacy of democratic leadership, a legacy that differed sharply from those of neighboring peoples with hierarchical models of chiefship (14). The South African San Council, first of these national bodies to be founded, declared its immediate intention to secure "access rights to heritage sites, building links with museums and parks, identifying other San groups in southern Africa and negotiating entrance to the House of Chiefs in South Africa."[18] The two sides of Ethnicity, Inc., the incorporation of identity and the commodification of culture, were both implicated in the genesis of a newly institutionalized "Bushman" political identity.

Richard Dixey had surely been disingenuous in asserting that the "Bushmen" were extinct. The advantages to Phytofarm of his claim were obvious enough.[19] When the South African San Council protested to the CSIR, its representatives conceded that an injustice had indeed been done, that indigenous rights had been violated, and that some restitution was in order. Dixey confessed "embarrassment" at his earlier statements.

He was delighted, he said, that "these Bushmen . . . [were] still around"; he also insisted, indignantly, that *he* was being ripped off by other pharmaceutical manufacturers, which were using his company's trial results to market products that contained too little hoodia to be effective.[20] In the meantime, the San followed their complaint to the CSIR with a threat to file suit: they sought to recover some measure of benefit from the bonanza predicted for P57. After a flurry of acrimonious exchanges, the CSIR formally recognized that, by virtue of their traditional knowledge of the plant, the San were the rightful custodians of *Hoodia gordonii;* reciprocally, the San accepted that the CSIR had a right to patent P57, thereby protecting the work its scientists had done in isolating the bio-active component of the cactus. On this basis, a formal agreement was signed in March 2003; it stipulated that 6 percent of all royalty income was to be paid to the San Hoodia Trust. In endorsing the accord, the San Council said that these funds might help it buy back lost land;[21] a spokesperson for WIMSA later intimated that an initial sum of R600,000, then just shy of $100,000, had been distributed to the Trust.[22] Roger Chennells also expressed his approval: not only was the agreement a "significant step" toward profit-sharing, but it also showed how vernacular expertise could valuably be exploited in partnership with technologically-skilled national agencies.[23]

Not everyone was as enthusiastic. It was said at the time, for example, that some of the details of the deal between the CSIR and the drug companies remained confidential; also, that the agreement might not have laid out adequately the precise proportions of different kinds of income stream actually payable to the San. But spokespersons for the South African government hailed the agreement as a breakthrough in the difficult business of "attribut(ing) intellectual property to groups . . . as opposed to individuals."[24] This problem, they stressed, had been eased by the official adoption in 2004 of an Indigenous Knowledge Systems Policy, an initiative fostered by the efforts of the World Intellectual Property Organization, by the Convention of Biodiversity (see above), and by others to coordinate dialogue between developed and developing nations in respect of rights in intellectual property, genetic resources, and vernacular knowledge.[25] Again, the move was not uncontroversial. Representatives of Biowatch South Africa, a local NGO dedicated to investigating the commercialization of biodiversity, expressed concern: rather than respond to the country's unique cultural and biological heritage—by formulating a bold new approach to the marketing of indigenous expertise—the policy merely operated securely within existing intellectual property law. The latter, it added, has long been faulted for favoring state and corporate interests. And for failing to deal satisfactorily either with complex questions of collective ownership or with the innovative application of "traditional" cultural products and practices.[26]

Some time after the announcement of the accord between the San and the CSIR, Pfizer pulled out as licensee. It said that P57 was proving too difficult to synthesize and manufacture in pill form. This has not stopped several other companies from marketing what they claim to be hoodia supplements, however, gracing them with names, like *Bushman's Secret,* that seem quite shamelessly to offer the consumer exotic, purloined knowledge. *Bushman's Secret,* also the title of a critical documentary on the topic (see n.22), has a logo that features a brilliantly flowering cactus against desert dunes; it is advertised by its makers, Medical Supplies International SA, as a "synergistic natural appetite management blend," whose major components are chromium and calcium pyruvate, not hoodia. All unauthorized products that include the cactus among their ingredients violate the international benefit-sharing guidelines governing traditional knowledge and natural resources laid out by the Convention for Biological Diversity; consequently, efforts are being made to tighten up regulatory measures and put a stop to piracy.[27] This may turn out to be a daunting task. Already the enormous surge in collecting has placed the plant on South Africa's endangered species list; so much so, that the South African (and Namibian) authorities—once again, the state makes its regulatory role apparent—insist that all exports be accompanied by a CITES certificate, CITES being the Convention on International Trade in Endangered Species of Wild Fauna and Flora. There have even been calls for a total ban on allowing hoodia to leave the country until illegal harvesting can be controlled.[28] Meanwhile, Phytofarm has teamed up with Unilever, the latter replacing Pfizer as licensee of P57, in the quest to market the substance in its natural from. It has proclaimed its intention to have "meal-replacement" products on supermarket shelves by 2008; at the time of writing, it was about to unveil a major publicity campaign. The company has also set about establishing *xhoba* plantations in South Africa, aiming to bring "100s of acres" under cultivation in the near future.[29] What is more, the San Hoodia Trust, set up to manage incoming funds under the aegis of WIMSA, has received its first royalties and has begun to address the problems of distributing them among San in South Africa, Namibia, and Botswana. It plans to divide the revenue into quarters, Roger Chennells told us, retaining 25 percent for its own administrative costs and passing on the rest, equally, to the other three existing San Councils, one per country. It has also initiated its own lawsuits against illicit producers, of which it is aware of at least twenty-six. Taken together, all this suggests that the San *people,* as ethno-corporation, is taking increasingly articulate shape.[30]

As it happens, Richard Dixey had not been altogether wrong—or alone—in speaking of the demise of the San in the late 1990s. Not long after, in 2005, Survival International, having involved itself deeply in the struggle over the removal of Basarwa from the Central Kalahari Game Reserve, declared, ominously, that "the last chapter in the 200-year-old genocide of the Bushmen" was underway in Botswana (but cf. Wilmsen 2008).[31] The San may not have been extinct *sensu stricto,* but their *socio*cide—or, more properly, *ethno*cide—*was* quite far advanced. Having been cast out of the social ecology which had framed their existence for as long as there is historical record, "they" did not evince much by way of collective being. Aside from struggling remnants of older bands, they had dispersed either into the impoverished racial spaces of South African "colouredness" or into the farm-worker and indigent underclasses of Botswana and Namibia.[32] But the assertion of intellectual property— coupled, significantly, with the land claims that occurred in tandem with it—has had the effect of sedimenting and articulating San "identity." And of giving it ever "thicker," ever more textured substance.

One symptom of this, which by now should not surprise us, has been an increase in conflicts arising out of people accusing each other of "not being San":[33] out of, so to speak, bloody-mindedness over the measure of blood required for a genealogically legitimate claim to belong. In several places there have been efforts to denounce "fake bushmen" (Robins 2003:12), to "out" them in both senses of the term; for example, after his exit from Kagga Kamma, Dawid Kruiper accused its proprietors of "passing off Coloureds as Bushmen" for tourists who knew no better.[34] The question of consanguinity has also infused the attempts of self-designated "traditionalists" to distinguish themselves from their "adulterated," Westernized kin, especially where access to shared resources are involved: hence, for example, the struggle over the Community Property Association set up, in the Northern Cape Province of South Africa, to manage the land restituted to the ǂKhomani along the edges of the Kgalagadi Transfrontier Park—which "non-traditionalists" appear at the moment to control (Chennells 2006:20).

At the same time, more positively, the "thickening" of ethnic identity here has manifested itself in a campaign to revive San languages, reversing a long history of decline in the numbers of surviving speakers; also in the collection of genealogies, for which youth are being trained, in order to create a population register. In addition, the South African San Institute has actively concerned itself with "the development of [vernacular] culture, the management of cultural resources, and the encouragement of cultural practices," particularly among those who had left them behind; to this end, courses on "skills based in indigenous knowledge systems" have been provided for people resettled on the Kalahari fringe. SASI has also initiated a "cultural resources auditing and management" exercise; designed indigenously controlled "income generation projects that use cultural and intellectual [capital] in a sustainable manner"; and set in motion a legal program to "create an appropriate rights base" for the San, thereby to protect their interests. Interests like the revenue from *xhoba,* the hoodia cactus. And like !Xaus Lodge, a luxury game camp in the Kgalagadi Transfrontier Park owned by, and operated for, the ǂKhomani and Mier. Here paying guests are "drawn into the fascinating rituals, traditions and historical cultures of the Bushmen," accompany "the legendary 'hunter gatherers' as they track through the desert following the spoor of animals [and] identify plants they can eat or harvest for medicinal purposes," and listen to "their legends of the night sky, their health secrets and the history of their culture and existence."[35] Thus it is that a band of San who, just a few years ago, performed themselves as menial employees of Kagga Kamma (above, p. 10), now do so as "proprietors" in the service economy, specializing in the sale of their own brand of exotic experience. They may or may not still see themselves as "animals of nature." But they certainly *have* become entrepreneurs of culture, entrepreneurs for and of themselves. *!Xaus,* as in *!Xaus* Lodge, incidentally, translates as "heart."

In sum, the "newly empowered San" are being encouraged, from within and outside, "to channel their cultural heritage into useful modern day crafts"—and into enterprises—"that provide them with dignity and capital"; this in the words of Betta Steyn, director of Khomani Sisen ("We Work"), a project dedicated to the creation of "income generating opportunities for the descendants of the 'First People' of southern Africa [by making and marketing] products inspired by ancient Bushman traditions."[36] The "channel[ing of] cultural heritage" in pursuit of "dignity and capital" has had some unexpected uptake: Sanscape One, for instance, a collaboration in which a few of the "world's best and most diverse producers and remix artists" were invited to render "raw and undiluted" recordings of the healing songs of the San into "an album which . . . highlights [their] plight." If, we would add, in a rather Sanitized version,[37] "[their] plight" being described without any historical nuance whatever. In similar vein, if not by precisely the same means, Art of Africa, a commercial venture in South Africa with the subtitle *Bushmen Art,* is intended both as "an income generating initiative"—that term again—and as a way for the former hunter-gatherers "to rediscover their identity." With its flagship gallery located opposite the Iziko South African Museum in Cape Town, a national institution that once upon a time exhibited Bushmen in primitivist diorama, the company supplies a small coterie of artists with materials and then markets their work. It takes care to explain that, after costs and a profit margin are deducted, the remaining income is divided between the (un-named) NGO that runs the operation in situ and the producers themselves; the latter receive 70 percent, of which they give up most "to support the community," this being a "sharing society." The nobility of the exercise, though, is said to lie in the fact that the artists "have taken the burden of [becoming] the record keepers of their race," of its "painful and abusive past," their paintings being an illustration of "the heart and soul" of their people. True, it is impossible "to insinuate a direct thread between the work produced today and the rock art of several thousand years ago." But that does not vitiate the point of this "journey," whose object for the San is to "preserve a rich cultural heritage" by "evok[ing] past memories . . . [through] visualization, trance, dancing . . . and group therapy sessions."[38]

Such assertions of San-ness put pressure on "the natives" to enact a legible form of primordialism. Some of them, encouraged by zealous NGOs, have responded willingly. Thus, when the ǂKhomani won their land claim back in 1999, it was assumed by many local observers that they would "[slip] back into their ancient lifestyle." But their *real* challenge, said Mandla Seleoane of the South African Human Sciences Research Council, was to "bring their knowledge . . . to the surface" and negotiate "a sustainable link to mainstream knowledge systems."[39] It is a challenge that SASI has itself taken up. "The commercial value of heritage," stated its Annual Review for 2001–2, "requires indigenous people to protect this body of knowledge as a newly appreciated asset."[40] Note how, wittingly or not, those who advocate empowerment by resort to alienable heritage tend to employ the lexicon of intellectual property. They prefer talk of "knowledge" (local, translatable know-how *about* the world) to "culture" (particular ways of being-and-acting *in* the world). From this perspective, "culturalist" conceptions of identity exoticize in the wrong way, invoking pristine archetypes that ignore dynamic, untidy realities of life on the ground (Sylvain 2005:362; cf. Robins 2001); among them, the fact that San—most of whom live as menial workers on farms—have few rights of any kind. Which is why WIMSA (recall, the Working Group of Indigenous Minorities in Southern Africa) has come to espouse a modern indigeneity that involves *both* the husbanding of "indigenous knowledge systems" and the "creation of a cyber economy in the Kalahari,"[41] *both* a putatively primordial patrimony and evolving, alienable cultural practices. Their endeavors have been assisted by the promulgation in 2004 of an Indigenous Knowledge Systems Policy aimed at nurturing the "holders and practitioners" of that knowledge "as living libraries" (see above).[42] There are signs, moreover, that its idiom is infusing everyday talk, especially at moments when San strive to craft a means of survival by presenting what remains of their "ancient life-style" in terms recognizable to others. "My language was twisted out of me," says Dawid Kruiper, pulling on his ear to show how colonial bosses insisted that San workers spoke only Afrikaans, now their lingua franca. "But my knowledge (kennis) of nature is lodged deep inside of me, and cannot [rightfully] be taken away."[43] Kennis, here, has come to connote both naturally endowed ingenuity—Kruiper, recall, sees himself as a "child of nature"—and inherited expertise, both of them marketable assets.

Talk of San "empowerment" by means of cultural property may leave unanswered the vexed question of who exactly is being empowered—and in what manner.[44] But there is undeniable evidence of a "growing sense of San pride." Also of a direct connection between "the xhoba pills," land claims, and the construction of a collective future.[45] When we asked Roger Chennells whether a new ethnic identity had emerged out of the process of incorporation, he answered in the affirmative. Emphatically so. Notwithstanding the autonomic tendency to speak of Sanness as if it always-already existed, there is strong ground for his view. The presumption that "the San" actually had a shared identity—or an ethno-sociology—prior to the colonial dispersal of a complex, linguistically diverse population of hunter-gatherers is highly problematic. Who or what "they" were or were not remains a matter of bitter scholarly contention.[46] Nor only of scholarly contention. Of practical ethno-politics as well. Back in 1999, Chennells had stressed the necessity "to make . . . a reality [of] the myth that we . . . created in order to win the land claim"; the myth, that is, "that there is a community of ‡Khomani San" (Robins 2003:13; emphasis in the original). And this pertains to just one "Bushman" grouping, not "the San" at large. He went on to remark that some of the voting members of this "potential entity" did "not know what it meant to be San"; many were unsure whether to "join the club."[47] As the South African Human Rights Commission (2004:5) was to observe five years later, the ‡Khomani land claim "involved reinventing a community from dispersed San descendants." Even here it is unclear what, for purposes of reinvention, "San" denotes: again, sans historical substance, it bespeaks no more than a spectral, speculative connection to peoples said once to have inhabited the Kalahari and its fringes, peoples about whose collective self-identifications little is known for certain. To the degree that the ethnic term has a genealogy at all, its broader frame of reference is *Khoisan,* an early twentieth-century ethnological label for non-Bantu-speaking "societies" (cf. Schapera 1930). It is one from which San leaders now seek to disentangle themselves—because it "waters down" their distinctive heritage.[48]

The fact that "the San" may be a relatively recent social construction matters not at all any more, at least not outside the academy. Their putative presence in the past has sedimented into an assertive, future-oriented ethno-corporation. What is more, "San" has become a term of *self*-reference. It describes an imagined cultural community, a *nasie* ("nation"; cf. Sylvain 2005:362) that is itself transnational, straddling three of the countries of the subcontinent. Securing title to territory, as we have seen, has been integral to its (re)birth. Said Thabo Mbeki, as he put his presidential signature to the historic ǂKhomani restitution accord, the "return" of the land would do more than merely enable the "ingathering" of a people scattered across rural ghettos, white farms, and impoverished communal areas. It would also allow collective dreams "to take root" (Mgoqi n.d.; cf. Robins 2001:834). Similarly Roy Sesana, speaking for the two hundred and forty-three Bushmen who charged the Botswana government with removing them forcibly from their central Kalahari home: "Land is the first building block of one's culture [; . . . it] makes the person what he is. It is what he does with [territory] that defines his identity. It connects him to his past . . . to the ancestors."[49] Which, recall, is more or less what Moringe Parkipuny said of the Maasai (above, p. 81).

But the role of land in materializing the imagined *nasie,* fundamental as it may be to its mythic and moral rebirth, is turning out to be more complicated than either Thabo Mbeki or Roy Sesana might have anticipated. The process of restitution has embraced only a small proportion of those who now identify as San. Few have taken up residence or sustain themselves on that land. Yet fewer still are thought likely to do so in times to come. Those ǂKhomani who did "return" to the Andriesvale-Askam region of the Northern Cape after 1999 (see chapter 2, n.15), says the South African Human Rights Commission (2004:5), suffer dire poverty and ongoing police harassment; the state, it adds, has failed entirely to provide services or to support the community in its resettlement.[50] ǂKhomani may now be proprietors of the fancy !Xaus Lodge, transient residence for affluent visitors, but their own living conditions remain abject in the extreme. Much the same is true, as we have seen, of the Bushmen recently allowed to return to the Central Kalahari Game Reserve in Botswana. Not only is their own situation precarious, but, according to outside observers, it would "take major investment to make the park viable for tourism":

animal populations are allegedly down to a bare 5 percent of their levels of three decades ago, having been decimated by government-built fences, which cut beasts off from their migration routes and water sources.[51] Little chance any time soon, then, of a Kalahari Sun resort—in the mode of either the Mohegan Sun in Connecticut or Sun City in South Africa— although there *has* been muted talk of rights to mineral wealth in the dim and distant future.

Land may be the "first building block of . . . culture." But a "sustainable" San identity has come to rest, more proximately, upon ethno-business driven by intellectual property. Most of all, by *xhoba*. While a few of the former foragers have begun to cultivate the cactus on their own reclaimed soil, its real promise lies in revenues from others who plant or process it, thereby adding value elsewhere to its raw potential. In addition to its patent agreement with the Council for Scientific and Industrial Research (and, through it, with the licensees, Phytofarm and Unilever), WIMSA has also signed a benefit-sharing accord with the (predominantly white) Southern African Hoodia Growers (Pty) Ltd., which has undertaken to "market [its] products with a clear logo showing that the San have received a benefit . . ."[52] Deals of this sort, it has been said, could well "decide the fate [of the Bushmen] as a people."[53] Some of them, we have seen, entertain the hope that the new wealth will enable a buy-back of more of their "ancestral" land, thus to restore their "life, rights, traditions and *nasiegheid*" (nationhood). Hoodia, it seems, has become a panacea for peoplehood. And all the cultural aspirations made manifest in the various plans, programs, and projects of the San Institute. Whether it will actually realize that hope, of course, remains uncertain.

The dream of repossessing ancestral real estate completes a historical cycle of the long run. Territory, the link between past and future, is the sovereign ground, metaphorical as much as material, on which a putatively "primordial," enterprise-honed identity may congeal, on which culture may be "thickened," on which nationhood may "take place." And on which it may husband its affective economy. The link between hoodia and the land, whether or not the former actually grows on the latter, has become metonymic for many San themselves of their prospects of survival. As a concrete abstraction, the cactus portends its own fragility in the heat of the market, a market fraught with all the temptations and the risks of rapacious exploitation. If it is harvested too greedily, says Ouma /Una, an elderly San woman, if it is chopped out without care or respect, "the plant will be finished, and we'll be extinct along with it."[54] The Land of the Rising San would be emptied of life for once and for all.

The hoodia saga appears to be blazing a trail for others in southern

Africa. In March 2007, the local press announced that "several rural Venda communities" in Limpopo Province are about to "be thrust headlong into the First World economy, thanks to *mpesu* tree bark," an especially powerful aphrodisiac hitherto unknown to outsiders. Dubbed the "African Viagra"—*xhoba*, remember, was held to have similar attributes—it is said to have been successfully tested at the University of Pretoria. The "pharmaceutical companies," declared the *Sunday Times*, will soon "fight . . . for the right to develop" *mpesu* as a commercial product. Already, however, Venda efforts to enter the market in cultural bio-products, and to navigate the ethno-economy, are mired in dispute.[55] Over land.

The story continues. . . .

The Second: Of Mines and Men, or The Story of a South African Firm

The second of our Tales involves the Bafokeng, a Tswana nation situated in the North West Province of South Africa. We introduced them earlier: they are the people made wealthy by platinum, the people whose kings are spoken of as CEOs, the people who are actually referred to by the mining industry and the mass media as "Bafokeng, Inc."[56] And, sometimes, as "the Richest Tribe in Africa" (see, e.g., Manson and Mbenga 2003; Kriel n.d.). Their preferred self-designation, however, is "Royal Bafokeng Nation" (*morafe*). The history of their incorporation, an extraordinary epic by any measure, has its genesis more than a century-and-a-half ago, long before the dawn of the Age of Platinum.

It begins with land. Specifically, with the loss of Bafokeng territory to the expansion of white settlers from the late 1830s onwards. These settlers were part of the northward migration of some ten thousand Boers, forebears of the modern Afrikaners; apartheid historiography typically ascribes their so-called *Great Trek* to an heroic effort to escape British colonial control. Its motivation and consequences are still a matter of bitter contention and will no doubt be debated for as long as the "new" South Africa takes to re-write its past from the vantage of the postcolony. But what *is* indisputable is that, between the early 1840s and the mid-1860s, the Bafokeng, whose ethno-history goes back to the twelfth century (Bozzoli 1991:29; Kriel n.d:14; Mokgatle 1971; Breutz 1953), were rendered effectively landless. The modes of expropriation deployed by the Boers will be readily familiar to anyone with even a rudimentary knowledge of other settler colonialisms: a proclamation of suzerainty over large tracts of land by right of conquest after the defeat of "warlike" tribes in the region (Theal 1893); the reduction of the commonage of local peoples to privately owned farms; and the enactment of racially grounded laws, under the First Boer Constitution of the Transvaal Republic (1844), that debarred "natives" from "any right to possess immovable property in freehold" (Royal Bafokeng Nation 2003.).[57]

So bereft were Bafokeng of a *lebensraum* that, by the late 1860s, in order to survive at all as a chiefdom, they were compelled to rent farms from the very people who had dispossessed them. J. S. Bergh (2005), who has documented their territorial travails *in extenso*—and whose narrative tallies quite closely with one prepared for the Nation by its Legal and Corporate Affairs Department (Royal Bafokeng Nation 2003)—recounts how their ruler, Chief Mokgatle Thethe, came to realize that, if his people were ever to repossess their land or to have a future as an independent polity, they would have to find means to buy it back (cf. also Cook n.d.[a]:5–6). As Ngwenya (2000:124) has suggested, the Bafokeng, who by this time had considerable experience with the cash economy, Christianity, and colonialism, were decidedly forward-looking in their understanding of the changing face of the subcontinent. With the connivance of Christian evangelists—a Hermannsburg mission had been established in 1867— Chief Mokgatle went quietly about buying up settler farms. To avoid legal restrictions imposed by the Transvaal Republic on African land ownership, the chief elicited the proxy of two of the German missionaries: the farms were registered in their names, primarily in that of the Reverend Christoph Penzhorn.[58] In order to pay for them, the Bafokeng relied on income earned as agricultural laborers on white farms. Patently, however, this source of capital accumulation was never going to be sufficient unto their ambitions, a cold fact that might have put an end to the scheme. But, toward the end of the 1860s, diamonds were discovered in the South African heartland, not too far to the south. With the rapid growth of the diggings in and around Kimberley, Mokgatle seized the opportunity to send young men as contract workers, had them deposit a portion of their wages—£5 (GBP) per contract to be precise—into a designated fund, and used the cash to execute a long string of real estate transactions (Coertze 1990:40; Ngwenya 2000:124; Bergh 2005).

The "question of native property rights in land" (Stals 1972) was to arise yet again, albeit in passing, after what is often referred to as "the First Anglo-Boer War" or the "Anglo-Transvaal War" (1880–1881)—which ended in victory for the Afrikaners, in the return to them of control over the Transvaal, and in raised anxieties on the part of indigenous communities about the security of their real estate. But the Pretoria Convention of 1881, signed in the wake of the British defeat, sustained the changes that had been enacted by the previous administration: under article 13, "natives" would still be "allowed to acquire land," with the provision that its "grant or transfer" would "in every case be made to and registered in the name of the Native Location Commission . . . in trust for such natives." Later, the Native Location Commission gave way, as trustee, to the Superintendent of Native Affairs (Bergh 2005:113). Interestingly, in the historical consciousness of Bafokeng, the ensuing decade, the 1880s, are recollected as a time of security and relative economic prosperity (Bozzoli 1991:41–42).

There are a number of addenda to this early part of the story, some minor and some major, but none of them alter its gist from the vantage of Chief Mokgatle's people: another war between Britain and the Boers, further changes of regime, a slight amendment in title whereby the superintendent became the commissioner of Native affairs, a hiccup or two in the transfer of the titles held by the missionaries, and in 1913, the notorious Native Land Act, which made it extremely difficult for blacks to acquire any more freehold (Plaatje 1916; cf. Cook n.d.[a]:6). Through all of this, however, Bafokeng territory—some twenty-two farms purchased in the nineteenth century, another eleven in the twentieth (Manson and Mbenga 2003:25)—continued to be recognized as "immovable property" owned outright by "the tribe" under the trusteeship of the state. It was to lay the foundation for the emergence, many decades later, of the Royal Bafokeng Nation *qua* "ethnic corporation" (Cook and Harding n.d.:3). A consolidated land mass of some two thousand square kilometers, roughly the size of Rhode Island, that territory today is home to approximately three hundred thousand people living in twenty-nine villages. As in all Tswana polities, belonging here is reckoned in the first instance by patrilineal descent, although outsiders may be and have long been absorbed into the *morafe* at the pleasure of its ruler (Schapera 1952).

The late colonial history of South Africa was to present the Bafokeng with new difficulties arising out of their real estate, although their nineteenth-century exertions—by establishing them "as a private, corporate owner"—would enable them to defend it when the going got tough (Cook n.d.[a]:6 et passim). In 1924, the Merensky Reef was discovered beneath their territory: a layer of rock in the Bushveld Igneous Complex, it is said to contain much of the world's supply of platinum group metals, along with rich deposits of chromite and graphite (Cawthorn 1999; Viljoen 1999). The announcement led to a frantic scramble for mineral rights, to a lot of unscrupulous deal making, and in the end, to resort to law on the part of Bafokeng to safeguard their interests (Manson and Mbenga 2003:27). This time, however, it was not the state that turned out to be the enemy. As the secretary of mines put it in an official memorandum, there was no question that "the ownership of both surface and mineral rights of the land in question . . . vests in the said Bafokeng Tribe, [which] land therefore ranks as private land for the purposes of the mineral laws" (Royal Bafokeng Nation 2003). Under the Native Trust and Land Act of 1936, prospecting on ground owned by "natives" could only be conducted with permission of the minister of Native affairs. But, according to the historical accounting of the Royal Bafokeng Nation itself, government never dealt with the negotiation of mineral rights, or anything else regarding tribal terrain, in a manner contrary to its wishes. Not, at least, until the late 1980s. Of which more in a moment.

For all the scramble for contracts, little platinum mining was actually done until the 1960s, apparently because it was expensive and technically difficult. But advances in modes of extraction and rises in the price of the metal, especially with its use in exhaust pollution control, changed that. In 1968, as Manson and Mbenga (2003:27f) and Cook (n.d.[a], n.d.[b]) tell it—we composite their accounts for present purposes—Impala Prospecting Company, a subsidiary of Gencor, itself a major player in the emerging "Afrikaner capitalist class," entered into a prospecting accord with the Bafokeng. Nine years later, having concluded that the venture would be profitable and having gone through the bureaucratic steps to obtain the necessary permits, Impala Platinum ("Implats") took up leases on two mining areas. Under the contract, which was negotiated on behalf of the Bafokeng by a minister of the national government, putatively with their approval, the "tribe" was to be paid 13 percent of the taxable income that accrued to each operation. Such royalty agreements are notoriously open to manipulation on the part of mining companies: apart from all else, they can determine distributions by calculating their "taxable income" in a variety of ways. In the event, the Bafokeng only received their first revenues in 1978. Moreover, their remuneration was fairly paltry relative to shareholder dividends. By the mid-1980s, their king, Edward Lebone Molotlegi I—who, as it happens, we ourselves came to know well in the late 1960s—was far from satisfied with the prevailing arrangements. When the company approached him in 1985 with a request to open up a third area, known as "the Deeps," he demanded an adjustment to the contract. Implats agreed to raise royalties to just under 15 percent and, after a prolonged exchange about previous compensation, added a one-off payment of R4.5 million.

At more or less the same juncture, King Lebone concluded a deal with another company, Bafokeng Minerals, of which the Bafokeng and their ruler owned 25 percent, for the right to mine the new site. This led to conflict with Impala, which appealed to the Bophuthatswana government—

the administration of the ethnic "homeland" (bantustan) created for the Tswana in the 1970s by the apartheid regime[59]—to support it in its dealings with the monarch. Initially, the difference was over valuable geological research findings about platinum deposits in the area that Bafokeng Minerals wanted from Implats in order to open its operation at "the Deeps." But it hardened into a struggle over mineral rights *tout court* between the "tribe" on one hand and the mining company and bantustan authorities on the other. Inevitably, all parties resorted to lawfare.[60] The outcome was devastating to the Bafokeng. The judge ruled, perversely, that, far from being "corporate private owners," they did not possess the land at all: that Lucas Mangope, president of Bophuthatswana, in his capacity as head of state, had taken over the authority to administer it from the former South African minister of Bantu affairs. Who had taken it over, some time in the past, from the commissioner of Native affairs, who had taken it over from the superintendent of Native affairs, who had taken it over from the Native Location Commission, which had taken it over from the "responsible representative" of the British government of the Transvaal, the first colonial trustee to hold the land that the Bafokeng had bought back for themselves after its expropriation. It did not help that King Lebone Molotlegi, as we knew from what he told us in the early 1970s, despised Mangope, the "Dog of the Boers" (Lawrence and Manson 1994). Further conflict between the two men, with the imbrication of the mining conglomerate, was inevitable. Inevitable, too, was the fact that the hostilities would implicate the corporate standing of the Bafokeng *morafe*.

And then there was an attempted coup.

In early 1988, an effort was made to overthrow President Mangope by the leader of the opposition People's Progressive Party of Bophuthatswana, Rocky Malebana-Metsing. As he explained to an amnesty hearing of the South African Truth and Reconciliation Commission in 2001, the object was to put an end to "the tyranny of [a] state which *inter alia* refused to grant its citizens civil liberties and basic human rights."[61] In fact, the rebels disapproved of the very existence of Bophuthatswana (Jones 1999:600). The coup failed, however, not least because Malebana-Metsing, who wanted to avoid bloodshed, forewarned the South African authorities about it, asking them not to intervene. Which, of course, they did: they dispatched their military. As a result, the uprising was quelled with, well, dispatch. Speaking retrospectively of the incident, many Tswana joked to us about the humiliations inflicted on Mangope: stories were told, most of them unverified, of how he and his white mistress were hauled, in pajamas, from their bed at a local resort—owned, incidentally, by Sol Kerzner, the white South African casino-capitalist of Mohegan Sun fame in the

USA (see above, p. 72). But, for the Bafokeng, and for Bafokeng, Inc., the failed rebellion had a deep down side. Perhaps because its instigators were all allegedly from this "tribe"—whose ruling lineage was known never to have favored the creation of a Tswana homeland (Cook n.d.[b])—the commissioner of police accused King Lebone of being a "pioneer of the coup" (Manson and Mbenga 2003:31). Serially harassed, interrogated, briefly incarcerated, and under sustained threat, he fled to Botswana.

In the vacuum opened up by his absence, Mangope connived to have Lebone's compliant younger brother, Mokgwaro, installed as ruler, to sideline the powerful wife of the exiled king by resort to repeated intimidation, and in 1990, to sign a contract on behalf of the Bafokeng with Implats. According to the annual report of the company, that agreement gave it the right to mine existing areas until the platinum was exhausted; also to prospect, and later to acquire a lease for, "the Deeps," paying a 16 percent royalty on taxable income when the site was developed. The Bafokeng, in return, acquired the right to purchase up to 7 percent of equity in Impala (:33–37).[62] What followed was a decade of exquisitely Byzantine lawfare. King Lebone and his people took action against Bophuthatswana and Implats—both of whom retaliated by whatever means they could. These struggles were played out against the backdrop of the end of apartheid, a second, successful uprising against Mangope, the return and death of the monarch, and a corporate merger between Impala and Lonrho, the large British company. And they entailed a bewildering rush of suits and countersuits as the litigants fought over court jurisdictions, the legitimacy of the Bophuthatswana bench, arcane special pleas, and technical issues of *local standi, res judicata,* and the like. Boardroom guerilla tactics and media campaigns added to the noise. So did labile share prices and extralegal attempts to negotiate new mining contracts.

Suffice it to say that, in 1999, a settlement was finally reached.[63] It specified that the Bafokeng would receive 22 percent of taxable income on operations in all areas; that a minimum of 1 percent of the gross selling price of all metals mined on their terrain would be paid to them; that they would be allocated a million shares in Impala Platinum Holdings, an equity stake worth R100 million; and, finally, that they could nominate a person to the board of the company. This, after the strenuous efforts of Implats to contest their ownership of the land, to subvert them as an active corporate partner, and to minimize any and all payments to them, was a comprehensive victory for the Bafokeng. It had been a bitter battle, a battle not just about minerals but about racial capitalism itself. At the funeral of King Lebone I, Nelson Mandela called it a "landmark" in the "struggle of black people against . . . oppression."[64] The road if not to freedom then certainly to a platinum fiefdom had been long indeed. But, in the end, the money spent all those years ago to repossess the land had paid off handsomely. True, the social costs accrued along the way were exorbitant. So, too, were the costs of lawfare, largely because, under apartheid, the law was rarely fair. On the other hand, so adept at it did the Bafokeng become that, as one journalist put it, "their traditional weapon" is now litigation, "not the knobkerrie [club]."[65] Which is just as well, since they have also had to stave off the implementation of new statutes—a Mineral and Petroleum Resources and Development Act (2002), and other measures—whose objective, if not quite to nationalize the mining industry, is to "recognize the . . . right of the State to exercise sovereignty over all its mineral and petroleum resources."[66] Thus far the Bafokeng have been successful.

Since the watershed victory over Implats, the growth of Bafokeng, Inc.—the nation, that is, in its commercial aspect—has been little short of breathtaking. Already in 1999, *Enterprise,* an industry magazine, referred to this "ethnic corporation" (Cook n.d. [b]) as a "major business," reported its diversification into eight large-scale ventures, and commented approvingly on the management executives that it had hired.[67] Note here the simultaneous separation and blurring of *morafe* and company, at once the same thing and, sociologically and administratively, distinct; the point will turn out to be crucial. Soon after, *Mining Weekly,* noting that mineral royalties had paid for extensive infrastructure in the kingdom—such things as tarred roads and bridges, water reservoirs and reticulation, civic buildings and clinics, electricity and educational facilities—spoke of "the Bafokeng" as "a living example of African business acumen and black empowerment." It gave as collateral evidence the fact that, in order to create employment and to become self-sufficient over the long run, they had established such medium-size concerns as Bafokeng Civil Works, Bafokeng Brick and Tile, Bafokeng Chrome, Phokeng Bakery, and Bafokeng Plaza, a shopping center, and were actively looking for further business opportunities.[68]

Which they have found, in plenitude. The Royal Bafokeng Nation (RBN) has accumulated substantial stakes in, is paid royalties by, or otherwise benefits from a hugely complex array of enterprises. This goes back to before the legal settlement with Implats: in 1996, it bought its first large firm, Murray Construction—renamed Bafokeng Construction—and, with it, acquired several substantial contracts, including one to upgrade Durban Harbor and another to build the Bakwena Platinum Corridor, together worth R4.2 billion; the company was to be liquidated six years later in order to "distribute its assets among small businesses run by

members of the community, [thus] to make way for the emerging construction industry within [Bafokeng]."[69] In 1998, the RBN established a
profitable joint venture with Mobil Oil SA, a subsidiary of Exxon; registered as Phoka Petroleum, it was to distribute Mobil products in the North
West Province. A second partnership with Mobil, Geared Lubricants (Pty)
Ltd.—it specializes in "gear management" for mining and industry—followed in 2001.[70] That year also saw Bafokeng, Inc. purchase 22 percent of
the listed company SA Chrome and Alloys, an equity holding of R100 million; later, its stake was to grow to just under 35 percent —whereupon SA
Chrome became Merafe Resources.[71] *Merafe,* plural of *morafe,* is Setswana
for "nations." *Merafe* also has a joint venture with the signature Swiss corporation, Xstrata, premier producer of ferrochrome on the planet. Then,
in 2002, the RBN reached agreements with two mining conglomerates
to open up new operations—the first with Anglo-American Platinum
(AngloPlat), the world's largest platinum concern, the second with Rustenburg Platinum—in both of which it obtained a 50 percent share, each
valued at R2 billion. Not only that: the announcement of the Rustenburg
deal added that "the Bafokeng are now actively involved in the mining
industry and are no longer the passive recipients of royalties. [They] in-
tend to develop this involvement aggressively in the future . . ."[72] In that
same financial year, 2001–2, note, their holding in Implats yielded R80
million [c. $12 million].[73] By 2004, their mining contracts with their two
major partners, Implats and AngloPlats, netted them $65 million (Cook
2005a:129).

Nor is this the end of the story. Take 2005. In April, Royal Bafokeng Finance purchased 10 percent of SA Eagle Insurance from Zurich Financial
Services, a Swiss-based multinational;[74] in August, it took over 20 percent
of Astrapak, South Africa's second-largest packaging business,[75] and 51
percent of Concor Holdings, a concrete manufacturer;[76] in October, it acquired Fraser Alexander, a mining services company with operations both
in southern Africa and in Chile.[77] But December was even busier. First,
the Bafokeng assumed possession of 26 percent of MB Technologies, an IT
conglomerate.[78] Then, a week later, Royal Bafokeng Finances made its first
investment in agriculture, buying over 27 percent of Senwes, a large seed
vendor.[79] And finally, under the national policy of Black Economic Empowerment (BEE), it became the "empowerment partner" in Impala Refin-
ery Services, a subsidiary of Implats, taking a 49 percent stake, worth R5
billion, for R3.4 billion;[80] by these means was an affirmative action strategy intended to redress long-standing *racial* inequalities made to serve
specific *ethnic* interests. Nine months later, the RBN was to take yet another great leap forward, again at the hands of Implats, which decided to

pay it R10.6 billion, equivalent to all future platinum royalties owed. This was to be converted into 9.4 million shares, which made the Bafokeng the largest stockholder in the company (Cook and Harding n.d.:1).

There have been other deals. Our inventory is far from exhaustive.[81] A majority stake in a top-ranking Premier Soccer League team, to be renamed Platinum Stars,[82] is one of the latest of which we are aware.[83] But it is hard to keep up. The business of Bafokeng, Inc., its diversified portfolio recently estimated at R20 billion ($2.7 billion; Cook and Harding n.d.), seems to expand with every passing month. That business, the consolidated ethno-prise of the Royal Bafokeng Nation, has several branches, with a complex internal structure.

Government of the RBN, like the protection of its sovereign concerns, is vested in the kingship and its executive, legislative, and judicial institutions. In this regard, it is like all other Tswana polities. With one exception: *kgosi,* the vernacular term here for "king," is translated in those other polities as "chief." The difference, patently, reflects the singular wealth and stature of the Bafokeng. Their monarchy, a dynastic patriline, sits at the apex of a *morafe* consisting of seventy-two wards spread across the twenty-nine villages. Each falls under a hereditary headman (*kgosana*), who, in turn, is assisted by one or two "wardmen" (*bannakgotla*). These personages, together, compose a Council of Headmen, with which the king meets regularly to discuss public affairs. In the past, a smaller Tribal Council of some sixteen members, nominated by the headmen and appointed by the *kgosi,* served as a "policy and decision making body in relation to day to day operations" of governance (Royal Bafokeng Nation 2003). In 1996, however, it was replaced by an Executive Council made up of elected representatives from each of the villages; now, under the Traditional Leadership and Governance Framework Act (no. 41 of 2003), it has five regionally elected representatives and six named by the king.[84] The Executive Council and Council of Headmen combine in a Supreme Council that, formally, comprises the Bafokeng legislature (Cook n.d.[a]:4). It is charged with all major decision making, including "the disposition of tribal land or mineral rights" (Royal Bafokeng Nation 2003) and the approval of the annual budget of the *morafe.* In addition, a mass assembly, called *kgotha kgothe,* is summoned twice a year to deliberate on communal concerns. It is also a forum of public oversight: in the long-standing spirit of indigenous democracy, even the intricate financial maneuvers of the Bafokeng money managers—of whom more in a moment—are presented to this gathering for cross-questioning, comment, and critique. All of which makes *kgotha kgothe,* these days, appear for all the world like a corporate shareholder meeting. In a fairly literal manner of speaking, of course, it is.[85]

The bureaucratic side of everyday governance is entrusted to the Royal Bafokeng Administration. Until 2006, the RBA existed in parallel with a Royal Bafokeng Economic Board, which was charged with the task of development; lately, that task has passed to the Local Economic Development Department of the RBA. In addition, a Royal Bafokeng Institute was created in 2007. It has two missions: to improve the quality of education in the kingdom, and tellingly, to "consolidate [its] national identity." But the real corporate engine of Bafokeng, Inc., the source of its income stream, is Royal Bafokeng Holdings (Pty) Ltd. This ethno-national corporation, centered in Johannesburg, is run much like other global finance houses with fiduciary responsibility to its shareholders. While it reports to the *morafe* at *kgotha kgothe,* it is staffed by a CEO and money managers who would be at home in any boardroom in the world. Other than three white executives and Leruo, who is chairman of the company, its senior personnel include four Tswana directors. Of them, none are Bafokeng royals; they are lawyers and accountants, all trained in South Africa, with substantial business experience on the national scene. One, Steve Phiri, is also the highly successful CEO of Merafe Resources; another, Thabo Mokgatlha, is director of the Treasury Department of the Royal Bafokeng Nation, and, thus, the point of articulation between the income stream generated by Royal Bafokeng Holdings and the expenditure stream back to the *morafe.* In theory—there are many ambiguities in practice—that expenditure stream emanates from RBH, is directed to the Royal Bafokeng Administration under a budget approved by the Supreme Council, and is then allocated, via the Treasury Department, to the Local Economic Development Department, the Royal Bafokeng Institute, and various other official recipients and programs.

In overseeing the Nation's business operations, RBH is an umbrella for four subsidiaries—Royal Bafokeng Industrial Holdings, Royal Bafokeng Resources, Royal Bafokeng Management Services, and Royal Bafokeng Finance—each of which looks after the companies, investments, and interests relevant to its domain. Royal Bafokeng Capital, to add another branch to this corporate tree, is, according to its Web site, "a professional shareholder, [that] aims to become the corporate empowerment partner of choice for small- to medium-sized owner-operated and managed businesses." It is itself owned and operated by Royal Bafokeng Ventures, which, in turn, falls under Royal Bafokeng Finance. At one point in time, Royal Bafokeng Resources was said to be heading for a listing on the stock market as a *public* company.[86] Were it to do so, "the Bafokeng" would become the ultimate ethno-prise: one in whose finances, and futures, it would actually be possible to purchase shares.[87]

As this suggests, the Royal Bafokeng Nation has become an "ethnic brand" of sorts (Cook and Harding n.d.:22). It has also been the subject of professional corporate branding. As we mentioned much earlier, Enterprise IG has been "building an identity" for the RBN and, in particular, for three of the subsidiaries of Royal Bafokeng Holdings. The point? There are several. When it was designed, the logo of the Royal Bafokeng Economic Board, for example, was meant, explicitly, to "act as a catalyst for economic growth within the community," to perform "the promise of empowerment for a pioneering nation," and to represent "the intentions of the Bafokeng," fusing elements of indigeneity with the promise of responsible profit in such a way as to attract "investors, entrepreneurs and government." In this last respect, it has succeeded beyond all expectation: although not beyond garnering minority benefits, like BEE deals, Bafokeng business has clearly taken off into the realms of mainstream megaenterprise. But it remains rooted in communal capital; as the Royal Bafokeng Nation itself puts it, Bafokeng is "a traditional community that is leveraging corporate investments and participation in the bigger economy to meet its developmental needs, without losing its traditional footing" (Royal Bafokeng Nation 2007:9). That, precisely, is the logic of the logo. Its visual image, the crocodile, totem of the *morafe,* was chosen because ostensibly it symbolizes an "awakening in nature" and "the long journey of Bafokeng heritage." It is the "signature" of their corporate being, at once located in the vernacular yet "global [in its] feel."[88] Perhaps a tad too global: two multinational companies, Singapore Crocodile International and Lacoste clothing, are already engaged in an acrimonious legal tussle in the Chinese courts over rights to use the same animal in their trademarks.[89]

The question arises here—as everywhere with Ethnicity, Inc.—of who benefits from the ethno-branding, the incorporation of identity, the accumulation of capital. And what impact it has had on belonging. Thus far, the strategy of the Royal Bafokeng Nation has not been to distribute its income to its ethno-citizenry as individuals, families, kinship groups, or anything else. It has, instead, invested it and spent it in the name of the *morafe.* As Matome Modipa, then CEO of the Royal Bafokeng Economic Board, told the financial media in 2005, "This is a . . . community-driven operation. We are using the traditional model where everyone has a right to the [shared] wealth to ensure we grow our people."[90] Hence the strong focus on development and infrastructure. Also on job creation. Like the sponsoring, in 2004, of fifty youths to study for a Certificate of General

Travel under the Royal Bafokeng Skill Development and Job Creation Programme, thus to equip them to enter the tourist economy. And a bursary initiative, for which R30 million has been allocated, to support those who, after completing high school, seek further education or vocational training in anything from hairdressing to advanced physics.

There is, however, considerable debate within and beyond the RBN about the deployment and distribution of its assets. *The Policy Gap,* a study of the platinum boom in the North West published in August 2007 by the Bench Marks Foundation,[91] argues that, while the mining companies pump out huge amounts in dividends to shareholders across the world, and while some Bafokeng are much better off now, the vast majority endure "unacceptable" poverty: 39 percent are unemployed, almost 95 percent use pit latrines, less than 13 percent have electricity. What is more, the report says, mining operations have so damaged the ecology that it is impossible to subsist on agriculture any longer.[92] It might have added, as well, that educational facilities here are said to be among the very worst in the North West Province. No wonder one of Inge Kriel's (n.d.) informants spoke of their *morafe* as "a rich nation of poor people." Kriel puts joblessness even higher, at almost 50 percent. She says that most "ordinary" Bafokeng, aware that "the windfall is not trickling down," do not understand "the leadership's emphasis on investments in order to maximize their profits" (13). Nor, as other Tswana have commented to us, might they all grasp the complicated relationship between Bafokeng-as-nation and Bafokeng-as-corporation—a relationship with any number of gray areas—let alone who benefits from the ambiguity. Many of them think that, to the extent that there is "trickle down," it accrues mainly to those connected with the royal family and other power brokers. There is also a fairly common belief, usually expressed sotto voce, that the royals themselves are being enriched by Bafokeng, Inc., that income from RBH flows directly into their bank accounts or that they receive handsome stipends. This is in spite of the audit culture that has come to infuse Bafokeng, Inc., a culture that, even though it may not always be honored, places an almost obsessive stress on transparency;[93] also in spite of the fact that those Molotlegis involved in the affairs of the nation, primarily the king and his mother, appear to be paid relatively modest salaries, do not live extravagantly, are scarcely implicated in Bafokeng business except as fiduciary officers, and seem not to have squirreled away large sums of money for themselves. To be sure, Leruo's personal style owes much more to the politics of corporate responsibility than to the corporeal "politics of the belly" (Bayart 1993).

But the quiet skepticism among Bafokeng about the wealth of their ethno-nation—its true extent is hard to gauge—is not confined simply to the specter of royal riches. It also extends to the *Geist* of the *morafe:* "Not all Bafokeng approve of the trend towards positioning their king as a CEO, redefining them as shareholders, and running the community like a company," note Cook and Harding (n.d.:23). Of these clauses, the first, the "king as CEO," is especially likely to be troubling. It raises the possibility of a species of executive privilege quite foreign to the Tswana ideal of *bogosi yo bontle* ("good government"), an ideal captured in idioms of accountability: *Kgosi ke kgosi ka morafe,* all Tswana are fond of saying, "a king is king by grace of the people." Company executives, by contrast, are governed less by accountability than by accountancy, less by the sociomoral needs of a nation than by the amoral imperatives of profit. Which is why indigenous rulers in South Africa who have tried to merge the roles of "traditional" chief and business leader, like the Makuleke monarch encountered earlier (p. 14), have run into difficulties. And why Leruo, who appears keenly conscious of his mongrel office—almost but not quite an ordinary CEO, almost but not quite an ordinary king (see n. 56)—has to ply the gray area between antithetical modes of leadership, antithetical forms of legitimacy, antithetical imaginings of power.

More pragmatically, however, for him and for the financial managers of Bafokeng Inc., the answer to "a rich nation of poor people," and to populist skepticism in general, lies in Vision 2020. This is an ambitious plan to develop the *morafe* into a "self-sufficient," more fully employed, globally oriented nation by the end of the coming decade (Gray 2003:13–14); hence the reorganization of the Royal Bafokeng Administration, the creation of the new department within it devoted to development, the establishment of the Royal Bafokeng Institute, and the inauguration of various betterment programs. The king himself, keenly aware that the mineral wealth of the Merensky Reef is finite—he said as much in August 2007 to "the Bafokeng, our shareholders" in his message as chairman of the board of Royal Bafokeng Holdings (Molotlegi 2007b: 4–5)—clearly wants to make it all work. At once communally oriented *and* founded on a neoliberal faith in finance capital, Vision 2020 fuses his own two aspects as he presents himself to the world: part leopard-skinned "traditional" authority, part Armani-suited businessman, entirely a figure of Afromodernity. Whether or not it addresses the concerns of his people at large, Leruo's vision does have its patriotic Bafokeng supporters. Damaria Senne, for one. She writes a blog from Johannesburg, where she is now a journalist. Responding to an announcement that the *morafe* was soon to have IT services installed—the "tribe" is soon to be "wired," an e-newsletter is to be published, and e-governance is on the agenda for the future (Royal Bafokeng Nation 2007:13–14)—she enthused: "I'm very excited about the Royal Bafokeng Nation's plan to roll out network infrastructure and to provide free phone calls and cheap Internet access for the community I call home." This proved that its leaders had learned the importance of "holding onto the essence of who we are, learning from our tradition and culture, and using whatever resources are available to us to improve the lives of our people."[94] And to extend their ethno-citizenship into the cyber age.

"Our people." Implicit in the question of who benefits from the Wealth of the Ethno-nation is the prior one of who belongs to it. As we said, membership is conferred either by patrilineal descent or by in-migration, with the permission of the rulers of the *morafe;* allegiance to the king*ship* is stressed above all. In the past, entry and exit was fairly fluid and quite frequent. In common with the incorporation of identity elsewhere, however, the borders of Bafokeng appear to be a matter of rising concern. For one thing, the king himself has become anxious to "protect and enforce the ethnically-defined boundaries of the community for the purposes of controlling wealth" (Cook n.d.[b]); he speaks of the need to control "continued alien influx" (Molotlegi 2007c:9). But the question has also arisen with gathering force around the accommodation of non-Bafokeng who have entered the kingdom to work in the mineral economy. Most of these people, who are seen unambiguously as outsiders, have become rent-paying tenants to local families, some of whom have as many as fifteen living on their premises; others are nonpaying squatters, of whom many Bafokeng disapprove (Kriel n.d., passim). Despite the fact that it still remains possible to join the ethno-nation by formal means, the influx of strangers seems to be deepening lines of distinction around Bafokeng-ness.[95] But, because the distribution of ethno-wealth has remained communal thus far, those lines are less about individual being than about belonging, about the right to land, social resources, facilities, and the like. All the signs are that they will deepen yet further as the corporate history of Bafokeng, Inc. unfolds.

What is missing in all this? On the surface at least—Damaria Senne notwithstanding—it would seem to be the cultural element of Bafokeng cultural identity. With all the talk of Vision 2020, of finance capital and the stellar rise of Royal Bafokeng, Inc., of lawfare and long-term investment, discursive attention has been directed primarily at the business end of things. To the degree that *sefokeng,* vernacular lifeways, have featured at all, they have either been taken for granted and hence gone unspoken or they have been enunciated as very general, "thin" values, connoting little beyond such tropes as "heritage," the "community," or "wealth in people"; the sort of signifiers easily captured in Enterprise IG's logo-centric representations of Bafokeng-ness. Of late, however, there has been much more, and much more self-conscious, culture-speak. And practice.

Most notable in this respect was the enthronement of King Leruo in August 2003, a ritual moment that celebrated not merely the inauguration of a new reign but Bafokeng public ritual itself. In particular, the public ritualization of Bafokeng, Inc. The event did not try to recapitulate an ossified notion of custom. It was composed, instead, of a fusion of elements that evoked an *Afromodernist* culture under construction. Staged by VWV Group, a Johannesburg public relations firm in the "experiential marketing and communications industry" (*We Sell Greatness*),[96] its dramaturgical content was partly invented, partly assembled from a historically mediated "tradition," powerfully vernacular. The corporate side of that fusion was everywhere in evidence: the ceremony took place at the relatively new Bafokeng Sports Palace in front of an audience of sponsors, business associates, and other important personages. It had all the trappings of the unveiling of a new product line, including elaborate, distinctly nonindigenous flowers and foodstuffs in the VIP section, about which were strewn mining magazines (Cook and Harding n.d.:3–6); elsewhere in the Tswana world, the whole thing would have been held in the royal *kgotla* (court). The monarch had on a dark business suit, on top of which the vernacular side of things became visible. A leopard skin—the critical symbol of the rite, about whose colonial origins Leruo had cross-questioned us a couple of months earlier[97]—covered his upper body throughout. In fact, he first entered the ritual space with it already on, rather than, as is more often the case among Tswana, having it draped across his shoulders by his senior paternal uncle at the numinous climax of the installation (cf. Gulbrandsen 1995:424). What is more, he came into the stadium, his first public appearance in the ceremony, riding a donkey cart, expressly to perform his standing as servant of his people. There are many proverbs in Setswana that capture the submission of ruler to subjects (*moja morago kgosi,* "the king eats last"; *kgosi ke mosadi wa morafe,* "the king is wife of his nation," and, again, *kgosi ke kgosi ka morafe,* "a king is king by grace of the people"). Leruo's opening act, especially in light of his inner-outer costuming—augmented by a spear, a shield, and an axe—made visible his inscription, on this day at this time, in *sefokeng,* contemporary Bafokeng culture.

When he addressed the gathering—in particular, his own people and those VIPs who had come from the Ashanti, Sotho, Swazi, and Zulu royal families—King Leruo asked his subjects "not to abandon the ways of our forefathers" or to emulate those who "have, historically, denigrated our ways." He spoke of his regret that Bafokeng children were "not encouraged to learn about [their] culture [and] language"—and that they knew no better than to "scoff at [our] cultural practices." This echoes things he has said in other contexts as well, in which he has underscored the necessity of seeking solutions to the problems of the future in "African values," of relying on the technologies of "traditional governance," and of "reaffirming" Bafokeng heritage as the *morafe* "moves forward" into the global age of Afromodernity (see Gray 2003:14).[98] It also gives voice to what Cook and Harding (n.d.:22, 16) describe as a "longing" on the part of RBN leaders "for a more 'authentic' . . . aesthetic and affective attachment" to "culture" and "collective consciousness": We would "like to see our culture promoted more than it is," they were told during the visit of a Bafokeng delegation to the ritual-saturated Kingdom of Swaziland (13). Perhaps this is why, in its mission statement of 2007, the executive council of the RBN promised "to provide continued *promotion of respect and enhancement of our culture* and economic self sufficiency" (Royal Bafokeng Nation Executive Council 2007:4). The emphasis here, which we have added, was distinctly on *culture.*

King Leruo's mother, Mme Semane Molotlegi, the charismatic, forceful wife of King Lebone I, seems to have foreseen some of this. In 1999, she initiated a project under the banner *Maikgantsho,* "We Take Pride." Its objectives, she told the mining magazine *Enterprise,* were to foster the commitment of Bafokeng "to [their] culture and history," to "advance community development," to "create employment and small business opportunities," and to "promote tourism and reap its benefits." In other words, to put in place all the elements of Ethnicity, Inc. Pragmatically speaking, it consisted of two "initiatives," linked by a Craft Village Ramble. The more important of them was to be a Living History Village. It was to offer an "authentic representation of the ancient homestead of the Bafokeng Royal Family"; examples of vernacular household architecture; livestock pens in which indigenous breeds of stock would be on display; gardens in which "traditional" crops would be grown, stored, and prepared; and a *patlelo,* an arena at the royal court, at which would be performed songs, dances, and praise poetry. The other initiative was to be a Services Center, fringed by baobab trees and modeled on a highway oasis, at which would be sold African cuisine and crafts, heritage items, books, and other culturabilia. The ramble between the two was to be a paved walkway, one kilometer in extent, along which were to be dotted a number of "villages," each specializing in a local craft "using age-old methods and materials."[99]

Bafokeng, Inc., then, is reaching toward a sense of collective cultural being in order to fulfill itself, to suture the gap between the communal and the corporate, and to find ways of giving itself "thicker," more tangible, more emotionally compelling content. In part, this has been expressed in calls to recuperate things lost, to assure the future by recourse to the past. In part, it manifests itself in an anxious recognition: that the incorporation of an identity founded entirely on finance capital is not enough, that it raises deep existential questions, that the line between difference and indifference is gossamer thin. Which is why the invocation of "history and culture" saturates the discursive surfaces of public life here, why it seems necessary, as the charter of the new Royal Bafokeng Institute puts it, "to consolidate national identity." The point, we stress, is not that the Bafokeng monarchy and its money managers seek simply to bring "ancient" ways back to life, thus to give an outer costume of African custom to a thriving business. Nor is it just to sustain the profitable tension between ethno-capital and ordinary enterprise. The matter is much more complicated, much more affect-laden. And its temporality is very much of the present. "Tradition is not static," says Mme Molotlegi. "Everyone has to adapt."[100] To the global age, that is. The Age of Afromodernity, the Age of Ethnicity, Inc. Little wonder that, in 2003, King Leruo—an architect by training, and a pilot with an impressive capacity to look at the world from above—approached another architect, a young American with a practice in Singapore, to draw a physical plan for an "Afro-Modern" nation; specifically, a plan that would take vernacular forms and introject them into a futurescape, where possible recommissioning waste from the platinum mines. The young American was our son, Joshua Comaroff, who had spent the second year of his life living in a Tswana village just across the border.

Running the San and the Bafokeng together, the dialectic at the heart of Ethnicity, Inc., reveals itself clearly. Each of these cases evinces the seven things—or, rather, six plus one—foreshadowed in Native America, if not in precisely the same proportions. Or in precisely the same ways. (i) Membership in both has come to be defined genealogically in the first instance, with some measure of contestation over being, belonging, and boundaries either evident or imminent. (ii) In both, commerce has been instrumental either in crystallizing or in reproducing the sociological entities ("people," "nation," "community") in which cultural identity is presumed to inhere; in their ethno-genesis, that is, or their ethno-regeneration. (iii) In both, capital and legal expertise from outside have been crucial in conjuring corporate existence into being, in animating it, and in investing the difference in which it is rooted with value. (iv) In both instances, processes of incorporation were mandated, rhetorically and legally, by appeal to that difference, but as we see in the case of the Bafokeng did not necessarily originate in its cultural *content.* (v) Both have asserted their sovereignty against the state and have either litigated against it or threatened to do so. (vi) And in both, territory—the effort to possess and protect, to reclaim and control it—has been critical in establishing an identity economy, in laying down its material, legal, political, and affective foundations, and in interpolating them into the past in order to assert rights to a future.

Observe as well, in respect of these six dimensions, the important part played by the displacement of the political into the domain of the legal. San and Bafokeng alike have fought many of their battles by means of lawfare, not putting much faith—as they might once have done, and the Bafokeng once did—in representations to conventional legislative, bureaucratic, or executive authorities. *Per contra,* some of their toughest judicial struggles have been against those very authorities. What is more, it is in the course of such struggles, conducted at the interstices of tort, intellectual property, and constitutional law, that their corporate identities have taken manifest shape. In the process, too, each has, without necessarily being aware of it, naturalized the trope of identity around which their rights have come to adhere. This is particularly striking in the case of the San. It could be argued that the biochemical effects of *Hoodia gordonii* were not discovered by "*the* San" at all—who may or may not even have existed at the time—but by hunters of the Kalahari, a class once defined, if we may be so old-fashioned, by their relationship to a mode of production. The projection of an inherent right to intellectual property ("natural copyright"? *Koporaet?*) onto "the San," a putatively primordial "community," has had the effect of *ex*tinguishing a class of producers as it *dis*tinguishes a cultural identity—not incidentally, as it does so, giving ontological primacy to the idea of identity itself. Thus, to reiterate, does ID-ology clothe itself in a neoliberal sense of the natural, the ineluctable, the right-ful. And of private property as an elemental fact of being, individual and collective.

Which takes us to the seventh dimension of Ethnicity, Inc.: the dialectic itself.

Our Tale of Two Ethnicities demonstrates how and why it is that Ethnicity, Inc. rests on a counterpoint between the incorporation of identity and the commodification of culture. Whether the process starts with the incorporation of identity, as it did with the Bafokeng, or with the commodification of cultural property, as in the case of the San, it appears to evince a drive to complete itself in the other. Thus it is that a motley population of "Bushmen," once dispersed to the point of advanced ethnocide, has become "the San People," replete with a sense of its own ethno-sociology, its own will to governance, and its own institutions to make it all real. Thus it is that the Royal Bafokeng Nation, a *morafe* in which there is the felt lack of a public culture commensurate with its political-economic being-in-the-world, is (re)turning to the vernacular in pursuit of an African modernity to inhabit. Neither is surprising. After all, Ethnicity, Inc., to the extent that it founds claims to "inherent" rights and "natural" interests on the sovereignty of difference, *does* require both the incorporation of identity and a cultural substance of sorts to realize, recognize, and accomplish itself. In this respect, it is a living tautology: Without the first, it would have no sovereign materiality; without the second, it would be indistinguishable from any other species of business enterprise.

This is exactly what we saw foreshadowed in Native America. There, as in southern Africa, Ethnicity, Inc. tends to begin, materially, with land, thence to express itself in assertions of sovereignty, which, in turn, is deployed to secure legal rights over cultural property and to expand the means of capital accumulation, thus to invest in the future. The future of ethnicity, as Contralesa concluded in 2000 (above, p. 7), *does* seem to lie in the millennial promise of ethno-futures. But it is only when the two sides of Ethnicity, Inc. are brought together, when the corporate and the cultural meet under the sign of the commodity, that those futures come clearly into focus as a telos for times to come. Vision 2020, like 20/20 vision, is bifocal; which is why San and Bafokeng seek to render their corporate and cultural identities *manifestly* indivisible. At the same time, because the dialectic always remains open-ended, always underdetermined, never fully complete, not all ethnically defined populations are caught up in it to the same degree. Even where they are deeply immersed in it, as are the San and the Bafokeng, not everyone need be equally embraced by the process. Or even embraced at all. Not everyone need "join the club" or want to see "the community [as] a company." Neither need they envisage "the company" in precisely the same way: just as Bafokeng, Inc. is built up of a series of executive-driven businesses under the hierarchical leadership of the monarchy, so the San aspire to a kind of corporation that reflects vernacular patterns of mass participation and shared responsibility. Such things, finally, are decided as much by the unruly exigencies of history, by its exceptions and excesses and externalities, as by its most powerful, monolithic forces.

SIX

Nationality, Inc., Divinity, Inc., and Other Futures

Marx's once-scandalous thesis that governments are simple business agents for international capital is today [an] obvious fact on which "liberals" and "social-ists" agree. The absolute identification of politics with the management of capi-tal is no longer the shameful secret hidden behind the "forms" of democracy; it is the openly declared truth by which our governments acquire legitimacy.
JACQUES RANCIÈRE (1999:113)

Ethnicity, Inc., we have stressed, has old roots, many prece-dents, and a few unexpected incarnations, past and present. It most obvious foreshadowing, probably, lies in the Euro-modernist nation-state itself; Weber (1968:392), for one, treated ethnic and national affiliation as similar, alike con-ceptually suspect, "political artifacts" (cf. Bayart 2005:35). Ideal-typically, at least, the hyphenated polity embraced the *Geist* of a people, bound in indivisible cultural unity, under the "great arch" of corporate governance (cf. Corri-gan and Sayer 1985); although it drew its lifeblood from af-fective attachments cast in much the same terms as those of ethnicity, namely, the idiom of genealogy and the fic-tion of nation-as-family (Weber 1968:925; Smith 1986:21; Jusdanis 1998; Povinelli 2006:197). Difference was domes-ticated, brought under the arch, by the legal-rationalist language of universal citizenship, liberal democracy, and enlightened statecraft (Broch-Due 2005:13). This imagin-ing—strongest in Europe, with its powerful metropoles, more precarious elsewhere—has become severely strained of late (above, p. 46). It has been frayed by, among other things, the irruption of claims, made in the name of identity, that give lie to the conceit of a commonweal vested in cultural homogeneity and civic kinship. With this has come an upsurge in the appeal, across the world, of "ethno-nationalism" (Hobsbawm 1992:4; Connor 1994; Offe 1993; Tambiah 1996), a vision of political being that bases belonging not on universal citizenship or on a social contract, but on ascription, cultural particularity, and shared essence. From the vantage of liberal democracy, it has long been portrayed as a primitive and irrational principle of state-making, a "premodern" or "eastern" throwback (Plamenatz 1976).[1] But these days it appears ever more to be invading civic nationalism, making the ethnic culture of dominant autochthons stand, pars pro toto, for the collective being of increasingly fragmented, heterodox populations. In short, to the degree that ethno-nationalism is becoming a common feature of neoliberal times and is insinuating itself into the heart of the liberal nation-state, it is abetting the projection of Ethnicity, Inc. onto a broader plane, giving rise to what we may dub Nationality, Inc. The fact that, archaeologically, the modernist polity was erected on the dual foundations of cultural homogeneity and corporate governance has long predisposed it to this. But the rampant branding of cultural heritage, its rendition as alienable property, and the increasing distillation of both nation and state into the vocabulary of business enterprise, gives Nationality, Inc. a distinctly contemporary twist. Indeed, it opens up an illuminating window on what *both* state and nation, and their hyphe-nation, are becoming in the New Age of Capital.

Political Artifacts and Virtual Persons: The Rise of Corporate Mercantilism

A brief step backward first, however. Or, rather, steps back and forward again. Into the corporate past and present of Nationality, Incorporated.

Corporation—minimally "a number of [people] . . . legally authorized to act as a single individual, an artificial person" (Oxford University Press 1971, 1:563)—refers to an elemental form of human combination that, over the centuries, has assumed many guises and served diverse political, religious, and economic ends. Born of a jural artifice that renders social groups into fictional persons, it thrives on a productive abstraction: a species of fetish, it has no corporeal body but acts upon the world and pursues interests as though it were a being with its own identity, rights, and legal standing. This has ensured that it has long been attributed uncanny qualities, "unlimited" life, and a host of quasi-magical, monstrous powers.[2] Corporations "can live forever," says Bleifuss (1998). "They feel no pain, . . . do not need clean air to breathe, potable water to drink or healthy food to eat. Their only goal is to grow bigger and more powerful." Taking shape as if, in many respects, they were flesh and blood, they have the capacity to behave like states—to govern, plunder, and profit—with limited accountability or constraint.

In the Roman Empire, corporations were chartered by the state for specific purposes, in which shareholders invested private funds. This model, with some later Germanic modification, was the basis for the canon law that established the medieval church as a corporate structure: a body more than the sum of its members, it could persist beyond the demise of any or all of them. Prior to the seventeenth century, European corporations were non-profit entities mandated to build institutions, such as hospitals, for the public good (Korten 1995; Bleifuss 1998). Their modern counterparts, joint stock companies, drew on these foundations to create a mode of "pseudo-government" (Pomeranz 2000), being authorized by monarchs of the mercantile era to raise capital, hire mercenaries, and launch imperial campaigns beyond the reach of individual actors, even governments; vide the British, French, and Dutch East India Companies—or the Hudson's Bay and Massachusetts Bay Companies, those "other Leviathans" that first colonized North America, facilitating the birth of state and empire in its modern form (Kelly 1999). These were private ventures, putatively in the national interest; in fact, the division of power and spoils between nation and corporate capital has, since time immemorial, been a matter of moral and political contention. While European polities tended, in the latter half of the nineteenth century, to administer their colonial possessions themselves, they also granted corporations—now understood almost exclusively as for-profit enterprises—considerable legal autonomy, allowing them to define their own objectives, limiting the liability of their shareholders, and transferring control over them from government to the courts. The ultimate irony, on the face of it, lies in the protection afforded the modern firm by the Fourteenth Amendment of the US Constitution, according to which "no state shall deprive any person of life, liberty or property without due process of law." Originally adopted to protect emancipated slaves in the hostile South, it came to be applied to businesses: in a landmark decision in California in 1886,[3] the bench defined corporations as "persons," thereby limiting their tax obligations to those of individuals. It also struck down a number of additional regulations that had constrained the actions of companies.[4]

There were efforts to reverse these measures in the decades that followed. When the economic crisis of the 1930s unsettled the gospel of laissez-faire, for example, US courts revoked the use of the Fourteenth Amendment to exempt business from government regulation. In so doing, they noted that the Constitution was concerned with the protection of liberty, not the freedom of contract.[5] Successive labor struggles and the rise of the welfare state also led to efforts to render companies more accountable to the general good. But they retained their First Amendment rights as legal persons. Their autonomy was further enhanced in the late twentieth century with the rise of neoliberalism, which encouraged the outsourcing of the functions of state to the private sector. This has revitalized the early-modern role of corporations in running hospitals and prisons, even waging war—if with a more overtly privatized profit motive. Moreover, at a time when entrepreneurialism is coming to dominate human activity, their modus operandi is being emulated across the social spectrum: in churches, charities, voluntary associations, NGOs, social movements, government itself. "The original virtual person," notes Susan Silbey, is "the quintessential post-modern actor."[6]

Of course, liberal democratic states and civic authorities have also long understood *themselves* to be corporations in a more general sense—this being reflected, for instance, in the common use of the term for municipalities (Willcock 1827). It is still in use in the United Kingdom and India. Already in the early nineteenth century, English evangelists, bearers of the civilizing mission to Africa, Asia, and elsewhere, were wont to refer to the countries of the north, collectively, as a "body of *corporate* nations" (Comaroff and Comaroff 1992:122). What is more, the political and economic dimensions of their corporatism, despite their distinct institutions, rationales, and personnel, were often hard to separate, as manifest in the close collaboration, even overlap, of state and capital, public and private interest. Colonialism, a nationalist project at once governmental and fiscal, was, from beginning to end, from genesis to revelations, just such a collaboration. Mercantilism might have waned with the rise of modern European states and the hegemony of laissez-faire. But the protection of their own economies, and the effort to establish worldwide spheres of influence, remained an integral motive for late nineteenth-century empires. Counterintuitively, perhaps, the classical doctrine of free trade also essayed the absolute advantage of specialization, including national specialization. *Portuguese* wine, *English* cloth, and the like have long histories. So, too, do "flagship companies": firms that produce and purvey "signature" goods that bear the image and imprimatur of their countries of origin.

From the first, then, Euro-modern polities have sought to mark and to market their uniqueness, their essence as embodied in both utilitarian and aesthetic objects. And to profit from so doing. Over the *longue durée,* French champagne, Italian grappa, German cars, Swiss cheese, chocolate, watches, and army knives, English . . . china, among very many other things, have become *national* products. And products productive of nationhood. Meanwhile, protectionism—some have called it "corporate mercantilism" (Chomsky 2000: 156)—continues to infuse the neoliberal global economy, forging alliances between companies and governments; it has also set up regional zones of competitive advantage, among them, the European Union and NAFTA. One symptom of this revamped, late-modern mercantilism is the fact that many national products now bear trademarks that prevent others from using their names, even where those names have become generic. Non-French champagne has now to be sold under rather less-appealing logotypes, like the brutishly descriptive "sparkling wine." Not that this has gone uncontested. Gallic protectionism has spawned the patriotic ingenuity of others in pursuit of trade-market share: South African vintners, for example, have concocted *Method Cap Classique,* itself a romantic, cryptonational reference to their Fairest Cape, the Cape of Good Hope. They have also marketed a red *vin ordinaire* labeled *Goats Do Roam*—and have managed to defend it against legal attack from the outraged producers of *Côte du Rhone.* Their distinctly antipodean sense of humor, one might add, is somewhat drier than their wine.

Struggles over culturally inflected, trademarked commodities have sometimes led to lawfare between corporate nations. Thus, in 2004, Ethiopia and Brazil entered combat over a naturally low-caffeine coffee bean, one, it is said, with huge profit potential; even more, probably, than hoodia. The Ethiopians argued that it was first found on their terrain; commercial coffee, they reminded the world, had its origin in, and derived its name from, the Kaffa region in the southwest of their country. Brazil, itself a noted "coffee culture," asserted its ownership by virtue of having uncovered the chemical properties of this latest variety and of having set in motion its development for the market.[7] Another version, this, of the troubled question of patenting nature; another, too, of the tension between birthright and the rights accruing to human innovation. Significantly, both Ethiopia and Brazil saw their entitlement to the branded beverage not just as a means to feed their national treasury but also as an assertion of their nationhood. Which seems quite a stretch in light of the fact that the beans were initially collected by a United Nations scientific mission in 1964–65; "reproductions" then went back to Ethiopia, India, Portugal, Tanzania, and Costa Rica, whence the Brazilian seeds were obtained in 1973. What is more, the Brazilian "discovery" of the properties of the plant was owed to an individual, one Paulo Mazzafera of the

Universidade Estadual de Campinas.[8] In spite of all this, the battle for its possession, as intellectual property, remained one between two corporate nation-states, both proclaiming their uniqueness as justification. To our knowledge, the dispute has not been resolved.

Nation-branding: From Machiavelli to Milton Friedman

Lately, many nation-states have formally trademarked not just their "signature" commodities but themselves. Nation-branding is becoming a globally recognized practice with its own community of theorists, consultants, and media. Simon Anholt, an "expert in the field of *image makeovers for nation-states*," recently characterized it as "national identity in the service of enhanced competitiveness."[9] An especially notable instance is Argentina, which registered a new national brand in 2006.[10] Designed by Guillermo Brea, a professor in the Faculty of Architecture at the University of Buenos Aires, the logo consists of three horizontal, intertwining waves, in blue and black, issuing from a single point of origin. Explicitly intended for "multiple interpretation," it is meant to evoke social and historical change, the sensuality of the tango, and "energy, strength, happiness, passion, vitality." Its designer—whose formal title is "chair of institutional identity"—says of it:

Country Trademark . . . will be an object of ownership of a different and heterogeneous group made up of millions of people to whom representativity is owed, lightly touching aspects as sensitive as the notion of nationality. It must also operate with equal effectiveness in both a local environment and abroad, seeking integration and unity within diversity. It responds to both rational and emotional factors, fluctuating between what is ambition and [what] exists.

The . . . Country Trademark was developed [by] trying to synthesize the main attributes that make our identity as a country in harmony with the demands that the trademark must bear . . . On this basis a multivalent sign was built . . . [It] started from a non-essentialist view of identity, [which presumes that] identity is built dynamically.

. . . We, therefore, established the notion of Argentine identity as mosaic, as juxtaposition of facts and figures, as a synthetic product of the multiple and the diverse in permanent dialectics. [It is the] trademark of a young country, whose identity is in a boiling process of construction and projects itself towards the future . . . [It] mobilizes emotional identifications. It is simple, and balanced between what is commercial and tourist; the global abstraction and its local proximity. It rides between sobriety and joy, between expressiveness and reserve, between what is modern and conservative, temporizing the South American root with the European reproduction. . . .

Argentina-as-brand brings together, in manifest synthesis, many of the diacritica, and also the contradictions, of Ethnicity, Inc.—and projects them into corporate nationhood. For one thing, its impetus is to make nationality an object of "ownership," the property of those "millions of people" who share an "emotional identification" through it. For another, the substance of that identity is not merely wrought by and for its own citizens. It is meant as well for "commercial" engagement with the "tourist," as if it were in the interaction between here and elsewhere that Argentina recognizes itself and fixes its place in the world. For a third, it is based on its South American "root[s]," on something *essentially* indigenous, yet also on a "non-essentialist view" of being: on the productive coexistence, that is, of biosubstance and choice, of what we are ("what exists") and what, through "boiling . . . construction," we might become; on the past and on a future that sounds not unlike Vision 2020. For a fourth, it rides on a "permanent dialectic" of "global abstraction" and a "local environment," of the universal and the particular, the cosmopolitan and the exotic; this by interpellating its particularity into a planetary material and moral economy under the "multivalent sign" of its national brand, itself a claim to and a guarantor of its cultural property. For a fifth, it plays heavily on the doubling, at the core of identity, of the "rational" ("reserve," "sobriety") and the affective ("emotional identification," "joy"). For a sixth, it is saturated with imagery of entrepreneurial selfhood, at once individual and collective.

At the same time—which is where Nationality, Inc. is *not* the same as Ethnicity, Inc., where its more encompassing scale becomes salient—the identity at issue here is founded, quite expressly, on hetero-nationhood, on a recognition of irreducible difference within. In fact, while it does not say it in quite these terms, the enterprise presumes the policultural nature of Argentina. Hence the image of "Argentine identity as mosaic," as a "synthetic product of the multiple and the diverse," as the accomplishment of "unity within diversity"—all this being captured, metonymically, in the concept of a "Country Trademark."

The Argentinian case is a token of a type: of the emergent model of country-as-company, its branded identity wrought at the intersection of business, government, the academy, and civil society. On the face of it, it would seem that, outside the great cosmopoles of the north, the "type" manifests itself most visibly in nation-states that (i) while they style themselves as exotic and/or marginal in some respects, (ii) have fairly substantial capitalist economies, and (iii) seek to commodify their difference by building a market niche around it. This is aptly illustrated in South Africa by an initiative, quite as remarkable as the Argentinian one, on the part of *Design Indaba* magazine in 2005. Titled, in the upper case, *BRAND THE BELOVED COUNTRY,* a somewhat flip evocation of Alan Paton's fabled antiapartheid novel of the 1940s, it commissioned "three top design agencies to pitch on Brand South Africa *and its premise of 'Real Freedom'*" (emphasis added).[11] This self-declared "Labour of Love" made postcoloniality itself—by stressing the achievements of the postapartheid democracy—part of its commodity image. Like its Latin American counterpart, it fused affect and rationality, the abstract and the concrete, genetic rootedness and nonessentialism, and saturated them all with the spirit of entrepreneurialism. This at a time when, as we have noted, the sale of culture was replacing the sale of old-fashioned labor power; when arguments raged over a proposed boycott of stores selling cheap Chinese imports; when many products and services, tourism among them (Mathers and Landau 2007), began to bear the label "Proudly South African."

The point of the initiative, self-evidently, was to sell the country, its goods, and its goodness, to all manner of consumers, citizens and strangers alike. But it also marked a shift in the very conception of nationhood, one in which the commonweal itself congeals in the brand and *its* success or failure. That shift has been starkly exemplified in the political fortunes of South Africa's most controversial citizen, Jacob Zuma, former vice-president and a candidate for the presidency in 2008. Zuma divides the population: highly popular in many quarters, he has, notoriously, been tried for and acquitted of rape, and may yet be tried for corruption. Along the way, he has alienated a large number of people by his allegedly sexist and homophobic statements—often made in the name of "culture"—and by his cavalier actions in the face of the HIV/AIDS pandemic. Against this background, a panel of local experts of diverse ideological persuasions was brought together in January 2007 to discuss the future of governance in South Africa. It agreed, as did the media, that Zuma could well be eliminated from the presidential race. Not because he had become a polarizing, divisive figure, but because of "the damage his reputation would do to the *South African brand* both across Africa and on the international stage."[12] An older species of political language would have phrased this in another way: "Bring the country into disrepute," most likely. No more. The italicized linguistic elision here bespeaks the *ontological* reduction of the nation-state *per se* to a corporation, a branch bank in the world of global capital, "Brand South Africa." In this semantic economy, difference adds value. But it cannot diverge too far from palatable prototypes. Thus far, South Africa, once a pariah, has been transformed into a highly attractive combination of aesthetic exoticism, technical sophistication, and political redemption; it has found a market niche for its uniqueness and, for the moment, looks to be a safehaven for investment. From this vantage, the antics of Jacob Zuma are an uncomfortable portent: on one hand, they evoke the ghosts of a lingering authoritarian legacy; on the other, they are a reminder that the exotic can become truly unruly. Both are taken to be bad for the business that trades under the invisible yet ubiquitous banner of South Africa, Inc.

The modernist nation might always have been a brand-under-construction, always immanently, imminently corporate. But it is becoming ever more explicitly, affirmatively, assertively so as the idiom of ethnonationalism interpellates itself into the existential core of civic being, even in the European heartland. The rise of Nationality, Inc., has had some strange consequences. Witness Jonathan Franzen's brilliant fictional caricature of the d/evolution of Lithuania into a neoliberal nightmare—or, for some perhaps, nirvana—in *The Corrections* (2001). The story has two especially memorable moments. One is when the Bank of Lithuania is swallowed up, through a Byzantine series of transactions, by a suburban finance house in Atlanta, Georgia—which then liquidates the country's hard currency reserves, and with it the national economy, to cover losses incurred in a credit card launch (112–13). The other is when, under the impact of International Monetary Fund and World Bank policies, a venerable democratic political organization turns into the Free Market Party Company, and promises, as soon as it has bought enough votes to win an election, to make "Lithuania Incorporated" into a "For-Profit Nation-State," in which foreign investors would become equity shareholders and, thereby, part of a globally dispersed citizenry of Free-Market Patriots (128, 439).[13] The first of these two moments was to be echoed, five years later by an internationally syndicated cartoon that had a TV news anchor—in front of a huge illustrated map of Australia, across which is written MACQUARRIE BANK—announcing that "Today Australia was re-named after a takeover joint venture with a private equity firm."[14]

Fiction, or prediction? While he was its president, Silvio Berlusconi, CEO extraordinaire, referred to his country as *Azienda Italia,* "Italy, the Company" (Muehlebach 2007). In similar spirit, although with quite different objectives in mind, a prominent public intellectual and political analyst, Mutahi Ngunyi, wrote a "job description" for the new Kenyan president after his landslide election in 2003. It was published in all editions of *Sunday Nation,* the country's most widely read weekend newspaper:

We want the President to operate like the chief executive of a company and . . . to ensure that the country "makes profit." In this enterprise, the citizen would be a shareholder and would be required to invest an agreed amount of money in the form of
taxes. At the end of every year, the chief executive would be called to account for his
performance . . . Mr. Kibaki, we are not looking for a prince to pamper, we are looking for a chief executive who give us our money's worth, a good return on our investment in national resources.[15]

Azienda Kenya?

Azienda Britannica, too. By 2003, it had already become commonplace
to refer to the United Kingdom, colloquially, as "Britain, *PLC*"; PLC, an
acronym for "public limited company," is "inc." in another English. Less
colloquially, more formally, the marketing of heritage in the British Isles
is vested in the hands of a national ethno-prise registered as Heritage
Great Britain PLC.[16] The equation of nation with corporation, in this context, has proceeded quite far, to the extent that it has become implicated
in mass-mediated debates about the present and future of the country:
"Welcome to Britain PLC," blared a British broadsheet in September 2000,
above an extract of George Monbiot's *Captive State* (2000), a millennial
book of revelations that announced a corporate coup d'état in an Isle once
Sceptered, now somewhat septic.[17] By 2001 the coup was so complete, its
spirit so saturating that, just before the parliamentary elections of that
year, a report in the London *Observer* concluded, "[G]overnment [has] become a matter . . . of microeconomic management. [The Labour Party]
is set to be elected as managers of Her Majesty's Public Sector, PLC."[18] In
South Africa, too, similar things are being said: its ruling party has been
called "ANC Inc." (see n. 13) and its president, Thabo Mbeki, is sometimes
referred to as the nation's "chief executive."[19] Hence Rancière's (1999:113)
observation that the "identification of politics with the management of
capital is no longer [a] shameful secret," that it is "the openly declared
truth by which . . . governments acquire legitimacy." But, as we have tried
to show, there is more at issue than merely the emergence into unembar-
rassed, plain sight of a foundational alliance between the nation-state and
business. Statecraft itself has come to be modeled ever more openly on the
rhetoric and rationale of the for-profit corporation.

Here is the crux of the matter. Corporate nationhood may be remaking
countries, more or less, in the image of the limited liability company; in
some places it is doing so with astonishing abandon and almost no attention to social costs—or, worse yet, in denial of a "social" to which any costs
may be ascribed. But, even more, it has altered the very nature of neoliberal governance, and, with it, as we note at the start of this chapter, the hy-

phenation on which the modernist polity was founded. Where, under liberal democratic orthodoxy, that hyphenation marked the articulation of nation to state, state to nation—each the dialectical and historical condition of the other's making—the neoliberal turn has seen it mark not simply their disarticulation (Appadurai 1990) but a different species of connection between them: one that grows out of the logic of corporatism itself.

There is no need, in this context, to rehearse again all that has been said about the twenty-first-century state, about so-called "government at a distance," about the workings of biopower, neoliberal technologies of rule, population making, and the like. We are concerned here with just one dimension of all these things, namely, the rise of the post-Weberian state-as-metabusiness, as a franchise in the business of superintending and licensing business. To reiterate Rancière's (1999) point: it is not that the state has never, before now, been an active economic agent on its own account, a corporate actor *an und fur sich*. It is that this aspect of its everyday life-and-labor was submerged from sight, rendered translucent, by virtue of a liberal worldview that distinguished clearly between the domain of the economy and the domain of politics. From the vantage of that worldview, government assumed tutelary guardianship over the material and moral interests of the nation; from that vantage, too, Harvey (1990:108) notes, it represented itself as an ensemble of institutions whose *raison d'être* was to embody, serve, and protect a public good against the sectarian differences contained within it. From that vantage, it portrayed its relationship to capital as "mutually determining," as neither its master nor its medium (109).

That this self-representation may have distorted the historical relationship between state and economy, that the former has always had a much more intrusive stake in the latter, is the "shameful secret" of which Rancière spoke, the "secret" that has not merely been revealed to the plain light of day but has become a matter of positive assertion, a new truth for the Brave Neo World. It is also at the heart of the Great Neoliberal Transformation as Foucault (2004; see above) had it, the shift that produced the entrepreneurial self, the shift from an epoch in which the state "monitored" the workings of the economy to one in which "the market [is] itself the organizing . . . principle underlying the state." It is an epoch in which government actually *becomes* business, in which the presumptive line between polity and economy is largely obliterated. This is why so many ethno-corporations seek empowerment via capital as well as capitols. It is also why good government *itself* is measured in terms of asset management, of success in attracting enterprise, and of the capacity to accumulate (but *not*, beyond bare necessity or the dictates of emergency, to redistribute) wealth; this by deploying the national brand to maximum effect, by acting as an incorporated vendor, by commodifying the essence of the imagined community, by protecting its commonweal (*in extremis,* through lawfare), by creating the conditions for its entrepreneurial and ethno-preneurial subjects to realize their aspirations, by treating those subjects as, above all else, stakeholders in the corporate nation. And, in this last respect, by mobilizing—as ethno-preneurs also mobilize—the capacity of its cultural objects, as they enter the market, to (re)produce, congeal, and affirm national identity. In other words, by playing off exactly the same "permanent dialectic" of the abstract and the concrete, the rational and the affective, on which all identity economies are erected.

Good government in the Brave Neo World, insofar as it responds to the imperatives of capital, also has a supply side. This it tends to manage, in variable proportions across the world, by outsourcing many of its once-upon-a-time operations—and by buying them back as services in an all-pervasive service economy. In some places, those operations extend to the very things that constituted the modernist state in the first place, the state as imagined by Max Weber and much of orthodox political sociology: the exercise of "legitimate" violence, for one, in particular, in policing, security, intelligence, incarceration, and the conduct of war; for another, the management of bare life, including allocatory decisions over health, death, disaster relief, and provision to the indigent of basic means of survival, such as housing and care. In all of these spheres, complex collaborations of government and business have arisen, linked by a shared commitment to the primacy of the private sector, to market principles, and to corporate solutions. That commitment is evident, too, in such domains as the regulation of currencies, whose value, once fixed by national exchequers, now floats free, to be determined by the workings of finance capital. Whereas government in the past legitimated itself by promising to deliver more, it now flourishes by promising less. Or at least, by redirecting its attentions to securing zones of "liberty" in which the market may operate according to its "own" imperatives, in which citizens and communities are free to "take responsibility," in which the "investment [of] national resources" yields "a good return."

In sum, effective governance is to be achieved by fulfilling precisely the kinds of prescription that Mutahi Ngunyi wrote for Kenya in 2001, the one that called, on behalf of shareholder-citizens, for the prince of the polity to become chief executive of its economy. For Machiavelli to morph into Milton Friedman, or one of his Chicago School progeny. States may still speak the language of a common good. But the semantic loading of that language has changed. Increasingly, it displaces the onus of care, of tending the moral ecology of nationhood, from government to the private sector, encouraging firms to take a lead in social spending, in investing in the cultural wealth of the nation, in dealing with its immiserated and its indigent by means of their charity, often dressed up as entrepreneurial incentive programs. This, as widely noted, has produced an ethic subsumed under the term "corporate social responsibility" (CSR; cf. Shamir 2004). Spoken in the argot of altruism, CSR is typically portrayed to shareholders as sound fiduciary practice: a credit to company reputation, it converts into immaterial asset value that, expressly, feeds the bottom line. It has also been accompanied by concerted campaigns for the introduction of "soft law"; this being a euphemism for the idea that businesses be allowed to regulate themselves by arriving at and enforcing their own norms of good conduct. Which is a call for the state to cede its ultimate function: the rule of law. Soft law and corporate social responsibility, in other words, are founded on an argument for the subjection of governance to the market. And, in its extreme forms, for the unaccountability of corporate capital to anything but itself. It is an argument in which many ruling regimes—from Angola to India, the UK to the USA—have, to greater or lesser degree, become complicit in recent times.

CSR has a direct parallel outside of the business sector. Not only are "private" citizens being importuned to "take responsibility," to bear the risks of social existence, and to inhabit the world as entrepreneurial subjects. In many nation-states, they are entreated to do voluntary, unpaid labor, especially in the domains of health, crime, employment, and education; also in looking after the elderly, the young, the physically and mentally ill, the imprisoned, the paroled, the unwaged. In Britain, this labor, together with the associations and practices to which it has given rise, has become known, formally, as the Third Sector;[20] its US equivalent is the so-called Independent Sector. In the UK It has spawned a National Council for Voluntary Organizations and is being promoted by Westminster in an effort to draw upon "untapped sources of civic energy," thus to foster "social enterprise." This last phrase is important: neoliberal voluntarism is as deeply inscribed in the entrepreneurial subject as is business. It is intended to engender a sense of "grassroots endeavor" in the "service delivery" sector, so that volunteers might do the kinds of things that the state once did—and that citizens once expected it to do in return for their taxes—in efficient, cost-effective ways. What is more, as an aspiration rapidly being made real, this newly defined sector is envisaged, potentially, as a competitive source of those services, such that local government might "commission" suppliers from it to tender for contracts at lower bids than private firms—while, simultaneously, producing immaterial value in the form of "community cohesion, emotional satisfaction, . . . [and] "moral purpose." In Italy, too, as Andrea Muehlebach (2007) has shown, voluntarism has expanded greatly, most of all among those of the "third" age, the years between retirement and infirmity. It has become the object of legal regulation, has begotten a wide array of institutions and organizations, and has acquired an ideology founded on the worth and worthiness of *un*alienated toil—thus injecting into the economy a pool of willing *free* labor that, in a curious parody of Marx, revalues conventional work, typically for younger people, by making paid jobs more scarce. All this in the cause of a common national good, a good that redounds, self-evidently, to the gross benefit of *Azienda Italia,* if not to each and every one of its stakeholders, a.k.a. citizens.

The rise of neoliberal voluntarism in many places—Britain and Italy are anything but alone in this—transforms modernist conventions of *social* responsibility into postmodern idealizations of *ethical* responsibility. And, concomitantly, the social citizen into the ethical citizen (cf. Muehlebach 2007). This might seem to return us to classic liberal theory, to its conception of moral sentiments. But neoliberal ethics are focused less on securing a state that nurtures human freedom or equality than one that underwrites and abets the "entrepreneurial and competitive behaviour of economic-rational individuals" (above, p. 50). To the extent that we have entered the era of Corporate Government and Nationality, Inc., the Euro-modern Leviathan, as *deus ex machina,* appears to be an anachronism: cumbersome, heartless, inefficient, unresponsive. This historical shift, we would argue, cannot simply be put down to the triumph of crass utilitarianism, to human greed unbound, to capitalism at its most predatory. It arises, rather, out of the apotheosis of a particularly twenty-first century perception of being-in-the-world according to which humanity, identity, affect, government, morality, sociality, theology, ethical responsibility all express their *true,* "authentic" nature in the ineluctable will to an entrepreneurialism of the self and for the self, thus to manage life it-self. And so we come full circle. The historical process that began by making corporations into living, right-bearing persons ends by conjuring living, right-bearing persons into corporate-like "private contractors," human agents who own and market their skills, their heritage, their embodied capital.[21]

Variations on the Theme of Corporate Nationhood

Here, then, is where the parallel between Ethnicity, Inc., and Nationality, Inc., reaches bedrock. Both situate themselves in what, these days, is taken to be the true nature of people and things: in the forms of affect, interest, and ethical being that flow from the entrepreneurship of selves, singular and/or collective. In building their corporate identities on that "nature," both treat corporateness less as a metaphor of social organization—one, following Fortes (1953; see above), that sutured genealogically related human bodies into bodies politic—than as a concrete legal reality. Ethnicity may seem closer to the core of everyday life than does nationality, hence more substantial, more real. As we have already noted, nationhood has both to encompass internal heterodoxy and to subsume it within a superordinate one-ness, as a result of which it may submerge its *own* sense of ethno-cultural particularity in a civic conception of citizenship; which is how, for example, "Britishness" and liberal democracy, the particular and the universal, come to suffuse each other in the ideological scaffolding of the United Kingdom. But both ethnicity and nationality, in their contemporary guise, depend on the interplay of blood, culture, substance, sovereignty. And both may claim a natural copyright over their heritage-as-property: property that appears to be highly replicable without losing its aura; property whose commodification often adds value to, rather than cheapens, identity; property that, however widely it circulates at the behest of the market, typically resists the abstraction of its essence into pure exchange value or the reduction of its exuberant, messy particularity to bland ordinariness. Property, also, that fuses genetic endowment with human creativity, that may be protected by lawfare, that erases the distinction between economic, moral, and symbolic capital— and that, to the degree that it is a source of empowerment, transforms identity from the object of either a politics or an economics into the object of a political-economy.

At the same time, precisely because nationality differs in scale from ethnicity, the way in which states manage their corporate existence varies, especially with respect to the husbanding of their homegrown, branded commodities.

At one extreme are China and Russia, both of which seek to fuse market liberalization with highly centralized governance, thereby pushing Nationality, Inc., and government-as-business to unprecedented levels. In Russia, business and government have become so "intertwined" that, in June 2006, the US *Financial Times* suggested that its ruling elite had turned "Russia, Inc.," into a fully "corporate state."[22] Similar things have been said many times, both before and since. They are usually exemplified with reference to the rise of Gazprom, now the second largest energy supplier on the planet after Exxon Mobil.[23] The business, 51 percent owned by the Kremlin, is run under the close oversight of the presidency.

Vitaly Vasiliev, chief executive of Gazprom Marketing and Trading, has taken pains to claim that it is *not* a government enterprise but an ordinary "commercial company." Few are convinced. The chairman of its board at the time of writing was Dmitri Medvedev, who was also a deputy prime minister and was to become head of state after Putin. What is more, Gazprom is "part of a wider pattern of centralizing power in the hands of the President and his closest associates." By one account, some 40 percent of the economy—the figure seems steadily to be going up—is now under the management of state-controlled firms.[24] A few months after the *Financial Times* feature, the *Washington Post* carried a story under the banner headline "Kremlin Inc. Widening Control over Industry." It told of the takeover of a huge titanium plant and raised the possibility that renationalization might soon reach further into the energy sector, diamonds, metallurgy, and machine building. The burden of the piece was to make the argument that, in its effort to become a major player in various world markets, the Russian state was deploying economic power for political ends and political power for economic ends;[25] a prime case of "corporate mercantilism," this, in all but name. As important, its exertions have been intended, specifically, to *produce* patriotism. They seek to reassert difference, to revive an emotion-laden identity economy, and to foster the growth of a national brand—in the wake of what the ruling regime sees as the enervating, flattening effects of global capitalism in the years after the fall of the Soviet Union.

Not only is a sense of renewed pride being cultivated by Nationality, Inc. It is also being given affective voice in such things as the Young Democratic Antifascist Movement, Nashi, the "patriotic vanguard of a powerful new Russia."[26] Its cadres, we are told, see their futures if not in government itself, then in "state-owned companies such as Gazprom." For them, in other words, the route to a fully realized identity appears to lie in the nation-as-corporation: in the choice to express their essential Russian-ness by working for a private-sector firm that bears the brand of their country, a firm, moreover, that has become an instrument of its foreign policy—which, as the *Washington Post* implied in linking economic power to political ends here, is being conducted, under Russia, Inc., *primarily* by means of business.

Thus, to take an internationally notorious instance, in 2005 Gazprom, a major provider of natural gas to Ukraine, announced that it was to quadruple its prices with almost immediate effect. The Ukrainian government did not object to a raise *per se*—it had been paying well below the going rate—but to the suddenness with which the change was to be imposed. It responded by, among other things, proposing that the transit of Russian gas through its territory en route to Western Europe, previously remunerated in kind, now be paid for in hard currency. The ensuing conflict led to Gazprom cutting off all supplies to its neighbor in January 2006. After some hard bargaining, an agreement was reached and has subsequently been breeched; the politics of supply-and-sanction continue to this day. This has convinced many analysts in Europe that the Russians, who have insisted all along that their actions are motivated entirely by economics, have been using their brute resource power to impose their political will on a regime that has proven broadly unsympathetic to them. That has certainly been the case in the Kremlin's dealings with the USA. When tensions with President George Bush arose over trade and human rights at a G8 conference in July 2006—this after America had opposed Russia's membership in the World Trade Organization—President Putin ensured that US oil companies were kept out of a lucrative gas field then under development in the Barents Sea.[27]

Predictably, then, when Gazprom announced its intention to take over Centrica, the parent company of British Gas, disquiet was voiced in England, all the more so since the Russian "giant" had already purchased Pennine Natural Gas, a small retail firm in the same industry. According to one widely canvassed and hotly debated view, the Centrica initiative posed a threat to the *national* integrity and economic *sovereignty* of the United Kingdom.[28] At the time, to add further to local anxieties, Rosneft, the Russian *state* oil company, was in process of being listed on the London Stock Exchange; the chair of its board of directors, as the British media were quick to point out, was President Putin's deputy chief of staff.[29] To make matters even murkier, it was mired in dispute over having allegedly "stolen" Yuganskneftegaz, the operating arm of Yukos, a rival, privately founded oil company, and having laundered the proceeds at the behest of Russia, Inc. More recently, British anxieties over Russian fiscal expansionism has been echoed by the European Union. In the summer of 2007, it was announced that the EU was to "impose [controls] on state-owned funds"—they are referred to, tellingly, as sovereign wealth funds—that "take stakes in flagship European companies." The free flow of finance capital may be deemed an unvarnished good in the new global economy. But these funds "induce fear" because they are suspected of being, well, the *political* instruments of corporate states.[30] When they come from the likes of Abu Dhabi or Singapore, whose Government of Singapore Investment Corp. (GIC) is a wholly state-owned operation, they may or may not be a cause of great concern.[31] But they certainly are when they emanate from Russia or China.

Those two nations—two of the world's largest and the two with the longest histories of planned economies—have accomplished their own versions of country-as-company in a highly specific manner. Again, conjoining politics and economics in the effort to make manifest an expansive sense of their sovereignty, they have saturated their corporate enterprises with national identity; indeed, in Russia, state-owned conglomerates are regarded, explicitly, as both productive and expressive of that identity. And of its commonweal. While they may take over the flagship enterprises of others, their own are not for sale. Quite the opposite is true of Britain, PLC, which exemplifies the other extreme in the realization of Nationality, Inc. In this variant, there are no national concerns or state-owned shares in local establishments; those that existed in the past have been sold off, even those most closely associated with the functions of government, with the management of life and death, with the infrastructure of the polity and its well-being. What is more, there is no effort at all to protect home-grown firms. Although the ruling Labour Party repeatedly deploys the purported strength of the British economy in the cause of nationalism and encourages foreign investment to enrich its treasury, it derides any trace of economic patriotism vested in corporations—and evinces contempt for those countries that discourage the sale of their signature businesses. At its most laissez-faire, in fact, neoliberalism here tends to "[put] profit before nationality."[32]

Since the millennium, however, there has been a rising populist sense that Britain, PLC has not been careful enough in husbanding the national brand. It is one thing to market its commodities; that, in itself, would have no negative impact on their exchange value or their affective connection to the production of Britishness. But it is quite another to alienate the means of their manufacture or the intellectual property associated with them. Thus, in 2006, the *Guardian* declared that, with "well-known British [companies]" being sold to non-British conglomerates, it "feels as if the whole British economy is on offer to foreign bidders";[33] such icons as Manchester United, Rolls-Royce, Harrod's, and the British Airports Authority had already passed into the hands of outsiders. Hardly the removal of Lithuania, Inc. to Atlanta. But its effect on the public imagination also hints at sovereignty lost. Which is why, to return to the Russian front, the potential purchase by Gazprom of Centrica, parent company of *British* Gas, elicited so much anxiety. It called to consciousness the limits of laissez-faire, of "profit[ability] before nationality," for Nationality, Inc.

None of these British alienations—the sale, that is, of national assets to aliens—has occasioned nearly the same furor as that spawned in the USA when, in early 2006, President George W. Bush agreed to the takeover of six major harbors by the United Arab Emirate–based firm Dubai Ports World; ironically, although this was rarely mentioned, those harbors had not been managed before by an American company at all, but by P&O, once a "masthead" *British* concern. This deal certainly evoked widespread national *in*securities, those that, under the spectral effect of the so-called War on Terror, are fueled by anything with a Muslim fingerprint on it. But also, and as significantly, it raised uncomfortable questions, questions that pose themselves for Nationality, Inc. everywhere: What ought the proportional relationship be between "free" trade and a national interest that, for many citizens, is not always reducible to the purely economic? How easy is it, in this climate, to separate public from private interest, especially beyond the secure confines of Euro-America? These conundrums have arisen before in the USA, of course: trivially, when, for example, a Japanese conglomerate once tried to purchase a major league baseball team; more seriously, when Middle Eastern interests have sought to "buy into" the heartland of the US industrial economy—and when the Chinese oil company CNOOC Ltd. attempted to take over California's Unocal in 2005, an effort that elicited a "howl of protest from Washington lawmakers."[34]

If China and Russia represent one extreme variant of Nationality, Inc. and Britain the other, most countries have arrived at some compromise between them; although such things, by their very nature, are labile. The USA is a case in point: hence the Dubai Ports World imbroglio and others like it. So are France and Canada. And South Africa. All of them protect their national brands, often by recourse to lawfare; all of them take corporate nationhood, axiomatically, as central to the mandate of governance; all of them assert cultural difference as a basis for their material sovereignty—even if it is culture in the "thin" form, in the expression of very general values, of which we spoke earlier. And all of them are composed of local regions which, positioned between Ethnicity, Inc. and Nationality, Inc., *also* interpolate themselves into the identity economy. Locality, Inc.? We have already encountered this in Britain, with Scotland and Wales. In Russia, the analogue is Tatarstan, among the most economically developed zones within the Federation. Located in the Volga region, less than 1000 kilometers east of Moscow, it declared its own sovereign autonomy in 1990 amidst the demise of the USSR. At first, the Kremlin rejected the initiative out of hand, but later it agreed to a bilateral power-sharing treaty that gave the republic a large measure of self-determination; its administration seized the opportunity to privatize and promote the Tatar economy, not least by selling its "low-risk," human resource–rich *cultural* environment to foreign investors.[35] Similarly, in Canada, Ontario advertised itself in the *Economist* of June 2006 as "one of the fastest growing economies" on the planet, "predicted to outpace Germany, France, and Japan this year," with a gross domestic profit "already greater than Switzerland's or Sweden's"—enough "to *make any nation proud*" in a region that "isn't even a country."[36] And in South Africa, Mpumalanga, one of the provinces, has placed double-page spreads in major local newspapers.[37] This province, "the cradle of human life in Africa," is seeking to "find its own *corporate identity*" by "Reclaiming the Past and Redefining the Future." To this end it has designed a heritage project to prove, ethno-archaeologically, that it has enough of cultural and historical interest to be worthy of a tourist industry (plate 8). And, hence, of venture capital.

Divinity, Inc.?

Ethnicity, Inc.—or, more capaciously, Identity, Inc.—appears, in sum, to be a hyperextension of an older, modernist phenomenon, a phenomenon in the process of metamorphosing and migrating to places it has not been before: into diverse subnational, national, and transnational domains of being. Even, and more complexly, into the domain of religion, itself often taken to be the ontological core of a cultural politics of affect, identity, and sometimes nationhood. It has been said that the Roman Catholic Church is among the oldest businesses—indeed, global businesses—on the planet. That, patently, refers to its *institutional* existence, which was integrally tied to the consolidation of the corporation as a constitutional form in the Middle Ages (above, p. 119). But something more complicated, something more metaphysically grounded, appears also to be happening these days: the commodification of the *numinous essence* of faith. Even in the least expected of places. Like Islam, whose signs, practices, tenets, and truths seem hardly the stuff of intellectual property. Not so.

In the 1970s in Pakistan, *ulema,* the orthodox Muslim religious authorities, took action against the Ahmadis, an offshoot movement whose members they believed to be heretics and with whom they had long been in conflict. This they did by means of the law: they sought an injunction against the alleged apostates to prevent them from holding Muslim rites, from calling their place of worship a *masjid* or constructing one that resembled a mosque, and from using various terms reserved for the Holy Prophet. These, they said, were the distinctive Sha'ir ("signs") of Islam and, therefore, belonged solely to "proper" Muslims (Ahmed 2006:19–24, 40–45). The court found in favor of the *ulema,* but the Ahmadi defendants turned to the Lahore High Court, which heard their appeal in 1978.[38] In this context, counsel for the *ulema* argued "that Muslim-ness was the exclusive property of Muslims alone [and] that certain Muslim terminology was analogous to copyright and trademarks." Consequently, their improper use amounted to "an infringement of the rights" of Muslims (21); of Islam, Inc., that is, albeit, we may add, a non-profit Inc. The presiding judge remained unconvinced. Not on the substantive ground that the signs and practices of Islam might be considered intellectual property, but on a technicality derived from the positive law: that the argument of the *ulema* might only have *legal* force in a civil suit in which they could show that a material loss had been incurred (41). Significantly, though, in 1993, in a Pakistan Supreme Court case[39] that addressed the constitutional bases of Muslim identity, the same argument was *accepted* by a majority of the justices. According to Ahmed (2006:41–42), the "court realized the potential property characteristics of legal identity, in this case of Muslims, by arguing that certain signs were not just distinctive characteristics and practices but the exclusive property of Islam."

Thus was identity, "Muslim-ness," transformed "into property, something that could be owned, possessed and bounded off from others . . ." (Ahmed 2006:41–42), just as its faith-based financial practices, under the terms of Sharia law, are now an integral element of the global economy.[40] In some religions, the gods themselves appear to have a corporate identity of sorts. In 1986, when the Indian national government sued for the return of a twelfth-century bronze Shiva—the figure had been looted from a village in Pathur under somewhat obscure conditions—"*it did so on behalf of the offended god himself.*" The God, in other words, was the "named . . . plaintiff in the case" (Keefe 2007: 60–61; emphasis added). Thus does a deity become incorporated and the corporate become deified. Thus does a God become the ultimate "legal person."

Parallels to these cases are popping up in unexpected places. The same Roger Chennells who acted on behalf of the San was invited in 2007 to attend a Rastafarian forum in Jamaica, timed to coincide with a Nyahbingi ceremony held to honor the birthday of His Imperial Majesty (HIM), Haile Selassie. Chennells had come to the attention of his West Indian hosts through the mediation of a European NGO concerned with indigenous cultural rights; he was approached by representatives of the Ten Rastafarian Mansions, all of whom had evinced a desire to put a stop to the "increasing theft" of their "sacred property and symbols"—the songs, signs, and emblems they take to be His sanctified legacy. But they had not been able to do anything about it: although the Divine Conquering Emperor had decreed that his followers speak with "one voice," they had been too divided among themselves to do so (Chennells n.d.[a], n.d.[b]). Until now. Drawing on the procedures of incorporation that had led to the formation of WIMSA—the institution that had made it possible for San to reclaim their heritage and take control over their indigenous knowledge—Chennells set about drawing the ten dissenting Mansions together into a single International Rastafari Council under a newly drafted constitution. Without unity, it was emphasized, "the entire cause would be lost." Herein lay the first step in the "long journey" to protect their heritage, assert their legal and moral rights, and prevent further "use and abuse" by others of the culture, soon to become intellectual property, of the Brotherhood (Chennells n.d. [a]). The Rastafarians of Jamaica, it appears, have found one voice at last. It speaks, sings, and prays in the language of Divinity, Incorporated.

———————

So it is that we return to where we began, with the articulation—the manifest expression, the joining together—of culture to property, past to future, being to business, entrepreneurialism to ethno-preneurialism. The permanent, unresolved, often aspirational dialectic that connects the incorporation of identity to the commodification of difference looks to be extending in all directions. Ethnicity, Inc., Nationality, Inc., Locality, Inc., Divinity, Inc., and other Incs. yet unnamed.[41] Not all at the same rate, as we have stressed. Nor all in the same manner. Nor, patently, all with the same intentions. Nor, apparently, all with the same historical consequences. But at an exponential rate, and often to unanticipated places. Which leads us, in turn, to a number of conclusions.

SEVEN

Conclusion

We have come *not* to praise Ethnicity, Inc. Neither do we extol empowerment that hinges largely on the commodification of culture under the Empire of the Market. We are likewise vexed by the naturalization of cultural identity, by the radical challenge it poses to other explanatory epistemes, by its silent erosion of prior principles of mobilization and politicization. At the same time, we recognize, and have sought to make sense of, its appeal: of the promise of Ethnicity, Inc. to unlock new forms of self-realization, sentiment, entitlement, enrichment. This notwithstanding the fact that it carries within it a host of costs and contradictions: that it has *both* insurgent possibility *and* a tendency to deepen prevailing lines of inequality, the capacity *both* to enable *and* to disable, the power *both* to animate and to annihilate. Some of those costs and contradictions, as any number of critical anthropologies have pointed out, flow from the growing hegemony of the global intellectual property regime. And from the impulse to reduce culture to a "naturally" copyrighted possession. They are underscored, made undeniably poignant, by an all-too-concrete reality: that, in many desperately poor parts of the world, the attenuation of other modes of producing incomes has left the sale of cultural products, and of the simulacra of ethnicized selfhood, one of the only viable means of survival. Whether or not this is turned, imaginatively, into an act of *positive* choice, into a *positive* assertion of identity—let alone into a sustainable basis of communal life—is another matter entirely (cf. Rasool 2006), a matter, as it turns out, of historical contingency.

It is not our intention here, either, to enter a critique of the conditions that have given rise to Ethnicity, Inc., or to evaluate its implications of the longer run. True, we have suggested that the identity economy feeds, and feeds off, a deep ambivalence in modern life: a sense of exile from "authentic" being that seeks to requite itself in encounters with "authentic" otherness—albeit in consumable form. And that it is likely to do so with ever more, mass-mediated intensity. But such things are better dealt with in another kind of work. Our more modest objective here has been to identify, to scrutinize and anatomize, an emerging historical phenomenon: one that, being scattered and dispersed, has escaped systematic scholarly treatment—not least because the enduring concern with manifest *political* expressions of ethnic consciousness continues to draw attention away from (i) its ontological reconstruction in the unfolding political and ethical economy of the present and (ii) the affective dimensions of its commodification. Also, from the connection between these two things.

So let us reprise our argument one last time.

Ethnicity, Inc.—in its mature form, a projection of the entrepreneurial subject of neoliberalism onto the plane of collective existence—emerges out of a loose, labile dialectic: a contrapuntal interplay of, on one hand, the incorporation of identity and, on the other, the commodification of culture. While it may begin in either of these "moments"—recall the contrast between the San and the Bafokeng, or between different Native American peoples—each, over time, appears to seek to complete itself in the other. But in diverse ways and by diverse routes. In short, the *form* of this dialectic may be broadly similar everywhere. And it may evince the common features spelled out in chapter 4: such things as a fixation on belonging and its boundaries, the intervention of capital from outside, a counterintuitive connection between enterprise and ethno-genesis, the assertion of sovereignty against the state, the foundational salience of territory, and the frequent resort to lawfare. But its *substance* varies widely with respect to all of these things. And with respect to the rate at which it works itself out, to the part played in it by "externalities," to the proportional weight of the two sides of the dialectic, to the manner in which they interpolate themselves into the "local" context in which they come to be embedded, and, finally, to the extent to which the process actually *does* complete itself—the extent, that is, that difference is elaborated into a fully fledged identity economy. Apart from all else, that process is always prone to intervention by the regimes, institutions, and practices of a capitalism whose own history-in-the-present is under construction; also of the state, itself undergoing transformation as it is called upon to regulate Ethnicity, Inc., sometimes by choice, sometimes necessity. The open-endedness of the process is owed, as well, to the fact that the forces of abstraction entailed both in the incorporation of identity and in the commodification of culture are mediated by the pragmatics of everyday life. Here, on the ground of concrete existence, living human subjects inflect, and are inflected by, the generalizing tendencies of the market. It is by such means that culture and commodification constitute each other—in coproduction, as it were.[1] We have tried to illustrate, by recourse to ethnographic instances drawn from far and wide, precisely how they play off one another in shaping ethnic futures. And the futures of ethnicity.

This, in turn, takes us back to the questions posed at the close of chapter 2. What, precisely, is the part played by the rise of neoliberalism, broadly conceived, in the incorporation of identity? Who, if we may be so unsubtle, are its primary beneficiaries? Who suffers it, and in what measure? What are the implications of Ethnicity, Inc. for everyday ethno-politics, not least those conducted by violent means? Also, for the affect archetypically held to lie at the core of ethnic consciousness? Are any regions and reaches of the new global order likely to escape the processes narrated here?

The answer to the first of these questions, patently, has been the *leitmotif* of our account. While the incorporation of identity and the commodification of culture—or, at least, elements of both—predate the present moment, their maturation into Ethnicity, Inc., as we know it today, is intimately linked to the contemporary history of capital: to its spawning of the entrepreneurial (singular) and ethno-preneurial (collective) subject; to the hegemony of a voracious intellectual property regime that has reduced hitherto unprecedented, and entirely unforeseen, domains of biological and cultural being to alienable rights, immaterial assets, private effects; to the globalization of economies of difference and desire; to the judicialization of political and social life on a scale unimaginable before now. And to a whole lot else besides.

That is the easy one. More difficult is the question of who benefits, who suffers, and in what proportions. Precisely because Ethnicity, Inc. is born of a complex, open-ended dialectic, its political, economic, and ethical consequences remain highly uncertain. As uncertain, in fact, as the promises of neoliberalism itself. For many advocates (and, to be perfectly frank, for many anthropologists) of indigenous populations, the possibilities opened up by the identity economy for previously immiserated, violated peoples—peoples who are still disempowered and often desperate—appear almost alchemic. Who could, would, should gainsay Native Americans, the San, autochthonous South Africans, or anyone else the right to an income from casino capitalism, cultural tourism, and/or other means of selling their difference? But it is yet to be seen whether ethno-prise actually *will* increase the general prosperity, the common-weal, of those who look to it for a panacea—or whether it will exacerbate, even reinvent, long-standing forms of extraction and inequality. As Mathers and Landau (2007:253) note, to take just one example, the *raison d'être* of "Proudly South African" tourism is ostensibly to "empower . . . disadvantaged South Africans." But it relies "heavily on colonial imagery that is inherently (if implicitly) racist." And its bounty is *very* uneven, compounding rather than erasing old cleavages of color and class. Similarly casino capitalism in the USA: not only have its profit-sharing arrangements accrued disproportionate returns to a few "alien" venture capitalists. Its legal underpinnings have also conduced to make the sovereign aspirations of some First Peoples—and therefore their political being—an object of real estate and other transactions whose active "partners" are often non-Indians. The Pomo may be especially notable for this fact, but they are far from the only indigenes whose territorial integrity has been bought for them under conditions that might broadly be described as neocolonial. To be sure, it was the specter of sovereignty compromised that persuaded the Navajo to hold out against casino capitalism for a long time, preferring, when they did enter the identity economy, to commodify their cultural products rather than merely their legal status.

Ethnicity, Inc. has, without doubt, opened up new means of producing value, of claiming recognition, of asserting sovereignty, of giving affective voice to belonging; this, not infrequently, in the all-but-total absence of alternatives. What is more, as we have argued, ethno-commodities are queer things: their mass marketing is as likely to animate cultural identities as to devalue the difference on which they are founded—although, in the process, they may reformulate identity *sui generis* in important respects. But those commodities are also vulnerable to the vagaries of commerce, which demands that the alienation of heritage ride a delicate balance between exoticism and banalization—an equation that often requires "natives" to perform themselves in such a way as to make their indigeneity legible to the consumer of otherness. On occasion, the costs of so doing are held to be too high, the risk of loss too great. "We can't organize ourselves to be only a tourist destination," a senior Lovedu royal told writer Liz McGregor (2007:27), speaking of Modjadji, the famed "Realm of the Rain-Queen" in South Africa (Krige and Krige 1943); Modjadi I, the original Lovedu monarch, as it happens, was the mythical *She* of Rider Haggard's fabulist African tale, now an Oxford World Classic (1991 [1887]).[2] "It would be too expensive a price to pay. We have a tradition that is very strong and if you dump it, you don't have it any more." Nor is this the only perceived peril. Once established, as many entrants into the identity economy discover, ethnic commerce typically sharpens the line of division between enrichment and exclusion: hence the "outing" by some San of "fake Bushmen," the concern of the Bafokeng king about the influx of outsiders, the Native Americans suddenly excised from tribal membership. The Difference Business, which is frequently commandeered by big players from both inside and out, everywhere underwrites new divisions and inequities: lines of cleavage that render invisible, or only just translucent, those whose claims to belonging and material benefit are erased by the process of incorporation itself. Therein lies the immanent contradiction, the Janus face, of Ethnicity, Inc. Also of Nationality, Inc., Divinity, Inc., and Locality, Inc.

Talk of the undersides of Ethnicity, Inc. points toward the question of ethno-politics; specifically, the ethno-politics of violence. Does the incorporation of identity not bear within it a dark energy, the potential to foment division, dissension, even homicidal hatreds? How, more generally, does the commodification of cultural being relate to the kinds of violent confrontation so often associated with assertions of ethnic consciousness, belonging, and birthright?

The short answer is that Ethnicity, Inc. may spawn violence of its own accord or it may come to insinuate itself into already-existing conflicts. It may also displace those conflicts into commerce, sublimating the exercise of force by directing it toward other sorts of transaction. The long answer, inevitably, is more complicated. In so far as the politics of identity assumes diverse guises, it rarely reduces to a simple utility function: to equate ethno-belonging with the pursuit of brute power or unmediated interest—whether it be by means of law or war, combat or corporate enterprise—is to confuse its strategic with its existential dimensions. And to ignore the ways in which it intersects with other modes of social, ethical, and aesthetic being, thus to "elevat[e] physical into moral necessity" (Schiller (2004[1795]:28). Even when ethnicity presents itself as a *causus belli,* it cannot be taken at face value. "[T]he tendency to privilege [it] in the storyline of violent encounters by participants and spectators alike," writes Broch-Due (2005:6) of contemporary Africa, "should not blind us to the fact that ethnicity is not [an] isolated fact of . . . existence."[3] To the contrary: once it takes on concrete form, it has an almost uncanny capacity to naturalize cultural identities at the expense of other kinds of collective consciousness, to conjure up communities of belonging and invest them with affect, to incite passions and primordialist fantasies, to valorize the vernacular, its practices and its commodities, to fashion a perceptual universe in which otherness appears as immanently antagonistic.

And, sometimes, to do all of these things in varying proportions. To invoke again a point made by Bayart (2005:40): ethnicity is "simultaneously a principle of exclusion and even death, and the vehicle of a new moral economy of the *polis*." Nor only a moral economy. Also, indivisibly hyphenated, a political-economy.

Exploring that economy has been a critical concern in this essay. It is only by understanding how and why identity congeals into property—into a species of capital vested in the entrepreneurial subject, singular and collective—that we may fully grasp emerging patterns of selfhood and sociality at the dawn of the twenty-first century. This is all the more so as difference, made manifest in and through culture, is increasingly commodified, and, reciprocally, as commodities are rendered cultural, experiential, affective. All the more so, as well, under historical conditions that unmoor the struggle for survival from received forms of wage labor and material being-in-the-world, and redirect it toward the alienation of the immaterial—epitomized in the branding and marketing of just the sorts of value that accrue to the identity economy and to those best positioned within it. The means and ends of that economy, even where they do not involve resort to arms, are often violent in their own way, especially in their modes of exclusion and erasure. Not for nothing has trade, like politics and lawfare and a few things besides, been dubbed "war by other means." Like the Clausewitzian phrase itself, this is hardly new. Neither is it confined to ethno-prise. But the same historical forces that have honed the consciousness of difference across the globe, and have made it the ground of so many recent struggles over sovereignty, territory, resources, and rights, have heightened its availability, too, as a basis for incorporation and commodification.

The problem, though, persists. What are the conditions that might predispose a people to pursue their objectives, their manifest destiny, through business rather than bloodshed, polite commerce rather than political coercion? When are they likely to traffic rather than fight with their enemy-others? There is no obvious answer to this conundrum, at least not just yet. It seems to depend on historical contingencies and on the ecologies of difference to which they give rise. There is no easy answer, either, to the obverse question: In what circumstances will people kill, commit atrocities, or surrender their own lives under the sign of identity? This one, though, has drawn much greater attention from the social sciences.[4] A number of prognostic "factors" have been said to portend the outbreak of identity-based violence: among them, the changing composition and settlement patterns of ethnic populations; radical impoverishment and contestation over resources; the ambitions of charismatic leaders; and the decay of the state (see, e.g., Toft 2003; Kaufman 2001; Broch-Due 2005). But such things have proven to have little predictive value. Outbreaks of ethnocidal strife continue to take scholars by surprise, even when, with hindsight, they appear to have been overdetermined. Nor, by inversion, do these "factors" tell us when it is that ethnocide might morph into ethno-prise. Which can happen in the most unexpected of theaters, like the Balkans or East Africa, in which murderous conflicts—conflicts with political and material roots in the relatively recent past—are typically blamed on ancient, incorrigible ethnic hatreds.

Where struggles of this sort dissolve into identity economics, they sometimes turn carnage into commerce, perdition into patrimony. Take Rwanda, now ruled by a "Tutsi ethnocracy" (Tiemessen 2004). Here heritage tourism is being vigorously encouraged under the logo "Discover a New African Dawn."[5] It has willing consumers, "international visitors [who] want to witness the . . . authentic remains of the violence" (Cook 2005b:293). Killing fields feature prominently. In Kigali, at the Gisozi Memorial, "vivid images" and "horrifying video clips" trace the history of mass murder in "macabre detail." Other towns have also opened up massacre sites, partly as places of preservation and recuperation, partly as stops on the travel itineraries of foreigners—many of them on their way to other national attractions, like the tropical habitats of wild mountain gorillas. Perhaps the most dramatic commemorative center in the country was originally established by a British charity, partly funded by the UK government. It is in the south, at Murambi Technical School, whose classrooms are gruesome "reminders of one of the worst acts of genocide in modern times." Here, in 1994, fifty thousand Tutsis seeking refuge were killed by Hutu militias. Many of their bodies—having been preserved in lime, allegedly at the request of survivors—are on view, ostensibly placed where they died. One room "is filled with hundreds of skulls and piles of bones, while another contains the children, some with their petrified arms raised up to fend off the blows that killed them."[6] The place has become an object of controversy: a number of Rwandans have criticized the Aegis Trust for presenting an unremittingly monstrous, one-sided account of the genocide and for failing to provide a culturally sensitive monument to the slaughter of a million people.[7] For their part, some visitors express dismay at being brought here on regular guided tours; others seem to take it in stride.[8] All of them, though, are "encouraged to leave donations," which are "shared between the guide and the other local people who help to maintain the site" (Cook 2005b:301).

In sum, ethnicity can make capital even out of its own capacity for destruction. There is no telling where a market, however modest its magnitude, might be cultivated. Hence our stress on historical contingency. At the very least, ethno-incorporation rides on a number of indeterminacies. Ecology, in all its arbitrariness, is clearly significant: the fortuitous presence of platinum, coal, endangered species, medicinal flora, rare fauna, sunshine. So, too, is geographic location: the happy proximity to sea or ruins, accessibility to mass transport and mobile consuming populations. Structural conditions also have a palpable impact: minimal order, more- or less-regulated markets, security of investment, governmental regimes conducive to the identity economy, the availability of venture capital, the presence of nongovernmental agencies concerned with minority rights. It is such contingencies, after all, that enable the Mohegan Sun to flourish in Connecticut but disable the development of a Kalahari Sun in the sandy desert reaches of central Botswana (above, p. 97). On the debit side, as well, is the unruly, sometimes violent play of political processes of the larger scale. In 1999, for example, a growing local tourist industry in Western Uganda was killed off when foreign visitors, on a trip to view gorillas in the Bwindi Impenetrable Forest, encountered guerillas of a more deadly kind:[9] *Interahamwe* "rebels"—who had been deeply implicated in the Rwandan genocide in 1994, whose victims lie unburied at Murambi School, and who now operate as a murky force in the combat zones along the frontiers of central and east Africa—gunned down eight tourists from England, the USA, and New Zealand. At the same time, those combat zones may themselves be sites of ethnically controlled extractive economies, economies in which the trade of gemstones, precious metals, chemicals, and drugs exists in savage symbiosis with struggles over political sovereignty (see, e.g., Mbembe 2110:87).

Contingencies aside, ethno-incorporation, as we have seen, often walks a fine line between the tame and the wild, accessibility and remoteness, sameness and singularity. Difference, by its very nature, is relative and relational: distinctive when measured against the unmarked mainstream, its successful commodification is most likely among populations defined unambiguously as cultural minorities, old or new, disadvantaged or otherwise. And it is put at risk when their uniqueness begins to dissolve. Which has happened where Native American business has challenged "ordinary" US corporations too effectively at their own game; also where the identity-based brand become bland, its distinction extinguished. Conversely, former "peoples without culture"—culture, that is, in the quotidian, lower case—have become much more prone to stress the particularity of their lifeways, their patrimony, even their species-being. *Vide* the escalation in the making, marking, and marketing of ethnic otherness at the heart of the global north, which seems, in this respect, to be evolving toward the global south: the Celtic, Breton, and Andalusian folk musics produced, ever more expansively and expensively, by cosmopolitan natives; or the British "stately home," which retails the aristocratic as exotic; or countless historical theaters, like colonial Williamsburg, where the re-enacted past becomes another, more colorful country. Yet here, too, there are limits. No amount of energy, or ingenuity, has managed to turn dreary postindustrial towns in upstate New York, northern England, and the former German East into heritage sites with customer appeal.

Does this mean that some ethnically marked subjects and their objects are more *intrinsically* favored, more susceptible to commodification, than are others? Again, generalities are qualified by the exigencies of the particular. Attractiveness is very much in the (carefully conditioned) eye of the (historically situated) beholder. And market-worthiness rides on its back. The huge profitability of the hoodia, that "very ugly" cactus, is directly tied to the sociosexual aesthetic of slenderness in a world currently obsessed with it. What is more, the manufacture of ethno-commodities—and, with it, their vernacular "beauty"—is sometimes born of, or inflected by, the serendipities of commerce. Fifteen or so years ago, we visited our favorite Tswana potter in the rural North West Province. Immediately plain to us was the fact that her comely clay beer-pots, once upon a time manufactured primarily for domestic use, were about half the size they had been a decade before. "Why?" we asked. She shook her head at us. Was it not obvious? Her wares were now made to fit into the over-head compartments of the jets that bear her buyers homeward. Their new compactness, she thought, had made them lovelier. Less whimsical are forms of ethno-prise fueled by patently voyeuristic fashionabilities; among them, so-called "poverty tourism,"[10] designed for the consumption of the economically advantaged, in which the immiseration on display is often ethnicized. In South Africa, where overseas visitors are taken in ever increasing numbers to desperately poor urban townships, their itineraries include "traditional" beer drinks, visits to the interiors of homes, and stops at "authentic" healers, communal water taps, and food stalls that sell such indigenous delicacies as "walkie-talkies" (chicken heads-and-feet) to "natives" who, as it happens, can afford nothing better; all of which smacks of the atmospherics of an archetypical cultural village tour.

With a frisson of danger.

South African townships, notoriously, carry the cachet of being crime-ridden, violent, unruly; visitors are sometimes held up at gunpoint—as, in December 2005, was an entire busload of German . . . travel agents.[11] Excursions to them marry cultural tourism to the "extreme" tourism that takes "freak-chic" voyagers into war zones, prisons, favellas, and despoiled inner cities. While, for the most part, Ethnicity Inc.—especially in its more elaborate, highly capitalized forms—tends to flourish in secure social ecologies, it may also profit in the interstices between the rough and the smooth, the wild and the predictable. But not too rough, nor too wild. Such things are labile, of course: ethnic markets, and the fortunes of those who depend on them, *do* fall victim to shifting geographies of political instability and terror, as did Ugandan gorilla tourism to guerilla predation. This fact was archly captured, some years back, by a South Africa satirist, Mark Banks. In a sketch entitled "Shrieko Tours," Banks manages a travel business that guarantees its overseas clients their very own, entirely authentic experience of local (for which read "African") customary practices. Like a mugging. Not that they should worry: their adventures come with a license to shoot "unprotected" local species—which include indigenous (i.e., black) citizens, but *not* "endangered" wildlife.[12] All of which acts out the absurdities of consumer life-as-usual in violent trouble zones. It also makes plain the obscene undersides of a commerce in exotic, exciting, but ultimately safe, encounters with the dispossessed and desperate "others" of the earth. And the fact that, in the traffic in difference, culture-as-commodity may expand onto even the most inhospitable of terrains. In one form or another, it appears, Ethnicity, Inc. can turn up, if not everywhere, then almost anywhere. For, existentially speaking, it appears to be driven by a burgeoning desire at once to endorse difference and to transcend it, the desire to touch for an instant the elusive otherness that we are too late, too settled, too detached fully to embrace.

———

It is not usual, as well-advised graduate students are told, to introduce fresh data into the conclusion of a book. We have just broken that rule. But we have done so to make a point. As we write, Ethnicity, Inc. gathers momentum, morphs, moves off in unexpected directions. In short, we are narrating a story as yet far from concluded, a story that takes on more plot twists, more *dramatis personae,* with every passing day. Were we writing this tomorrow, there would be yet another paragraph to pen, another footnote to fill in, another surprise to document. We could, for example, tell of a saga presently unfolding in Bogotá, Colombia. Here the Asociación de Cabildos Indigenas, an organization of urban ethnic groupings, is trying to unite Kichwa, Ambika-Pijao, and Muiscas—communities not legally "ethnic" because they do not possess their own territories in the city—into a political coalition. Why? In order to build an "indigenous shopping mall." As Ati Quigua, a local leader, explains, the point is "to . . . generate resources, income and sustainable projects to improve the quality of life of this population." But "what would an indigenous mall actually look like?" asks ethnographer, Diana Bocarejo (2007), given that the plan is to house all the usual major stores in a somewhat conventional, high-end retail palace. Architecturally, the answer is plain: says Ms. Quigua, the object of the building itself is to "symbolize indigeneity." But there is more to it. As a Kichwa notable added, the "project helps us have a . . . space where we can display our cosmology . . . [I]t will narrate the history of the place, there will be small plazas where we will do, as they say in North America, our *pow wow,* what we call a *minga.*'" There will also be theaters in which to "perform our dances, our rituals . . . where people," not least tourists, "can be with us." Where better for commodified custom and custom-made commodities to converge, and to infuse each other, than a shopping mall? Where better "to anchor and fix modern indigeneity?"[13]

As all of this makes plain, the peoples of "traditional" Africa, Latin America, the USA, and Asia—whether they speak the language of blood or business, or a creole of both—constantly find new, often ingenious ways to partake of the identity economy. What is more, in deploying their "traditions" to this end, they have become thoroughly modern, if each in their own ways. Or, like that Indian tribe of which we spoke in chapter 4, they pass by the modern and leap directly into the Pomo—which, above all, distorts, exaggerates, and sometimes renders absurd, the lineaments of modernity. We may or may not like what Ethnicity, Inc. promises as a future. But we are going to have to live with it, and, even more, to fashion a critical scholarship to deal with its ambiguous promises, its material and moral vision for times to come, the deep affective attachments it engenders.

We have been at pains to show that, in as much as Ethnicity, Inc. is a historical process in the making, it manifests itself across a very broad spectrum indeed. Take the less-than-obvious case of Namibia, a postcolony with less than two million people, a large unemployed rural population, an indigenous citizenry fractiously ethnicized by its colonial masters, and "real Africanity" for sale (plate 9). At one extreme are Herero women attired in highly ornate "traditional" costume (Hendrickson 1996:223–26)—in fact, the garb of early Christian converts, which consists of Victorian-style dresses of dark cotton print topped by extravagant headgear shaped like the squared-off horns of oxen—who offer their Herero-ness to the alien photographic eye for a few Namibian dollars. Interestingly, they often hold a small doll that replicates themselves exactly, as if to tender, alongside their embodied, exoticized identity, a miniaturized simulacrum, thus to alienate their ethnic substance, but not their selves, in condensed form (see plate 10).[14] At the other extreme are those San included in the formal process of corporate ethnicization founded on *Hoodia gordonii*. In the middle are small Damara communities that eke out a living by selling for a pittance objects that, fancifully or otherwise, they take to be their ethnic products; like the members of the eleven-household patriclan living at Blaauwkrans—off the rutted, dusty C39 that links the small regional center of Khorixas to Torra Bay, on the barren Skeleton Coast—who have erected rickety roadside stalls, heralded by hand-painted signs to their "Graft Market" (*sic*). Here travelers, most of whom speed by in their four-wheel-drive vehicles, are implored to buy such diverse objects as sketchbooks made from the dung of the desert elephants living in the area, jewelry of reeds and beads, and "semi-precious" stones, gathered in the nearby foothills (plate 11a). The jewelry and stones are fairly common throughout central Namibia. Nonetheless, the vendors insist on these being "Damara" things (plate 11b). And the things on which their survival as Damara, in this place, depends.[15] As in Namibia, so in many other places. If anything, the spectrum across which Ethnicity, Inc. is taking shape is widening all the time—in proportion to the imaginative, affective, and material possibilities that it opens up.

But *why*, finally, is Ethnicity, Inc. so obviously on the rise? Why now? The simple answer is that "to fit into a consumer economy," especially an economy in which social identity is almost wholly mediated through processes of commodification, "ethnicity must [itself] become a commodity" (Bankston and Henry 2000:403, 385). More subtly, perhaps, it is because the identity economy is itself a congealed product—a fusion both hot and cold, if you will—of three elemental features of the neoliberal moment: the apotheosis of intellectual property and the more-or-less coercive reduction of culture to it; the displacement of politics into the realm of the law; and the growing naturalization of the trope of identity—especially cultural identity, at once essentialized and made the subject of choice, construction, consumption—as *the* taken-for-granted domain of collective action in the Age of Entrepreneurialism and Human Capital. Herein lies a critical Station of the Cross on the Road, if not to Damascus, then to a Brave Neo World.

Acknowledgments

This volume is intended as a provocation, an unconventional piece of anthropology by means of which to reground a familiar topic, an effort to think about, and theorize, a global phenomenon from the vantage of the global south. It began its public life in 2002 with an event entitled, rather grandly, the *Stiftungsgastprofesseur Wissenschaft und Gessellschaft* der Deutschen Bank AG Lecture, Johann Wolfgang Goethe University of Frankfurt, Germany. We would like to record our appreciation to both its sponsor and to our very gracious hosts on that occasion. Since then, we have presented versions of *Ethnicity, Inc.* in a number of places—among them, Princeton University, the University of Illinois, the University of Pennsylvania, the University of Vienna, the Universities of the Witwatersrand, the Western Cape, and Stellenbosch in South Africa, the Van Leer Foundation and Ben Gurion University in Israel, the Max Planck Institute for Social Anthropology at Halle, Indiana University, the American Ethnological Society, and the American Bar Foundation— where it elicited insightful comment from Bonnie Honig, Andre Gingrich, Carol Greenhouse, and many others, all of whom are owed a deep debt of gratitude. So, too, is Maureen Anderson, our long-time research assistant, who continues to give us her unstinting support and the benefits of an imaginative scholarly mind; Rita Guenther, of the National Academy of Sciences, who took a personal interest in the study, and found us any number of interesting examples with which to enrich it; and Jessica Cattelino, our former colleague, whose unusually perceptive research on Seminole Indians and casino capitalism in Florida has close, very suggestive parallels to our own. Several doctoral students at the University of Chicago have also made distinctive contributions: Rob Blunt, who has taken an interest in the project from the start, and alerted us to the case of MEGA/GEMA in Kenya, outlined in the prologue; Caroline Brown, whose work on Alaskan Natives helped us to broaden our study in its initial stages; Susan S. Gooding, who wrote an exceptionally insightful commentary on our analysis of North American Indian casino capitalism; Bianca Dahl, who went through the manuscript with an unusually perceptive eye for detail; and Lisa Simeone, who gave us the gift of an extraordinarily rich, acutely critical reading of the manuscript in its all-but-final stages. Several close friends and colleagues in South Africa are also owed fulsome acknowledgment, most notably, David Bunn, formerly of the University of the Witwatersand, who first introduced us to the worlds of Makuleke and Hamakuya; Steven Robins, of the University of Stellenbosch, who taught us a great deal about modern San and Makuleke history; Roger Chennells, a distinguished human rights lawyer also based in Stellenbosch, without whose very generous cooperation the account of the San and the hoodia cactus would have been much less nuanced; and, most of all, Susan E. Cook, of the University of Pretoria, a comrade-ethnographer in the North West Province of South Africa, whose highly sensitive writings on Bafokeng, Inc. and corporate ethnicity—which, as our citations make plain, infuse our own—are sure to leave their own mark on the social sciences in years to come.

We would also like to thank Jutta Dobler, who made the memorable photograph of Selma Helao and her Herero doll in Namibia (plate 10), Marie-Jean Butler, who is responsible for the striking image of Makuleke Cultural Village (plate 7), and *Cultural Survival* for the right to include an excerpt from "Tourism Opens New Doors, Creates New Challenges, for Traditional Healers in Peru" by Rachel Proctor (2001). We reproduce plate 2, "Platinum Prince: Meet the New 'CEO' of Bafokeng Inc.," with the kind permission of Kenneth Creamer; its source is Creamer Media's Mining Weekly at www.miningweekly.co.za. Kgosi Leruo generously has allowed us to use the portrait of his late brother in plate 1. Our perennial debts of gratitude are also acknowledged to the Lichtstern Fund, Department of Anthropology, University of Chicago, and to the American Bar Foundation, without whose financial support this book, like so much of our other work, could not have been undertaken.

Notes

1. North Catalonia, Catalogne-Nord, is in the Pyrénéen-Orientales in France, south of the Languedoc. It is separated from the rest of Catalonia by the Franco-Spanish frontier. In 2004, its population was 410,000. For anthropological accounts of North Catalonian identity, see, for example, O'Brien (1990, 1993).
2. This passage is drawn from three sources, http://www.catalogne-nord.com/ang/economy4.htm, http://www.catalogne-nord.com/ang/thecatalanidentity1.htm, and http://www.catalogne-nord.com/ang/thecatalanidentity4.htm, all accessed 8 August 2006.
3. Somewhere between 28,000 and 35,000 Shipibo live in Peruvian Amazon in scattered communities along the Ucayali River. They are typically characterized in media accounts as desperately poor, famous for their ceramic and textile designs, and tenacious in adhering to cultural practices of the past. For an older anthropological account of their "tourist art," see Lathrap (1976).
4. See http://www.shipiboway.org, accessed 9 August 2006.
5. The phrase "close distance" was used by Walter Benjamin (1968 [1936]); see also Mazzarella (2003:256–57) and below.
6. See http://www.megawelfare.org/index.htm and http://www.megawelfare.org/mega%20holding.htm, accessed 14 August 2006.
7. Philip Schlesinger, "Democratic Devolution in the UK: Scotland's Quiet Revolution," *Le Monde diplomatique*, English edition, April 1998; http://www.mondediplo.com/1998/04/09scot, accessed 8 August 2006.

8. Craig Cowbrough, "New Global Image for Scotland's Life Science Community," *Scottish Enterprise*, 9 April 2006; http://www.scottish-enterprise.com/sedotcom_home/about-us/se-whatwedo/news-se-about-us/news-se-about-us-details.htm?articleid=156511, accessed 10 August 2006.

CHAPTER TWO

1. See "Traditional Leaders to Form Private Firm for Investment," *Business Day* (South Africa), 10 October 2000; http://www.businessday.co.za/Articles/TarkArticle.aspx?ID=286941, accessed 31 October 2002.
2. A National Conference on Traditional Leadership, Midrand, 17–18 August 2000, Department of Provincial and Local Government. It should be noted that the assembled royals declined to take part in the proceedings, refusing, as plenipotentiaries, to talk to anyone other than the state president. We attended the conference at the formal invitation of the minister for provincial and local government, the Hon. F. S. Mufamadi, and wish to thank him and the ministry staff for making our presence possible.
3. Mawande Jubasi and Thabo Mkhize, "Unite against ANC Treachery—Buthelezi," *Sunday Times* (South Africa), 4 August 2002, 4. This quotation is from a speech in which Buthelezi sought to consolidate Zulu support in the "fight for the autonomy of the[ir] kingdom."
4. *Special Report of the Auditor-General on an Investigation at the South African Telecommunications Regulatory Authority*, 10 February 2000 (RP 47/2000), lists Contralesa Development Trust as part of the Cell C consortium but notes that it was not yet registered as a company; registration was to occur a few months later. An on-line copy of the report is available at http://www.agsa.co.za/Reports/special/Special/RP47_2000.pdf#s, accessed 3 July 2006.
5. The merger was between Fluxrab Investments no. 90 (Pty) Ltd, the acquiring firm, and Metcash Trading Africa Ltd. and Metcash Aviation (Pty.) Ltd., the firms being taken over. The merger was approved; see http://www.comptrib.co.za/decidedcases/html/49LMJun04.htm, accessed 4 July 2006. Black Economic Empowerment (BEE), governed by the Broad-Based Black Economic Empowerment Act (no. 53 of 2003, signed into effect by the president in January 2004), has as its object the growth of black involvement in the national economy—especially by changing the "racial composition of ownership and management structures and in the skilled occupations of existing and new enterprises" (South Africa 2004:3); it also requires that local companies comply with its regulations if they wish to do any business with the state or its agencies.
6. See "Contralesa Buys Stake in Engineering Firm," *South African Business*, 16 November 2004. The *South African Business* archive attributes the article to the *Mail & Guardian*, 22 August 2006; see http://www.mg.co.za/articlepage.aspx?area'/breaking_news/breaking_news__business&articleid=142038, accessed 10 July 2006.

7. See *Investor Wire*, 11 October 2005; http://www.investorwire.co.za/ViewStory .asp?SID=060059059063008, accessed 1 July 2006.

8. Elsewhere (2001), we note that casino capitalism is typically associated with less-than-respectable forms of accumulation, not least those through which quasi-sovereign minorities sometimes find means to enrich themselves. In South Africa at the time Setumo made his fortune, casinos were confined to the ethnic "homelands" erected by the apartheid regime and were operated by white firms under government license.

9. *Kgosi* in Setswana is usually translated as "chief." Among Bafokeng, however, it tends to be rendered as "king," itself an assertion of ethnic power. We are grateful to Dr. Susan Cook, who told us of Leruo's visit to Brown University in October 2002 and who alerted us to the edition of *Enterprise* that carried the supplement. Dr. Cook is presently doing highly original work on "corporate ethnicity"—her term—among Bafokeng; ours and hers, to which we shall return, have long informed each other.

10. Martin Creamer, *Mining Weekly* 6, no. 41, (November 2000), 17–23; see http://www.miningweekly.co.za, accessed 1 August 2002.

11. Tswagare Namane, "Searching for Tswana Heritage," *Mail* (South Africa), 4 March 1994, 8. The *Mail* (formerly the *Mafeking Mail*) is published in Mafikeng-Mmabatho, the provincial capital. We should like to thank its editor, Martin McGie, for allowing us open access to its archive.

12. Victor Azarya (2004:passim) has made the telling point that, for some ethnic groups, commodifying their marginality—as much as their culture—has also become a means to enter the global tourist economy.

13. "Unwitting" because Xie (2003:6) does not himself put these three statements together explicitly or stress their connection; we have extracted and reassembled them from a longer passage.

14. In a later essay, Kirshenblatt-Gimblett (2006:163–64) identifies the emergence of three species of heritage—the tangible, the intangible, and the natural—itself partly an effect of UNESCO efforts to protect them on a global scale. We are concerned here primarily with intangible heritage.

15. In 1999, the ǂKhomani San successfully reclaimed territory in the Andriesvale-Askam area of the Northern Cape Province under the national Land Reform Programme provided for by the Restitution of Land Rights Act 22 of 1994; they subsequently resettled there (South African Human Rights Commission 2004:5).

16. Gordon (2002:228), who also quotes this statement, adds that it "is rapidly becoming canonic."

17. See http://www.northonline.sccd.ctc.edu/christen/safrica.KK.artist.html, accessed 20 October 2006. For an account of Kagga Kamma from the perspective of its proprietors, see http://www.kaggakamma.co.za/en/ history.html, accessed 12 April 2006.

18. The sentences quoted from White (1991) were originally written in the present tense. We have rendered them in the past to account for the fact that the

‡Khomani San no longer live, or perform themselves, at Kagga Kamma. But allegedly "fake" Bushmen now do; see below.

19. According to authoritative sources, a staggering 80 percent of the two hundred and fifty licensed tour operators in Cape Town—one of the most frequented tourist destinations in the world at the time of writing—do cultural tours; see Caryn Dolley, "Business 'Back to Normal' after Tour Groups Robbed," *Cape Times*, 4 December 2006, 3. Note, too, that we have used the term "Brave Neo South Africa" elsewhere with reference to the postcolony (Comaroff and Comaroff 2004; 2006), and in the subtitle to a book currently in preparation (n.d. [a]).

20. As Kirshenblatt-Gimblett (1998:163) reminds us, cultural villages have a long history. And they are to be found all over the world. In southern Africa, too, a few predate the 1980s. But it is since the early 1990s they have multiplied most conspicuously and have become a recognized form of local enterprise.

21. The series, *Shaka Zulu*, was screened by the South African Broadcasting Corporation in 1986 and rebroadcast in 2001. It attracted a great deal of media attention on both occasions.

22. The South African Heritage Resources Agency is "custodian of the national estate." Its express mission is to manage all aspects of the country's heritage, including its import and export. See http://www.sahra.org.za, accessed 11 November 2006.

23. See http://www.zulu.org.za, accessed 20 November 2006. This URL automatically opens up another: http://www.kzn.org.za/kzn/. Despite its headline, the text advertises tourism in the province as a whole—ending, puzzlingly, with a repetition of the headline, "Welcome to South Africa's Zulu Kingdom: KwaZulu-Natal."

24. See, for example, *Sawubona*, the South African Airlines magazine, March 2007.

25. See http://www.kzn.org.za/kzn/kznta/96.xml, accessed 20 November 2006; emphasis added. The idea of KwaZulu-Natal itself as culture park becomes even less far-fetched by comparison with Swaziland, the adjoining nation-state to its north. "Swaziland is regarded by most outsiders as a kind of royal African theme park," wrote a well-known journalist not long ago; Peter Fabricius, "Welcome to Theme Park Swaziland, Unless Democracy Ruins It for King Mswati," *Cape Times*, 18 December 2006.

26. See Draft Constitution of the Province of Kwazulu-Natal, chapter 5, § 60.(1), http://www.ifp.org.za/Constitution/provKZNconstitution.htm, accessed 19 May 2008. This constitution was unanimously adopted by the legislature of the province in March 1996, but its certification by the Constitutional Court of South Africa, required under national law, was rejected on grounds that some of its clauses were incompatible with those of the national Bill of Rights. These did *not* include the paragraphs concerning the monarch, however. They were found to be consistent with § 160(3)(b) of the interim national constitution then in force; see Constitutional Court of South Africa, CCT

15/96, Certification of the Kwazulu-Natal Constitution (CCT 15/96) [1996] ZACC 17; 1996 (11) BCLR 1419; 1996 (4) SA 1098 (6 September 1996), § 3.

27. Samantha Enslin-Payne, "King Shaka Airport Gets the Thumbs Up in Time for World Cup," *Cape Times*, 14 August 2007, Business Report, 24.

28. See Craig Bishop, "Community Reserve Launched," *Natal Witness*, 15 October 2001; the version we cite—kindly made available to us by Ilana van Wyk of the University of Pretoria, to whom we wish to express our gratitude—is copied from the SA Media holdings of the University of the Free State (ref. no. 5653, topic 19).

29. Association for Rural Advancement, Kwa-Zulu-Natal, *The Investigation of the Effects of Conservation and Tourism on Land Tenure and Ownership Patterns in KwaZulu-Natal* (2004),125; http://www.afra.co.za/upload/files/AP18b.pdf, accessed 24 November 2006.

30. The objectives of these partnerships were outlined in an untitled presentation on behalf of the Makuleke by Mashangu Livingston Maluleke to the World Parks Congress, 2003. At the time it was marked "not for citation." However, its contents were summarized by several informants to John Comaroff during a visit to the area in March 2007; they are no longer confidential. We should like to thank David Bunn, our colleague and close friend, for first introducing this case to us (see acknowledgments).

31. For an account of a parallel, yet somewhat different, process among the Maasai in Kenya, see Azarya (2004:960–61); not only do "the Maasai of Kajiado and Narok local councils [receive] a share from entrance fees to Amboseli and Maasai-Mara National Parks, . . . [but a] small group of them have opened their own Kimana Community Wildlife Sanctuary and negotiated a deal with a British tour operator to build a luxury lodge on the premises and to channel tourists to the area."

32. The Outpost was established by the Mix, a Johannesburg company, and sold in November 2006 to the Outpost Co. Ltd. Both are owned by white South African businessmen. Our information on the resort derives from a visit to it in March 2007 and on an informal interview there with Ms. Alex Johnson, one of its senior managerial staff.

33. Much of our description of Pafuri Camp, and of the Wilderness Safari operation there, is based on a research visit in March 2007; we spoke at length there to Ms. Hanèl de Wet, manager of the camp, and, more briefly, to other staff members. Note that the same company runs other camps in southern Africa, also ostensibly for the benefit of local populations. The social and economic impact of such enterprises, however, has raised deep concern among critical scholars (see, e.g., van Wyk 2003; Matthers and Landau 2007).

34. These phrases are quoted from a publicity sheet given to tourists at both Pafuri Camp and Makuleke Cultural Village. We visited the latter in March 2008.

35. Interview with Innocent Mamatho (a pseudonym), an ex-ranger now in an environmental management position for SANParks, Thulamela, 5 March 2007; Mamatho describes his own ethnicity as Venda.

36. See Leon Marshall, "Locals Benefit from Pafuri's New Lodges," *Sunday Independent*, 24 July 2005, 9. Note that the Makuleke are also referred to in the media as the Maluleke. For scholarly accounts, see, for example, Steenkamp and Uhr (2000); De Villiers (1999); and Ramutsindela (2002, 2004).

37. We are grateful to Silvana Dantu of African Equations for an account of the company, which is run by an estimable group of women of color in Cape Town. We met Ms. Dantu and Shareen Parker, the director, in August 2002.

38. See http://www.enterpriseig.co.za/display/BrandsDetails.asp?BrandID=232, accessed 18 October 2006. Enterprise IG claimed to be developing brands for three Royal Bafokeng enterprises: the Royal Bafokeng Economic Board, Royal Bafokeng Finance, and Royal Bafokeng Resources.

39. These quotations are taken from www.brandchannel.com, in particular, from its capsule review of Halter (2000); see http://www.brandchannel.com/books_reviews.asp?sb_id=59, accessed 2 June 2002.

40. Bindu D. Menon, "Popular Crafts Put Buddha Back with Masses," *Economic Times*, 26 September 2006, 4. The report went on to add that "even [corporate] clients who opt for ultra modern offices . . . have some corner dedicated to ethnicity."

41. See http://listservicedirect.com, accessed 9 August 2006.

42. Rob Walker, "Branding by the Slice" *New York Times Magazine*, 11 February 2007, 28. The italics are ours, but the elision is in the original text.

43. According to Lowenthal (1998:4), the "preoccupation with heritage" in the United Kingdom—as in the USA and France—"dates from about 1980." Note, in this respect, the rise in the UK of the discipline of Heritage Studies from the 1990s onward (Howard 2003:vii, 4, 14ff). "Cultural tourism," so named, has also developed a cadre of professional practitioners—and a literature aimed at them (see, e.g., Walle 1998).

44. See, respectively, http://www.namaste-uk.com, http://www.punjabkitchen .co.uk; http://www.ethnic-interiors.com; http://www.ethnicbritain.co.uk; http://www.totallyjewishproperty.com/agents/; http://www.foodyorkshire .com/foodyorkshire/ view.asp?content_id=329&parent_id=5, http://www .ethnicity.uk.com; and http://www.prweb.com/releases/1999/11/prweb 10581.htm, all accessed 20 November 2007. On the same date, a Google search under "marketing ethnicity in England" yielded 12,500 hits.

45. For source material on "Asian business" in England, see the British Library Web site, http://www.bl.uk/collections/business/asianbusiness.html, accessed 10 November 2006.

46. Lillian Pizzichini, "Shaman on You," *Independent on Sunday* (*Real Life*), 3 May 1998, 5.

47. Chanock's comment is made in the context of a critique of the part played by "culture talk"—specifically, of the ontological reduction of difference to culture (cf. Mamdani 2000:2)—in the politics of the ex-colonial world. The

interpellation into his argument of "weapons of mass instruction" is our own; so, too, is the definition of branding in the next sentence, which goes somewhat further than his.

48. According to the South African Human Rights Commission, 215 initiates died and 118 suffered penile amputations in just one province, the Eastern Cape, between 2001 and July 2006; see, for example, "Ndebele Initiations Safe Because They Put Pride before Profit," *Cape Times*, 24 October 2006, 4. Significantly, in light of what follows, the secretary of an Ndebele initiation school, in another part of South Africa, blamed accidents on the "profit-orientation" of those in charge of the rituals.

49. According to Fraser McNeill (2007:92), the effort of Venda leaders to "pre-serve cultural activities" is part of an "ideological attempt to re-brand them." Their initiative has led to the founding, with the aid of the National Arts Council, of a "center for tradition" (*Dopeni Vhulungani Siala*) in the Tshivhase area; it advertises courses in such things as bead making and tradi-tional dance—each at a set fee. Participation in the *domba* female initiation costs R300. It is open to outsiders at an increased charge (McNeill, personal communication, June 2007).

50. We use "aura" in the sense intended by Benjamin (1936 [1968]; see chapter 1, n.5 above) to connote the awe or reverence experienced in the presence of unique, authentic works of art in the age of mechanical reproduction. That aura, Benjamin added, embodies an elusive quality that appears to be anni-hilated by mass production. We will return to it below.

51. Mark Anthony Neal, "Benjamin, Warhol and the Aura: Use-Value and Exchange-Value," *The Pinocchio Theory*, blog archive, 26 October, 2005; http://www.shaviro.com/Blog?p=453, accessed 10 July 2006.

CHAPTER THREE

1. In their influential essay on "The Culture Industry," Adorno and Horkheimer (1979[1945]) likened modern mass culture to factory production in its capac-ity to manufacture standardized commodities, goods whose consumption rendered the populace similarly standardized, subject to market-driven de-sire and docile in the face of exploitation.

2. Note in this respect the activities of organizations like Suoma Sami Nuorat, a Sami movement that protests the exploitation of their culture and its images by government and commercial tourist ventures in Finland. Its members have demonstrated at the Santa Claus Theme Park in Rovaniemi, capital of Lapland, and their internet "site of protest," *SSN*, lists a series of indignities, from "fake 'shamanistic' ceremonies" and Lappish "winter fantasias" to play-ing cards depicting jolly Sami characters as drunken, drugged, and deranged; http://boreale.konto.itv.se/rovaniemi.htm, accessed 8 December 2006.

3. Cited by Mazzarella (2004:357).

4. This may, in turn, have an equivocal effect on ethnic self-recognition. Roger Chennels (personal communication) reports overhearing teenagers on the margins of a newly declared San settlement in the Northern Cape debating whether or not to assume the "native" dress and identity to which they were entitled.

5. Benjamin, unlike Adorno, did not lament the "disintegration of the aura" (Buck-Morss 1989:416, n.133). He saw the "aesthetic aura" of objects as a subjective illusion—by contrast to their "metaphysical aura," which "shone forth" when their truth was exposed. For him, mass culture, the source of modernity's mystification, also generated the energy that could propel a revelatory politics of art.

6. On the growing salience of the power of capitalism to produce variety, see Mary Zournazi, "Interview with Brian Massumi," *Port* (n.d.); http://www .theport.tv/wp/pdf/pdf1.pdf, accessed 10 May 2007. Because no further details are available on this text—it has not, to our knowledge, been published elsewhere—we do not annotate it in our bibliography.

7. Thus, for example, a major international newspaper carried a story in 2007 of the efforts of hotel chains, including the largest, to brand their service— especially in Europe—with a view to "creating a unique experience that inspires loyalty in customers." One, *Le Méridien*, which is owned by Starwood Hotels and Resorts, a giant US firm, has gone as far as to hire a "cultural curator" whose objective is to use "new ideas in design and the use of scent, sound and light to lure guests . . . to its brand." See Matthew Saltmarsh, "Hotel Cornucopia," *Internation Herald Tribune*, 14–15 July 2007, 11–12.

8. Mary Zournazi, "Interview with Brian Massumi," *Port* (n.d.); http://www .theport.tv/wp/pdf/pdf1.pdf, accessed 10 May 2007.

9. As Phillips and Steiner (1999:3) note, the dualism between Culture and culture often proved unstable in practice, not least because, by the late eighteenth century, both had already begun to circulate as commodities in the capitalist economy.

10. Greaves (1994) is a source book for indigenous peoples on the protection of their intellectual property rights, produced under the aegis of the Society for Applied Anthropology. In fact, there is now a burgeoning social science literature at the intersection of critical analysis and advocacy (see, e.g., Coombe 1998, 1999; Posey and Dutfield 1996; and the citations in n. 11 below).

11. See, for example, Posey (1994:227-233), Greene (2004:213), Greaves (1994), and Kirshenblatt-Gimblett (2006). For the UNESCO *Convention for the Safeguarding of Intangible Cultural Heritage* (2003), see http://www.unesco.org/ culture/ich_ convention/index.php?pg'00006, accessed 7 December 2006. This convention built on a series of earlier agreements and declarations, notably the Universal Declaration on Human Rights (1948), the International Covenant on Economic, Social and Cultural Rights (1966), the International Covenant on Civil and Political Rights (1966), the UNESCO Recommendation on the Safeguarding of Traditional Culture and Folklore (1989),

the UNESCO Universal Declaration on Cultural Diversity (2001), and the Istanbul Declaration (2002). As this suggests, the recognition of indigenous peoples' rights to their vernacular knowledge has been a cumulative process, beginning after World War II and accelerating with the end of the Cold War.

12. The declaration emerged from the 1993 Rockefeller Conference, "Cultural Agency/Cultural Authority: Politics and Poetics of Intellectual Property in the Post-Colonial Era"; for its text and signatories, a diverse, interdisciplinary group of scholars, see http://www.cwru.edu/affil/sce/BellagioDec.html, accessed 23 March 2005.

13. Stephen Godfrey, "Canada Council Asks Whose Voice Is It Anyway?" *Globe and Mail*, 21 March 1992, C1, C15; cf. Coombe (1993:250).

14. This contrasts with the scenario drawn by Shweder (2003:13), which identifies two inimical "paths": the "postmodern" one, which "leads to "a free flow of everything," with "boundaries . . . down, everything . . . up for sale, and nothing . . . sacred"; and a "premodern" one, where "everything is private, secreted and shielded from the interest and interests of outsiders, and the intellectual and social commons have been destroyed."

15. Also, for example, by Watson and Solomon (2001), writing of Maori in New Zealand, especially in respect of the Waitangi Tribunal. We shall return to this case below in another connection.

16. Julian Dibbell, "We Pledge Allegiance to the Penguin," *Wired Magazine*, 12 November 2004; http://www.wired.com/wired/archive/12.11/, accessed 17 August 2006.

17. Popularly dubbed the "Minister of Counterculture," Gil is a signatory to the Royal Society of the Arts' Adelphi Charter on Creativity, Innovation and Intellectual Property, which "calls on governments to restrain corporations from further locking down their ownership of ideas." See "Gilberto Gil on Open Source, Copyright, and Network Society," *Arthur,* 18 January 2006; http://www.arthurmag.com/magpie/?p=1081, accessed 17 August 2006.

18. Trademarks, in turn, lay claim to phrases or names, although advertising logos might bear both trademark *and* copyright.

19. "Gilberto Gil on Open Source, Copyright and Network Society," *Arthur,* 18 January 2006; http://www.arthurmag.com/magpie/?p'1081, accessed 17 August 2006.

20. See Christina Stucky, "Rooibos Row More Than a Storm in a Teacup," *Sunday Independent*, 7 March 2004, 15.

21. Lathrap (1976:200; see chapter 1, n.3 above) shows that Shipibo ceramicists have long produced innovative work in response to commercial demand for their art. From his account, however—he had difficulty in eliciting narratives on innovation even from his closest informant in the 1950s and 1960s—it is clear that the self-conscious idea of actually *being* "an innovator" is relatively recent. It appears to have crystallized with the recent growth of the market in, and the marketing of, Shipibo arts and artifacts.

22. Randeria (2007:13) notes the Indian government's claim that its obligations

under the World Trade Organization's *Agreement on Trade-Related Aspects of Intellectual Property Rights* (*TRIPS*) run counter to those under the UN's *Convention on Biological Diversity* or the Food and Agriculture Organization's *International Undertaking on Plant Genetic Resources*, which excludes patents on life forms. She adds (14), also, that the Indian Biodiversity Act (2002) "seems to undo the protection against the patenting of life forms" included in the Plant Variety Protection and Farmer's Rights Act (2001).

23. In another version of this argument, Blu (1980:227) holds that "ethnicity" should be restricted to the analysis of social differentiation in the USA and not be used at all for comparative purposes.

24. The topic entered anthropological discourse somewhat later. In 1969, Frederick Barth (1969:9) wrote that ethnicity was of "great, but neglected, importance" to the discipline. Until quite late in the twentieth century, in fact, identity seems only to have become a "problem" in situations of historical change. As Abner Cohen (1974:ix) put it: "the tribes, villages, bands, and isolated communities . . . until recently our traditional subject-matter, are everywhere today becoming integral parts of new state structures and are thus being transformed into ethnic groupings."

25. The theoretical literature surrounding this question is huge; there is no need to annotate it here. In respect of Africa, however, Crawford Young's typology (see, e.g., 1993), which enumerates three approaches to the analysis of cultural identity—the primordialist, the constructivist, and the instrumentalist—is fairly representative of efforts to lay out the discursive field, although the constructivist and instrumentalist are often taken to be broadly the same thing.

26. It is a matter of note, too, that, in the face of such nightmares of the global age as "fundamentalist Islam," adjectives like "primitive" and "antimodern" have a habit of reappearing, even in the academy (cf. Mamdani 2004).

27. After Glazer and Moynihan (1970, 1975).

28. Marilyn Strathern (1996:38–45) makes a similar point, albeit in respect of kinship statuses, not cultural identity. These, she says—speaking of "Euro-America"—"bring out contradictory appeals to choice and to genes" (38). She also cites Janet Dolgin (1990:104) who, in speaking of motherhood in the USA, points to a fundamental tension between "biological certainties" and "negotiation and choice."

29. This, again, is why a theoretical synthesis that seeks the ontology of ethnic identity in a fusion of the primordial and the instrumental cannot explain ethnicity. It merely re-describes, at a higher level of abstraction, the phenomenon as it is lived and experienced. Which is precisely what needs to be explained. Put another way, the critical problem is to account for the doubling at the core of cultural identity, not to typify it.

30. See http://www.med.nyu.edu/genetics/research/jewish_origins.html, accessed 28 September 2006, emphasis added. The research is being conducted under the aegis of the NYU School of Medicine & Hospitals Center Human

Genetics Program. We are grateful to Nadia Abu El-Haj for allowing us to read and cite her manuscript.

31. For the fascinating case of Jewish ethnicity in France—especially among Sephardic Jews of North African origin, for many of whom identity is invested at once in physiognomy and in the choice of a clothing style (*chalala*)—see Arkin (n.d.).

32. These quotations come from two sources. One is the DNA Print Genomics Web site, at http://www.dnaprint.com/welcome/press/press_recent/2003/ march_6, accessed 8 July 2006. The other is Margaret Ann Mille, "DNA Print Sells Racial Tests to Public: The Company Says the Technology Has Forensic and Genealogical Applications," *Sarasota Herald-Tribune*, 19 September 2002, D1, whose quotations, in turn, are attributed to Tony Frudakis, CEO of DNA Print.

33. Amy Harmon, "The DNA Age: Seeking Ancestry in DNA Ties Uncovered by Tests," *New York Times,* 12 April 2006; http://www.nytimes.com/2006/04/ 12/us/12genes.html?ex=1302494400&en= 94e1fa50f8081d8e&ei=5090, accessed 24 November 2006. On its Web site, adds Harmon, DNA Print Genomics once urged people to use its services "whether [their] goal is to validate [their] eligibility for race-based college admissions or government."

34. For GeneTree, see http://www.genetree.com, accessed 7 July 2006. The quoted passage is from http://www.genetree.com/ancestral/index.php, accessed 7 July 2006. On GeneBased Systems, see http://www. genebase.com, accessed 7 July 2006. The prose on these sites is similar: "Find the race of your ancestors by discovering your haplogroup. Were they European, and if so, which haplogroup did they belong to? Do you have a Native American ancestry? What about African ancestry? Do you belong to the famous Jewish Cohanim line?" See http://www.dnaancestryproject.com, accessed 11 July 2006. The DNA Solutions Web site is to be found at http://www.dnasolutions .co.uk, accessed 11 July 2006.

35. Harmon, "The DNA Age." The same paper carried another report on the topic three months later, "For Sale: A DNA Test to Measure Racial Mix," *New York Times*, 8 July 2006; http://query.nytimes.com/gst/fullpage.html?sec =health&res=9B07E6DA1538F932A35753C1A9649C8B63, accessed 11 July 2006.

36. The story was published with some amusement in the African media; see, e.g., "Guinea-Bissau Euphoric to Claim Hollywood's 'Hoppy' Goldberg as One of its Own," Sapa, *Cape Times*, 8 February 2007, 2. The quoted phrases are from this account, which also reported that Oprah Winfrey's DNA test was done for a PBS special program; it "found that her genetic make-up is overwhelmingly Papel and Bayote," two Liberian "tribes."

37. In a review of recent ethnographies on Native America, Pauline Strong (2005:257) notes that "sovereignty, the politics of identity, and the federal recognition and acknowledgment processes have emerged as central

themes." What is true of much of the rest of the world—with respect to the stress on the political in studies of ethnicity—seems to obtain here as well.

38. The upper case and the italics are allusions to the (sub)title of the volume in which he reflects on the matter; see Castells (2004). All the emphases in quoted passages in this paragraph are our own.

39. The term itself is the abstract form of the noun *muntu* (sing., "person"; plural, *bantu*). It is cited frequently, along with dignity, as a justification for banishing capital punishment in one of the foundational cases of the Constitutional Court, *S v Makwanyane* (CCT 3/94). The phrase quoted here is from the judgment in that case (85), which also contains a telling passage, penned by Justice Yvonne Mokgoro: "one shared value and ideal that runs like a golden thread across cultural lines, is the value of *ubuntu*—a notion now coming to be generally articulated in this country" (101).

40. The quoted passage, interestingly, is from a mass-circulation women's magazine. See Charlene Rolls, "*Ubuntu*: For Sale or For Soul," *Fairlady* (October 2005), 52–56.

41. At the time, Gordon Brown was chancellor of the Exchequer; he became prime minister in June 2007. We paraphrase here from his lecture to a conference on "The Future of Britishness," organized by the Fabian Society of the United Kingdom (14 January, 2006); see http://www.fabian-society.org.uk/press_office/news_latest_all.asp?pressid=520, accessed 10 July 2006. In May 2006, the ruling Labour Party proposed introducing a compulsory course on "core British values" into the school curriculum for 11–16 year olds; see, for example, http://news.bbc.co.uk/1/hi/education/ 4771443.stm, accessed 10 July 2006. For an example of the coverage of Britishness in a school text, see Oakland (2006:68–72).

42. For a critique of Gordon Brown's lecture, see Henry Porter, "The British, Thank Goodness, Don't Talk About Their Values," *Observer*, 9 July 2006, 23; also an editorial in the *Independent*, "Concept of Britishness," reprinted in the *Cape Times*, 29 January 2007, 8, which referred to the concept of "Britishness" as "ugly and ill-defined."

43. We owe this observation to Professor James R. Wilkerson of the Institute of Anthropology, National Tsing Hua University, Taiwan (personal communication, 30 May 2007).

44. Anderson's *Imagined Communities* (1983) has had a major impact on the social sciences, it must be said. But it has also been subjected to extensive critique; see, for example, Kelly and Kaplan (2001).

45. Demographically speaking, Western nation-states are coming to replicate the heterogeneity typical of postcolonies. The diversity of the latter is owed to the fact that, historically, colonizers paid little heed, in carving out their "possessions" abroad, to their social and cultural viability; also to long-standing regimes of "divide and rule."

46. Cf. Rancière (1999:104), who notes that, in the contemporary age, "emancipation" is supposed to "liberate the new community as a multiplicity of local

rationalities and ethnic, sexual, religious, cultural, or aesthetic minorities, affirming their identity on the basis of the acknowledged contingency of all identity."

47. This is also true of countries, like Britain and New Zealand, that lack written constitutions, but whose legal cultures—if we may use the term loosely—have become more tolerant of heterogeneity.

48. Controversy still rages as we write. In late 2006, for example, Jack Straw, a cabinet minister, called for the removal of "full" veils by Muslim women in certain civic contexts; this in the cause of "community relations." His comments provoked a storm of protest. See "Remove Full Veils, Urges Straw," *BBC News*, 6 October 2006; http://news.bbc.co.uk/1/hi/uk_politics/5411954.stm, accessed 27 December 2006.

49. This was part of an official initiative, "Protect and Respect: Everybody Benefits." It also promised to consider allowing Rastafarian officers to wear dreadlocks, but a telephone inquiry to the British police in Manchester on 25 July 2007 left it unclear whether a decision had ever been taken on the matter; our repeated written enquiries also went unanswered. For a contemporary report on the Metropolitan Police *hijab*, see Nick Hopkins, "Met Lets Muslim Policewomen Don Headscarves," *Guardian*, 25 April 2001, 9.

50. The van Gogh murder is often coupled, in respect of changing attitudes toward difference in Holland, with the killing in 2002 of Pim Fortuyn, a controversial anti-immigrant, anti-Islam, openly gay politician. These events, the public outrage surrounding them, the xenophobia that followed, and Muslim reactions, have been documented innumerable times. For one notably well-balanced account, see Gamal Nkrumah, "How Holland Lost Its Innocence," *Al-Ahram Weekly On-line*, 717, 18–24 November 2004; http://weekly.ahram.org.eg/2004/717/in1.htm, accessed 3 March 2005.

51. See the *International Social Survey Programme 2003: National Identity II* (ISSP 2003); http://zacat.gesis.org/webview/index.jsp?object=http://zacat.gesis.org/obj/fStudy/ZA3910, accessed 13 December 2006. On Israel, in particular, see Ram (2000).

52. Gibson's study was widely reported in the South African media. The citations here are from an insightful analysis of that study; see Jan Hofmeyr, "Our Racially Divided City Can Ill Afford Another Fear-Based Election Campaign," *Cape Times*, 3 August 2005, 11.

53. Lemke worked from audiotapes lodged at the Foucault archive in Paris. This lecture and another, "Sécurité, territoire et population," delivered in 1978, were later published under the title *Naissance de la biopolitique: Cours au collège de France* (Foucault 2004).

54. Neoliberalism, in this argument, is specifically associated with Chicago School economics (Lemke 2001:197f.).

55. Mary Zournazi, "Interview with Brian Massumi," *Port* (n.d.); http://www.theport.tv/wp/pdf/pdf1.pdf, accessed 10 May, 2007.

56. The 2006 Nobel Peace Prize was awarded to Muhammad Yunus, founder of

the Grameen Bank and pioneer in the field of microfinance. For the most extensive media coverage of the subject, see "Millions for Millions," Conrad Bruck, *New Yorker*, 30 October 2006; http://www.newyorker.com/archive/2006/10/30/06103fa_fact1, accessed 29 July 2007. Yunus's approach to microfinance, as Bruck points out, is not the only one. It has its detractors—most notably Pierre Omidyar, another major figure in the field—and competing models.

57. The quoted phrases come from two pages of the National Productivity Institute Web site: its home page, http://www.npi.co.za/, and http://www.npi.co.za/pebble.asp?relid=231, on "How to be more productive," both accessed on 26 July 2007. Note that the NPI has a corporate Web address.

58. Bongani Mthethwa, "Zulu Culture Wears the Pants," *Sunday Times* (Johannesburg), 9 September 2007, 7.

59. We are compelled, in this section, to repeat things we have covered in our previous work (e.g., 2003a, 2006), although we do so in abbreviated and amended form.

60. See, for two early works that make the point, albeit somewhat crudely, Jay (1971) and Page (1972). For a recent piece of popular journalism from South Africa that draws the parallel between "tribes" and modern corporations in highly specific terms, see Jabulani Sikhakhane, "Tribal Spirit Lives on in the Modern Corporate Jungle," *Cape Times*, Business Report, 20 February 2007, 2.

61. Both cases have been extensively documented. For accounts published in Africa, see "Nandi to Sue Britain over Leader's Killing," *Daily Nation on the Web,* http://nationaudio.com/News/DailyNation/ Today/News/News150920037 .html, accessed 15 December 2004; and Solomon Muyita, "Ugandan Monarchy Applies to Sue Britain," *Daily Nation* (Kenya), 13 October 2004.

62. See *Roy Sesana, Keiwa Seitlhobogwa, and Others v Attorney General, for Republic of Botswana*, MISCA no. 52-2002, in the High Court at Lobatse. This case—whose judgment is long and fairly technical, and was based on a primordialist understanding of Basarwa life with its origins in the British colonial period (Edwin Wilmsen, personal communication)—has been widely reported across the world. It is also drawing a great deal of scholarly attention at present. Note that Botswana Bushmen are said to prefer this ethnic label to the others, like Basarwa or San, commonly used of them. For further examples of suits lodged against postcolonial states by ethnic groups, see Comaroff and Comaroff (2006).

63. This quotation and the one below on genetic tampering are from an interview with Maui Solomon, the barrister who represented the six tribes, published in *In Motion Magazine*, 22 April 2001; see http://www.inmotionmagazine.com/nztrip/ms1.html, accessed 10 January 2007.

64. It is not just governments that are being made answerable to history. Elsewhere (2006) we document suits against corporations, churches, and other institutions initiated by ethnic groups for alleged acts of violence committed against them in the past.

65. Note that, since we first used the term in the manner defined here, it has become part of public discourse in the USA, albeit in two different guises. One is associated with the administration of George W. Bush, by which it is deployed to describe "the strategy" by enemies of the USA "of using or misusing law as a substitute for traditional military means to achieve military objectives"; see Phillip Carter, "Legal Combat: Are Enemies Waging War in Our Courts?" *Slate,* 4 April 2005; http://slate.msn.com/id/ 2116169, accessed 20 May 2005. The other is the converse: it refers to a "carefully orchestrated Bush Administration policy" to discredit human rights ("habeas") lawyers who seek to protect clients from illegal detention, torture, and other acts that threaten their lives and violate their freedoms (Horton 2007:74).

66. See, for example, Peleikis (2006) for a revealing Lithuanian case.

67. The Makuleke leadership, with the help of the Legal Resources Center, is currently challenging the Communal Land Rights Act, claiming that it violates the constitution by reinforcing patriarchal traditional authorities to the detriment of women and ordinary residents on tribal land. See Christelle Terreblanche, "Controversial Land Rights Bill Delayed," *Sunday Tribune,* 26 November 2006, 24; Robins and van der Waal (n.d.).

68. *CILS in the News;* http://www.calindian.org/groundhog.fall2003.htm, accessed 7 December 2006.

69. Case no. 1999-CC-3096, Y*osefa Alomang, on behalf of herself and all others similarly situated, v Freeport-McMoRan, Inc., and Freeport-McMoRan Copper and Gold, Inc.,* brought in the Civil District Court for the Parish of Orleans in the State of Louisiana. On 21 February 1997, this lawsuit was dismissed on the grounds that it was an Indonesian matter. But it generated considerable public reaction within the US. See *Alomang v Freeport;* http://stats.utwatch .org/corporations/freeportfiles/alomang- filing.html, accessed 7 December 2006; also *Risky Business: The Grasberg Gold Mine. An Independent Annual Report on P.T. Freeport Indonesia, 1998.* Berkeley: Project Underground; http:// www.moles.org/Project Underground/downloads/risky_business.pdf, accessed 7 December 2006.

70. *CILS In the News,* Fall 2003; http://www.calindian.org/groundhog.fall2003 .htm, accessed 7 December 2006.

71. Jeffrey Rosen, "Supreme Court Inc.," *New York Times Magazine,* 16 March 2008; http://www.nytimes.com/ 2008/03/16/magazine/16supreme-t.html?_r =1&oref=slogin, accessed 17 March 2008.

CHAPTER FOUR

1. This statement was widely quoted. For one version, from a Native American source, see *Indian Country Today,* 19 December 2006; http://www .indiancountry.com/content.cfm?id=1096414204, accessed 9 July 2007. The title of the chapter, note, is an allusion to the Baffler's splendidly iconoclastic *Commodify Your Dissent* (Frank and Weiland 1997).

2. An online version of the act is to be found at http://www.infca.org/tribes/ IRA.htm, accessed 2 July 2007. All quotations from the IRA are taken from this source. For scholarly annotation and discussion of the law itself, see, for example, Deloria (2002), Taylor (1980), and Cohen (1941)—and, for one extended case study of its application, Biolsi (1992). We are grateful Susan S. Gooding (see below, acknowledgments) for alerting us to the terms of the act and to these writings; also to Brian Daniels, a doctoral student at the University of Pennsylvania, for helping us to broaden our understanding of the legal archaeology of incorporation among the First Peoples of the USA.

3. See Alaska Native Claims Settlement Act, 43 U.S.C. § 1606, Regional Corporations, (d), (f), and (g)(1)(A). Provision was also made under this chapter for the establishment of a thirteenth regional corporation to include nonresident natives.

4. See Alaska Native Claims Settlement Act, 43 U.S.C. § 1604, Enrollment(b) (1)–(4).

5. See Alaska Native Claims Settlement Act, 43 U.S.C. § 1602, Definitions (b).

6. See also "The Alaska Native Claims Settlement Act," *Alaska Native Knowledge Network,* University of Alaska, Fairbanks; http://www.ankn.uaf.edu/NPE/ ancsa.html, accessed 15 December 2006.

7. ANCSA instituted a twenty-year moratorium on sales of ANCSA shares to *non*-Natives, but the restrictions were to be loosened thereafter.

8. Caroline Brown (personal communication, circa May 2002). In addition to the primary sources cited, and Dombrowski (2001, 2002), this paragraph draws from an early draft of Brown's doctoral dissertation (Brown n.d.; see acknowledgments).

9. Dombrowski (2002:1064–65) notes that ANCSA opened up new divisions between shareholders and nonshareholders—and also between resident and nonresident members of village corporations. There were also great differences in the exploitable resources of different regions; those in resource-poor areas, he says, resent the corporate format of the settlement and favor the re-creation of tribal governing bodies. Dispute over the "profit-sharing" stipulations of the act has led to frequent litigation; much of the profit gleaned by successful corporations has found its way into the hands of non-native lawyers.

10. See the Sealaska Web site at http://www.sealaskaheritage.org/celebration/ about.htm, accessed 9 July 2007.

11. Again, Dombrowski (2002:1069f; cf. also 2001:257) provides telling detail here. He notes that converts to the Pentecostal and Evangelical churches— which are spreading across southeast Alaska, especially among marginal sectors of the population—have not merely denounced these "sinful" things; they have gone as far as to set fire to, among other things, the paraphernalia of the Celebration dance festivities and of the ANCSA corporations that support them.

12. We visited Mashantucket in September 2003; these very brief notes date from that visit.

13. The act states that tribes wishing to open gaming operations must negotiate with state governments under their prevailing regulations. It also set up the National Indian Gaming Commission, which established three classes of Indian gaming: class I, which covers "social" games of chance related to ceremonial activities, falls under tribal jurisdiction; class II, which includes games played by individuals against each other for a common prize (like bingo or card games), is regulated by states in conformity with their laws; class III, which involves "Las Vegas"–style gambling (roulette, slots, craps, etc.) that pit players against a house, is similarly controlled. State law varies widely: Nevada is highly permissive while Utah bars gambling entirely. All class III gaming requires that a specific compact agreement be issued by a state government to a tribal authority. The act has been criticized on many counts, from the imprecision of its framing to its breach of Indian sovereignty (see below; also Mezey 1996; Harvey 2000; Darian-Smith 2002).

14. Donald L. Bartlett and James B. Steele, "Playing the Political Slots: How Indian Casino Interests Have Learned the Art of Buying Influence in Washington," *Time,* 23 December 2002; http://www.time.com/time/magazine/ article/0,9171,1003911,00.html, accessed 22 December 2006.

15. Thus, for example, *Time* ran an extended report on the topic; see Donald L. Bartlett and James B. Steele, "Wheel of Misfortune: Special Report on Indian Casinos," 16 December 2002, 44–58. We refer to this report hereafter as "Wheel of Misfortune."

16. Adrian Sainz, "Seminole Tribe of Fla. Buying Hard Rock," *Yahoo! Finance,* 7 December 2006; http://biz.yahoo.com/ap/061207/hard_rock_cafe_seminole _tribe.html?.v=29, accessed 9 December 2006.

17. Lisa Simeone (personal communication, 5 April 2007), a University of Chicago student who had extensive dealings with Native American leaders while working for the US government, recalls often having heard them joke that "the wealthier the tribe, the higher the blood quota necessary to prove membership." Whether this is empirically true or not, it is very telling that Indian leaders should think it.

18. Our discussion of this and parallel cases here is informed by four sources: (i) Christine Graef, "Disenrollment: 'We're Not Alone Any More,'" *News from Indian Country: The Independent Native Journal,* 2002, http://www .indiancountrynews.com/fullstory.cfm?ID=272, accessed 1 December 2006; (ii) Louis Sahagun, "Battle over Rights to Casino-Fuelled Gravy Train Pits Grandparents against Kids," *Sunday Independent* (South Africa), 22 February 2004, 16; (iii) Emily Bazar, "Native American? The Tribe Says No," *USA Today,* 28 November 2006, http://www.usatoday.com/news/nation/ 2006-11-28-tribes-cover_x.htm, accessed 2 January 2006; and (iv) Deirdre Newman, "High Court Passes on Pechanga Case," *North Country Times,* 23 May 2006, http://www.pechanga-nsn.gov/page?pageId=431, accessed 1 February 2007.

19. It is held that 13 percent of casinos account for 66 percent of the overall

take. See, again, "Wheel of Misfortune," 46; also John M. Broder and Charlie LeDuff, "California Looks to Casinos for Revenue: New Deal with Indian Tribes Could Mean $1.5 Billion More a Year," *New York Times*, 2 February 2003, 14.

20. A poignant narrative of the history of the Lytton Band was given by Margie Mejia, tribal chairwoman, to the Senate Indian Affairs Committee on 5 April 2005; see http://indian.senate.gov/2005hrgs/ 040505hrg/mejia.pdf, accessed 7 July 2007. For purposes of this composite account, we rely on Mejia's testimony and several other sources, among them three pieces of investigative journalism: Pia Sarkar, "The Urban Gamble—Tribal Land Rush: Native Americans Bet Future on Bay Area Casinos," *San Francisco Chronicle,* 28 May 2001, A3; Zachary Coile, "San Pablo Indians, Feinstein Strike Deal that Keeps Casino from Growing," *San Francisco Chronicle*, 10 May 2007, B2; and Donald L. Bartlett and James B. Steele, "Who Gets the Money," *Time*, 8 December 2002, http://www.time.com/time/magazine/article/ 0,9171,397528-5,00 .html, accessed 14 July 2007. Wikipedia also has an extensive entry on the Lytton Band of Pomo Indians, but some of its content is disputed; see http://en.wikipedia.org/wiki/Lytton_ Band_of_Pomo_Indians, accessed 3 July 2007.

21. The legislation was inserted as a three-line amendment into an entirely unrelated budget bill voted on the last day of the 2000 congressional session. Its author was George Miller, a Democrat into whose congressional district San Pablo falls. See, for example, Richard Brenneman, "Governor's San Pablo Casino Deal Fulfills Hopes of GOP Operatives," *Berkeley Daily Planet*, 20 August 2004; http://www.berkeleydailyplanet.com/text/article.cfm?archiveDate =08-20-04&storyID=19452, accessed 14 July 2007.

22. It was most actively opposed by Harry Reid, Democratic senator from Nevada, who tried to reverse the amendment in the following congressional session; see "Governor's San Pablo Casino Deal Fulfills Hopes of GOP Operatives." A Republican congressman from Virginia, Frank Wolf, was quoted as calling the law a "disgrace"; see "Who Gets the Money."

23. See, for example, John M. Hubbell, "WASHINGTON—Indian Gambling Debate Comes to Capitol Hill: Lytton Band to Make Its Case for San Pablo Slots," *San Francisco Chronicle*, 5 April 2005, B1; also US Senator Dianne Feinstein home page, "Hearing Scheduled on Hearing Lytton Gaming Plan" (*sic*), 21 March 2005; http://feinstein.senate.gov/05releases/r-lytton-hrng.htm, accessed 20 December 2006.

24. James May, "Eight-Member Augustine Tribe Opens Casino," 30 July 2002; http://www.indiancountry.com/content.cfm?id=1028034940, accessed 10 July 2007. See also "Wheel of Misfortune," 46, 58 and *California Indians and Their Reservations*, a Web site maintained by the San Diego State University Library; http://infodome.sdsu.edu/research/guides/calindians/calinddict .shtml (last updated 4 June 2007), accessed 9 July 2007. These sources, from which all quotations in the paragraph are drawn, differ in the minutiae of

the story; we have composited what appears to be the most reliable overall account.

25. *California Indians and Their Reservations.*

26. Augustine Casino now has a Web site; see http://500nations.com/casinos/caAugustine.asp, accessed 12 July 2007.

27. Timothy Egan, "Lawsuit in California Asks, Whose Tribe Is It, Anyway?" *NYTimes.com,* 10 April 2002; http://www.citizensalliance.org/links/pages/news/National%20News/California.htm, accessed 19 December 2006.

28. James May, "Dispute Arises at Buena Vista Rancheria over Legal Heir," *Indian Country Today,* 25 October 2000; http://www.indiancountry.com/content.cfm?id=586, accessed 19 December 2006. A brief, somewhat patchy history of the Me-Wuk of Buena Vista is available at http://www.buenavistatribe.com/tribal_history.htm, accessed 12 July 2007.

29. "Lawsuit in California Asks, Whose Tribe Is It, Anyway?" See also Charlie LeDuff, "With Riches at Stake, Two Tribes Square Off," *New York Times,* 2 February 2002, 14.

30. "Rhonda Morningstar Pope's Biography," *Buena Vista Me-Wuk Indian Tribe* home page; http://www.buenavistatribe.com/rhonda_bio.htm, accessed 19 December 2006.

31. See Michael Fitzgerald, "Casino's Hose Aimed at Stockton," *Recordnet.com,* 26 October 2005; http://www.recordnet.com/apps/pbcs.dll/article?AID=/20051026/OPED0301/510260333/-, accessed 19 December 2006.

32. "Rhonda Morningstar Pope's Biography."

33. "Wheel of Misfortune," 46–47.

34. David Melmer, "*Time* Marches on Indian Country," *American Indian Nations,* 13 December 2002; http://www.americanindian.ucr.edu/discussions/gaming/articles/index.html, accessed 22 December 2006. Some critics accused Donald Barlett and James B. Steele, the authors of this feature, of fronting a scathing attack on "Indian people." Others, however, deemed the piece "competent."

35. See their Web site, http://www.paragongaming.com/about.html, accessed 12 July 2007.

36. See Brian Hickey, "High-Stakes Politics," *Philadelphia Weekly Online,* 21 March 2001; http://www.philadelphiaweekly.com/view.php?id=3631, accessed 14 July 2007.

37. The octogenarian Lim reportedly handed his financial operations to his son, Tan Sri Lim Kok Thay, in 2005. See "Lim Goh Tong"; http://en.wikipedia.org/wiki/Lim_Goh_Tong, accessed 19 December 2006.

38. "Wheel of Misfortune," 52f. The following material on Sol Kerzner is drawn from the same source.

39. See "Lyle Berman: There Is a Ramification for Every Decision," *Launch Poker*; http://www.launchpoker.com/players/poker_players/-lyle-berman-/, accessed 19 December 2006.

40. There are literally thousands of accounts of Sam Katz and the Lytton Band casino. A sample of those that we have found most useful are "High-Stakes Politics"; "Governor's San Pablo Casino Deal Fulfills Hopes of GOP Operatives"; "Who Gets the Money"; and "The Urban Gamble."

41. See "Who Gets the Money." All the passages in quotation marks in this paragraph are from the same source.

42. See, for example, Suzanne Malveaux et al., "Lobbyist Admits to Kickbacks, Fraud: Abramoff Agrees to Cooperate in Washington Corruption Probe," *CNN.com*, 3 January 2006; http://www.cnn.com/2006/POLITICS/01/03/abramoff.plea/index.html, accessed 19 December 2006.

43. Our use of this term parallels the notion of "biocapital" developed by Kaushik Sunder Rajan (2005), in which capital and biophysical life forms come to coproduce each other in new composite kinds of value.

44. The Lytton Band, obviously, does not conform to this generalization. Nor does the Wyandotte Tribe, which, backed by its own non-Indian financier, was permitted by the Bureau of Indian Affairs to build a casino on its land in downtown Kansas City, across the street from city hall. Kansas officials successfully contested the opening of the gaming house in a state court. But the 10th US Circuit Court of Appeals overturned the decision on two grounds, one of which was that the recognized sovereignty of the Wyandotte had been infringed; see Megan McCloskey, "Appeals Court Rules in Favor of Wyandotte Casino," *Indian Country Today,* 20 April 2006; http://www.indiancountry.com/content.cfm?id=1096412852, accessed 20 December 2006.

45. See http://www.buenavistatribe.com/tribal_events.htm, accessed 15 July 2007.

46. See http://www.pequotmuseum.org, accessed 20 December 2006, accessed 12 December 2006.

47. The *Urban Dictionary*, an online lexicon of slang, defines "Rez Car [piece of shit car]" as "a car that can be started with a screwdriver. Plastic covering one or more windows. Mirrors may be missing or secured with duct tape. Brake lights may be covered with red tape. Has a rag for a gas cap. Four bald tires. A car long passed its prime"; see http://www.urbandictionary.com/define.php?term'Rez+car+%5Bpiece +of +shit+car%5D, accessed 15 July 2007.

48. See *Meswaki Nation Times,* 4(5):10, 9 March 2007; http://www.meskwaki.org/newpages/newsletter/ V4I5.pdf, accessed 15 July 2007.

49. We owe the development of this point to an exchange with our colleague, Jessica Cattelino, whose highly original work on the topic is cited above. Says Cattelino (personal communication): "public debate overlooks the sovereign dimensions of Native American enterprise, which is seen to grow out of 'special rights' rather than sovereignty. The conflation of indigeneity with ethnicity has . . . trap[ped] Indians between the discourses and policies of multiculturalism and those of sovereignty-based rights."

50. The story of the agreement is best told, from the Navajo perspective, in Brenda Norrell, "Navajo Nation, Cuba Negotiate Trade Agreement," *Indian Country Today*, 31 August 2006; http://www.indiancountry.com/content .cfm?id=1096413568, accessed 17 July 2007. All quoted passages come from this report.

51. In June 2007, the House of Representatives passed the Lumbee Recognition Act in the face of long-standing opposition from the Cherokee and Tuscarora; the former, it seems, because, as a casino-owning tribe, they feared competition, the latter because they accuse the Lumbee of not being "real" Indians and of having stolen their heritage in order to seek sovereignty and its benefits. At the time of writing, however, the Senate had yet to vote on the legislation—which specifically *excludes* the Lumbee from building a casino. For a fairly full account of the Congressional process, see http://www .newsobserver.com/politics/ story/596206.html, accessed 2 August 2007.

52. Both Gray Davis and Arnold Schwarzenegger, as governors of California, sought to renegotiate the compact first signed by the state with Indian gaming tribes in 1999; that compact had secured a lower proportion of casino revenues than had those agreed by New York and Connecticut. In 2005, Schwarzenegger announced new compacts with five leading gaming tribes. They yielded more revenue, promised to establish detailed environmental, labor, and building codes, and agreed to abide by binding arbitration in certain kinds of disputes with local governments and customers. In return, the tribes retained a monopoly on casino gambling in the state and were allowed to exceed existing limits on the number of slots per establishment. See "Indian Gaming in California," Institute of Governmental Studies, University of California, Spring 2005, http://www.igs.berkeley.edu/library/htIndian Gaming.htm, accessed 26 December 2006; "California Looks to Casinos for Revenue," 14; Daniel B. Wood, "California Controversy: Gold Rush into Casinos," *Christian Science Monitor,* 31 August 2004, http://www.csmonitor.com/ 2004/0831/p02s01-usgn.htm, accessed 22 December 2006.

53. See Corey Kilgannon, "Son of Tribal Leader Held in Drug Raid in the Hamptons," *New York Times*, 20 April 2007, B6. The Shinnecocks, it appears, have begun legal proceedings in order to open a casino in the Hamptons.

54. James C. McKinley Jr., "End to State and Tribe Dispute Removes Obstacle to Casino," *New York Times*, 10 May 2003, A16.

55. See "Playing the Political Slots."

56. Testimony of Dr. James A. Thurber before the US Senate and Committee on Indian Affairs re Indian Tribes and the Federal Election Campaign Act, 8 February 2006; http://www.indian.senate.gov/2006hrgs/ 020806hrg/Thurber .pdf, accessed 22 December 2006.

57. Federal Election Commission press release, 8 February 2006; http://www .fec.gov/press/press2006/ 20060208testimony.html, accessed 22 December 2006.

58. "Playing the Political Slots."

59. While the Fair Political Practices Commission had expected the attorney-general of California to represent them in the suit, he declined. It has been noted that he had himself been a recipient of contributions from the Agua Caliente and other Indian bands; see "Playing the Political Slots."

60. One unreported donation was said to have been made to a committee supporting Proposition 51, a statewide ballot initiative that, had it succeeded, would have included funding a rail line from Los Angeles to Palm Springs, where the tribe operates a casino. See *Agua Caliente Band of Cahuilla Indians v. The Superior Court of Sacramento County* (Fair Political Practices Commission, Real Party in Interest) S123832 Ct. App. 3 C043716 Sacramento County Super. Ct. No. 02AS04545; http://www.fppc.ca.gov/litigation /34C6D84F .pdf, accessed 22 December 2006.

61. See *Agua Caliente Band of Cahuilla Indians v The Superior Court of Sacramento County* (Fair Political Practices Commission, Real Party in Interest), 3.

62. See *Agua Caliente Band of Cahuilla Indians v. The Superior Court of Sacramento County* (Fair Political Practices Commission, Real Party in Interest), 9.

63. "The Urban Gamble," A3.

64. Repatriation claims under NAGPRA, the Native American Graves Protection and Repatriation Act, can only be made by tribes already granted federal recognition. Reburial thus provides cultural reinforcement of their sovereignty. We thank Robert McLaughlin for his expert guidance on these issues.

65. For vernacular accounts of Wyandotte history, see their Web site; http:// www.wyandotte-nation.org/, accessed 19 July 2007.

66. Jennifer Auther, "Uses of Sacred Symbol Causes New Mexico Controversy," 14 September 1999; http://www.cnn.com/US/9909/14/new.mexico.flag/, accessed 20 July 2007. The preceding quote is from the same source.

67. This was reported on the Web site of the National Association of Tribal Historic Preservation Officers. See Reed Upton, "Zia Pueblo Receiving Money For Use Of Sun Symbol," 2 December 2005; http://www.nathpo.org/News/Legal/ News-Legal_Issues27.html, accessed 20 July 2007.

68. We owe this point to Susan Gooding (personal communication), from whom the quoted words also come. We are grateful to her, too, for alerting us to other, similar cases, among them, a Lakota effort "to grow and culturally brand hemp" and an Ojibwa initiative to brand and sell indigenous plant products "in the name," significantly, "of funding land buy-backs and alternative economic development."

CHAPTER FIVE

1. For example, Kenneth Good (e.g., 2003), a harsh critic of the Botswana government who was later expelled from the country, has suggested that the removal of the Basarwa had to do with a desire on the part of the state to develop diamond and uranium resources in the area (cf. also Taylor 2007:4). For

their part, the authorities claimed, among other things, that the Bushman do not belong in the Kalahari any more; that, as a historical result of changes in their life style, their presence interferes with the desert ecology and its conservation. For nuanced readings of the conflict, see Wilmsen (2008) and Taylor (2007).

2. See http://www.amnestyusa.org/artistsforamnesty/mar2004.html and http://www.landrightsfund.org/ content_projects.html, both accessed 1 July 2005.

3. For an account of the meeting between the San and Navajo leaders at Canyon de Chelly, see http://www.thetrackingproject.org/native.htm, accessed 2 August 2005.

4. This on the (technically correct) ground that the court decision allowed a "traditional" hunter-gatherer population to return to land on which it had formerly foraged—but required *neither* that a modern Bushman community be resettled on the terrain nor that essential services be provided; see also above, n. 1 and chapter 3, n. 62.

5. See John Grobler, "The San Are Losing Ground," *Mail & Guardian,* 24–30 November 2006, 27.

6. An account of the *60 Minutes* story, broadcast on 21 November 2004, may be found, under the title "African Plant May Help Fight Fat," at http://www.purehoodia.com/cbs_news.htm, accessed 15 June 2005.

7. See Tom Mangold, "Sampling the Kalahari Cactus Diet," *BBC News,* 30 May 2003; http://www. purehoodia.com/bbc.htm, accessed 12 June 2004.

8. See "Hoodia Life—The Fastest, Most Effective Weight Loss Supplement"; http://121. superpills.net, accessed 25 February 2006.

9. "Sampling the Kalahari Cactus Diet."

10. According to its Web site, the CSIR was "constituted by an Act of Parliament in 1945 as a science council. [It] undertakes directed and multidisciplinary research, technological innovation as well as industrial and scientific development to improve the quality of life of the country's people. . . . The CSIR's shareholder is the South African Parliament, held in proxy by the Minister of Science and Technology." See http://www.csir.co.za/about_us.html, accessed 12 November 2007.

11. See Antony Barnett, "In Africa the Hoodia Cactus Keeps Men Alive. Now Its Secret Is 'Stolen' to Make Us Thin," *Observer,* 17 June 2001; http://education.guardian.co.uk/print/0,,4205467-102275,00.html, accessed 31 October 2002.

12. One elder confided that "When the grandfathers eat the Xhoba, the grandmothers can't let them out of their sight." See Rory Carroll, "It's Green, Prickly and Sour, but This Plant Could Cure Obesity and Save an Ancient Way of Life," *The Guardian Unlimited,* 4 January 2003; http://education.guardian.co.uk./higher/research/story/0,, 869492,00.html, accessed 10 January 2007.

13. John Kamau, "How San Nearly Lost Their Heritage," *Daily Nation on the Web*, 11 April 2002; http://www.nationaudio.com/News/Daily/Nation/11042002/Comment/Comment22.html, accessed 13 October 2002.

14. As we note in our acknowledgments, we are especially grateful to Roger Chennells for his generosity in sharing with us a great deal of the information recorded here. John Comaroff first interviewed Chennells in Stellenbosch (South Africa), on 24 February 2005; we subsequently spoke to him, at length, several times during 2006–7.

15. The South African segment of the reserve was previously known as the Kalahari Gemsbok National Park. Critics have argued that the San "award" was not really a land grant: it merely acknowledged their historic connection with the region and permitted them access to it for ritual purposes, to gather natural resources, and to participate in development initiatives by selling crafts to tourists.

16. See the WIMSA Web page: http://www.san.org.za/wimsa/home.htm, accessed 10 January 2007.

17. This is clear from the SASI Annual Review, April 2001–March 2002. We have drawn extensively on that review for our account here; http://www.san.org.za/sasi/ann_rep_2002.htm, accessed 22 February 2005. See also Garland (1999) and Sylvain (2005) on Namibia.

18. "San Representation and Leadership," WIMSA; http://www.wimsanet.org/advnet_sanrep.asp, accessed 10 January 2007.

19. Lesley Stahl, "African Plants May Help Fight Fat," CBS Worldwide Inc., 21 November 2004; http://www.purehoodia.com/cbs_news.htm, accessed 21 November 2004.

20. "How San Nearly Lost Their Heritage."

21. See Melanie Gosling, "Hoodia 'Diet Plant' under Threat from Illegal Exports," *Cape Times,* 24 November 2006, 4; Tamar Kahn, "Prickly Dispute Finally Laid to Rest," *Business Day*, 22 March 2002, http://allafrica.com/stories/printable/200203220129.html, accessed 31 October 2002.

22. See *The Bushman's Secret,* a documentary by Rehad Desai, UHURU Productions, 2006; also "San Community Compensated for their Knowledge," *SABC,* 22 August 2002, wysiwyg://141/ http://www.sabcnews.co.za/ . . . e/print_whole_story/0,1093,41364,00.html, accessed 31 October 1002.

23. "Prickly Dispute Finally Laid to Rest."

24. "Prickly Dispute Finally Laid to Rest." This report also goes into some of the criticisms of the accord, as does, among others, "Hoodia 'Diet Plant' under Threat from Illegal Exports," 4.

25. See Indigenous Knowledge Systems Web site, Department of Science and Technology, Republic of South Africa; http://www.dst.gov.za/publications/reports/IKS_Policy%20PDF.pdf, accessed 2 January 2007.

26. See, again, "Prickly Dispute Finally Laid to Rest"; also Rachel Wynberg, "Indigenous Knowledge at Risk," *Weekly Mail & Guardian*, 18 December 1998, http://www.mg.co.za/articledirect.aspx?articleid=180483&area'%2farchives_print_edition%2f, accessed 12 January 2007.

27. Dominique Herman, "San Reap No Benefits as Companies Flout Law and Sell Fake or Illegal Hoodia Products," *Cape Times*, 13 March 2006, 3.

28. Mary Duenwald, "An Appetite Killer for a Killer Appetite? Not Yet," *New York Times,* 19 April 2005, D5; also "Hoodia 'Diet Plant' under Threat from Illegal Exports," 4.

29. See "African Plants May Help Fight Fat." The involvement of Unilever has also drawn criticism on the ground that, by some accounts, it has a poor record of honoring agreements with indigenous peoples; see *The Bushman's Secret.*

30. Roger Chennells (2007) has written a detailed account, "San Hoodia Case: A Report for *GenBenefit,*" as yet unpublished, that describes both the sociolegal environment in which this ethno-corporation has emerged and the institutional forms in which it is vested.

31. See Paul Kenyon, "Row over Bushmen 'Genocide,'" *BBC Radio 4's Crossing Continents,* 6 November 2005; http://news.bbc.co.uk/2/hi/programmes/crossing_continents/4404816.stm, accessed 13 December 2006. Wilmsen (2008) criticizes Survival International for sparing little effort to malign the Botswana government, largely in support of its own primordialist fantasy—derived, he says, from the romantic fiction of Laurens van der Post (1958, 1961)—which portrays the Bushmen as the "oldest form of human life on earth" and, hence, as worthy of protection.

32. For instance, speaking of the Omaheke San, Sylvain (2005:358f) reports that, while most differentiate themselves from non-San, many have intermarried; ethnicity among them, it seems, "is often reckoned opportunistically." The majority live as menial laborers on farms, although increasing numbers have landed up in areas set aside for indigent peoples, variously termed resettlement camps, squatter areas, cattle posts, or—in an older, colonial parlance—reserves.

33. SASI Annual Review, April 2001–March 2002, 8; http://www.san.org.za/sasi/ann_rep_2002.htm, accessed 31 October 2002. The other citations in this paragraph, unless otherwise specified, are taken from the same annual review, 4–9. See also Robins (2003:12f).

34. Before the land restitution of 1999 took them back to the Kalahari, as we note above, Kruiper's people had lived at Kagga Kamma, where they participated in a joint eco-tourist venture with its owners. The latter responded by saying that the coloureds had stepped in when the San left them in the lurch, that most were "married to Bushmen," and that their identity made no difference to visitors. But Kruiper insisted that his tradition was being "tampered with"; for its part, the San Institute claimed that this was a violation of "fair trade." See "Not the Real San, but Tourists Fooled," *IOL,* 30 June 1999; http://www.iol.co.za/index.php?set_id=1&click_id-13&art_id=ct19990630230014436K500156, accessed 23 January 2007.

35. See http://www.sanparks.org/about/news/2007/july/kgalagadi.php, accessed 11 August 2007. !Xaus Lodge opened in July 2007.

36. The quotation from Steyn in the first part of the sentence is from Vicki Robinson, "Newly Empowered San 'Must Learn to Redefine Their Freedom,'"

Sunday Independent, 8 September 2002, 10; the passage describing the project is from the Ezase Afrika Trading Web site, its page on "Cultural Industries," at http://www.ezaseafrika.co.za/cultural.htm#Sisen, accessed 13 August 2007.

37. Spanning a range of electronic music, the album has tracks with titles like "Kalamari Warriors"—no mispelling this, its subtitle is "Squiddly Mix"—and features "leaders in the drum 'n bass, trance, ambient and deephouse" genres. See Niall McNulty, "Ancient San Healing Songs Cross Cultures," *Cape Times*, 24 April 2002, 4. As of August 2007, the CD was still being advertised on kalahari.net (M.E.L.T. is the label, product number, ELM8037). The quoted passages are derived from both the newspaper article and the CD cover—which notes that all revenue from the project goes to WIMSA.

38. All the quoted material is taken from a photocopied handout, "Art of Africa: Frequently asked Questions regarding Bushmen Art," which we obtained from a visit to a branch of the gallery at Huguenot Square, Huguenot Road, Franschhoek, Cape Province, on 16 August 2007. The company also produces glossy brochures. Its Web address is http://www.theartofafrica.co.za.

39. See "Newly Empowered San 'Must Learn to Redefine Their Freedom,'" 10.

40. SASI Annual Review, April 2001–March 2002; http://www.san.org.za/sasi/ann_rep_2002.htm, accessed 31 October 2002 (emphasis added). See also ‡Oma and Thoma (2002).

41. SASI Annual Review, April 2001-March 2002; http://www.san.org.za/sasi/ann_rep_2002.htm, accessed 31 October 2002.

42. Speech by Minister Mosibudi Mangena at the Dinner of the South African Development Community Workshop on Indigenous Knowledge Systems held in Pretoria, 7 June 2004. See South African Government Information, http://www.info.gov.za/speeches/2004/04062109451001.htm, accessed 29 August 2007.

43. See *The Bushman's Secret*.

44. The same is true, more generally, of "development" initiatives among "the Bushmen" under the aegis of the various NGOs in this field; see Garland (1999).

45. See Gavin Evans, "'Extinct' San Reap Rewards," *Mail & Guardian*, 3–9 January 2003, 12.

46. The so-called Kalahari (Bushmen) debate concerns the way in which economy, society, and culture among the San-speaking peoples are to be characterized: whether these peoples ought to be seen as "prehistoric" hunters and gatherers, having been "authentically" such since time immemorial (e.g., Lee and Devore 1968; Lee 1992, 2002; Lee and Guenther 1993, 1995), or whether, as revisionist scholars argue (e.g., Wilmsen 1989, 1993; Wilmsen and Denbow 1990), their predicament is a relatively recent historical effect of their relations with other populations in the region. For overviews of the debate, especially in contemporary archaeology, see, for example, Smith (1996), Sadr (1997), and Kent (2002).

47. Roger Chennells (personal communication) recalls an exchange between two teenagers about the pros and cons of accepting San identity. One said that he was not about to jump about in animal skins; his mate retorted that the solution was to sport a bit of skin "as an accessory"—and an alibi.

48. SASI Annual Review, April 2001–March 2002; http://www.san.org.za/sasi/ann_rep_2002.htm, accessed 31 October 2002.

49. See Rampholo Molefhe, "Defender of His People's Rights," *Mmegi Online*, 2 July 2004; http://www.mmegi.bw/2004/July/Friday2/7262190111769.html, accessed 1 February 2007.

50. See South African Human Rights Commission (SAHRC), "Human Rights Violations in the Khomani San Community," 3 March 2005; http://www.info.gov.za/speeches/2005/05030409451004.htm, accessed 24 January 2006.

51. See Alex Duval Smith, "Kalahari Bushmen Win Ancestral Land Case," *Independent Online*, 14 December 2006; http://news.independent.co.uk/world/africa/article2073037.ece, accessed 22 January 2007.

52. This "benefit sharing agreement and joint venture," as mandated by the South African Biodiversity Act (10 of 2004), was signed on 15 March 2007; under clause 6, "Payment," it laid down that the San would be paid "the amount of R24 per kilogram of dry *Hoodia* to be exported." In August 2007, the Hoodia Growers Association of Namibia announced that it would begin to export on a substantial scale by 2008. It did not, however, say whether it had an agreement with WIMSA; see "Namibia: Country to Export Hoodia," *New Era* (Windhoek), All.Africa.com. http://allafrica.com/stories/200708160788.html, accessed 20 August 2007.

53. See *The Bushman's Secret*. Roger Chennells (personal communication) has termed it "the horse that is galloping fastest."

54. See *The Bushman's Secret*. /Una is pronounced *Koona*.

55. See Andrew W. Donaldson, "Sex Tourists Set to Go Barking Mad," *Sunday Times*, 25 March 2007, 2.

56. See Lani Holtzhausen, "Bafokeng Will Diversify Income, Says New 'CEO,'" *Mining Weekly*, 17–23 November 2000, 2–3. This report suggests that the present king, Leruo Molotlegi, "views himself not as royalty, but as the CEO of Bafokeng Inc., an apt description of a nation that has built up considerable wealth on the back of its platinum interests." Susan Cook, an anthropologist who has worked among Bafokeng for many years and enjoys the confidence of Leruo (see above, chapter 2, n. 9; below, acknowledgments), suggests otherwise (personal communication): the young king, she says, sees himself *both* as royal leader of his people *and* as a thoroughly modern business figure. John Comaroff came away with the same impression on first meeting him in 2003. We return to this point in the text below.

57. In 1858, the legislature of the Transvaal considered permitting the sale of land by Boers to blacks, with title being held by government. After a commission had looked into the proposal, it was resolved in 1871 to allow

for the (conditional) acquisition of real estate by "kaffir tribes." But the resolution never became law. The proscription against purchase remained in force—despite efforts of Bafokeng to reverse it—until 1877, when Britain annexed the Transvaal (Royal Bafokeng Nation 2003); see below.

58. Mokgatle's efforts to purchase the land also appear to have depended on the patronage and the paternalism of the legendary Boer leader, Paul Kruger, with whom he clearly had a complicated relationship (Bergh 2005:95, 102–112; Bozzoli 1991:35). For whatever reasons—they are not entirely clear—Kruger seems to have enabled the Bafokeng chief to evade the strict letter of the law.

59. There is a large literature on the history of Bophuthatswana, most of it in scholarly articles. For those unfamiliar with South Africa, Jones (1999) and Lawrence and Manson (1994) provide informative, if not exhaustive, overviews.

60. For the case record, see *Bafokeng Tribe (Applicant) v. Impala Ltd., Bophuthatswana Ministers of Departments of Energy Affairs and Land Affairs, and President of the Republic of South Africa (Respondents)* in the High Court of South Africa (Bophuthatswana Provincial Division), no. 1716/95.

61. Truth and Reconciliation Commission, Amnesty Committee, application in terms of section 18 of the Promotion of National Unity and Reconciliation Act, no. 34 of 1995, Peter Ishmael Rocky Malebana-Metsing, applicant (AM7674/97), 27 February 2001, AC/2001/077.

62. Interestingly, Mangope's machinations, and his collusion with the mining conglomerate, paralleled a broadly similar incident in the USA in the 1920s: in that one, when Navajo leaders rejected requests from Standard Oil for exploration leases on their terrain, they were summarily deposed and replaced by an acquiescent "Navajo Governing Council" at the order of the secretary of the interior (Gooding 2006).

63. For the announcement, dated 8 February 2002, see http://www.implats.co .za/press/press21.html, accessed 15 November 2002.

64. This quote is taken from a speech at Emory University, 5 May 2006, by King Leruo Molotlegi. It was entitled "Navigating the New South Africa: Notes from the Royal Bafokeng Kingdom."

65. "Bafokeng Will Diversify Income, Says New 'CEO,'",2.

66. See Mike G. C. Wilson, "South Africa's Geological Gifts," *Geotimes*, December 2003; http://www. geotimes.org/dec03/feature_SAfrica.html, accessed 25 August 2007.

67. See "The King Who Slays Holy Cows" and "The Future Lies in Diversifying," *Enterprise* (supplement), September 1999, 2–4, 17–18.

68. "Bafokeng Will Diversify Income, Says New 'CEO'"; see also Paula Gray, "People of the Dew," *Leadership*, August 2003, 10–16.

69. See Carli Lourens, "Bafokeng Construction to Close Shop This Year," *Business Day*, 19 August 2002, electronic edition; http://www.asaqs.co.za/ news/240802.htm, accessed 3 September 2007. As it turns out, there has

not been much take up of small business opportunities—or any great signs of a new entrepreneurial spirit—among ordinary Bafokeng as yet, for all the ethno-preneurialism of the RBN (Susan Cook, personal communication).

70. Both were announced on http://www.Mbendi.co.za, an African business site. For the first deal, in which the Bafokeng were the majority shareholder, see "Mobil and Royal Bafokeng in Joint Venture," 9 September 1998; for the second, "Mobil Oil South Africa and The Royal Bafokeng Administration Clinch Shareholding Deal," 1 June 2000.

71. See Ilja Graulich, "Bafokeng Nation Extends Portfolio," *Business Day*, 28 February 2001, electronic edition; David McKay, "Bafokeng's Cunning Plan," *Miningmx*, 13 October 2004; http://www.miningmx.com/mining_fin/388082.htm, accessed 11 November 2005.

72. Both agreements were signed in August 2002. On the first, see Rob Rose, "Bafokeng and Angloplat in R4bn Deal," *Business Day*, 12 August 2002, electronic edition. The details of the second were announced electronically on 15 October 2002 by Bell Dewar and Hall, legal advisors to the Bafokeng; see http://www.belldewar.co.za/news/articles_financiallaw/finlaw_article_20020815.htm.

73. See Julie Bain, "Royal Bafokeng Nation May Eventually Seek to List Extensive Mining Interests," *Business Day*, 30 August 2002, electronic edition.

74. See "Sale of a 10% Stake of SA Eagle in Support of Black Economic Empowerment in South Africa," *Zurich Financial Services*, http://www.zurich.com/main/mediarelations/mediareleases/2005/english/ article, accessed 22 August 2007; "Zurich in South Africa," *Zurich Financial Services*, http://www.saeagle.co. za/media_relations_release_ 130405.php, accessed 22 August 2007.

75. See, for example, Wiseman Khuzwayo, "Astrapak Investors Agree to Sell Twenty Per Cent of Equity to Royal Bafokeng Finance," *Cape Times*, Business Report, 13 January 2005, 1.

76. See, for example, "Concor and Bafokeng Nation in BEE Deal," *Engineering News*, 11 August 2005; http://www.engineeringnews.co.za/article.php?a_id=72070, accessed 28 August.

77. See "Bafokeng Buys Fraser Alexander," iAfrica.com., 6 Oct 2005; http://business.iafrica.com/ news/498147.htm, accessed 28 August 2007.

78. See Sapa, "Royal Bafokeng Takes 26% Stake in MB Technologies," *Mail & Guardian Online*, 1 December 2005, http://www.mg.co.za/articlePage.aspx?articleid=258212&area=/breaking_news/breaking_ news__business/, accessed 28 August 2007; "Royal Bafokeng Buys Majority Stake in MB Technologies," *Engineering News*, 1 March 2007, http://www.engineeringnews.co.za/article.php?a_id=102942, accessed 30 August 2007.

79. See, for example, Neesa Moodley, "Bafokeng, Senwes Conclude BEE Deal," *Business Report*, 8 December 2005; http://www.busrep.co.za/index.php?fSectionId=552&fSetId=662&fArticleId=3026586, accessed 26 August 2007.

80. See Nicky Smith, "Bafokeng Score with R3.4bn Impala Deal," *Cape Times,* Business Report, 15 December 2005, 17.

81. See http://www.mbendi.co.za/orgs/csuh.htm, accessed 30 August 2007, which lists a number of additional interests credited to Royal Bafokeng Holdings. Our object, however, is not to be exhaustive; it is merely to make plain the sheer scale and the rapid growth of Bafokeng, Inc.

82. See, for example, Sikonathi Mantshantsha, "Royal Bafokeng Buys PSL Club," *News 24,* 24 May 2007; http://www.news24.com/News24/Sport/Soccer/ 0,,2-9-840_2118756,00.html, accessed 28 August 2007.

83. Another very recent venture—with Yomhlaba Resources, a coal mining company—was approved by the Competition Tribunal of South Africa in June 2007. See http://www.comptrib.co.za/%5Ccomptrib%5Ccomptribdocs %5C675%5C29LMMar07.pdf, accessed 27 August 2007.

84. The intent of the act is, inter alia, "to provide for the recognition of traditional communities; to provide for the establishment and recognition of traditional councils; [and] to provide a statutory framework for leadership positions within the institution of traditional leadership." See http://www.info .gov.za/gazette/acts/ 2003/a41-03.pdf, accessed 15 July 2007.

85. We are grateful to Susan Cook (see also above, n.56 and below, acknowledgments) for acting as a sounding board and a source of information as we compiled this summary account of the internal governance and corporate structure of Bafokeng, Inc.; all errors or anachronisms, of course, are our own.

86. See "Royal Bafokeng Nation May Eventually Seek to List Extensive Mining Interests."

87. In February 2006, one of the executives of Royal Bafokeng Holdings, Gillian Kettaneh, who is responsible for legal and corporate affairs, told us that this was not a priority at the time. It may, however, change in future.

88. The three Enterprise IG Web sites from which this text is composited are http://www.enterpriseig.co. za/display/BrandsDetails.asp?BrandID=230, http://www.enterpriseig.co.za/display/BrandsDetails.asp?BrandID=231, and http://www.enterpriseig.co.za/display/BrandsDetails.asp?BrandID=232, accessed 8 October 2006. The *Annual Review 2006* of Royal Bafokeng Holdings, on its inside cover, adds that "the crocodile is recognised for having stood the test of time; for its strength and resilience during hardship; and for its reputation as a caring, nurturing parent—all qualities with which both the RBN and RBH enjoy being associated" (Royal Bafokeng Holdings 2007). People who live in Africa, most of whom think of the crocodile as a vicious killer, might be surprised at the bit about nurture, care, and parenting.

89. See Yin Ping, "Crocodile Rock," *ChinaDaily.com,* 5 September 2007; http:// www.chinadaily.com.cn/ bizchina/2006-02/13/content_535160.htm, accessed 5 September 2007.

90. "Bafokeng Want Everyone to Share in the Community's Wealth," *Business Report,* 1 May 2005; http://www.busrep.co.za/index.php?fSectionId=569 &fSetId=662&fArticleId=2503692, accessed 2 August 2007.

91. The document, *The Policy Gap: A Review of the Corporate Social Responsibility Programmes of the Platinum Mining Industry in the North West Province*, is available at http://www.bench-marks.org/ downloads/070625_platinum _research_summary.pdf, accessed 27 August 2007. The Bench Marks Foundation is a church-based organization.

92. King Leruo has also expressed his concern at the ecological damage done by the mines; see Molotlegi (2007a:5).

93. For just one example, see King Leruo's "Message from *Kgosi*" to the Royal Bafokeng Nation in 2007, in which he speaks of the necessity of "governance" always being "transparent, efficient, accountable, and effective" (Molotlegi 2007a:4).

94. See http://damariasenne.blogspot.com/2007/04/royal-bafokeng-na tions-ict-plan.html, posted 17 April 2007, accessed 29 August 2007.

95. Kriel (n.d.) stresses that Bafokeng is at once "inclusionary" and "exclusionary" but implies that its boundaries are more open than Cook (n.d.[b]) suggests. However, her data show that the king is indeed anxious about the influx of "people who are not Bafokeng" (12); that those Bafokeng who are unconcerned about the presence of non-Bafokeng may be precisely the ones for whom they are a source of income (14); that nonpaying squatters are not just unwelcome, but are seen as uncivil ("rough"; 9); and that the subject seems to provoke feelings of ambivalence in almost everyone (passim).

96. See http://www.bizcommunity.com/Company/196/82/100308.html, accessed 30 August 2007.

97. This occurred in an informal discussion over lunch at King Leruo's home in Phokeng in July 2003; present were John Comaroff, Joshua Comaroff, and Susan Cook.

98. In similar vein, Susan Cook, in an email to us written in February 2006, observed that, when he addressed the Asantahene from Ghana in Phokeng, King Leruo spoke repeatedly and emphatically about the significance of culture.

99. "Taking Pride in Their Heritage," *Enterprise* (supplement), September 1999, 14. In the *Kgotha Kgothe 2007 Report* (Royal Bafokeng Nation 2007:32), this project appears under tourism. It lists the initiatives in a slightly different manner to those originally described by Mme Molotlegi and reports that the scheme was at the tender evaluation stage in August 2007.

100. Michael Dynes, "Platinum King's Riches Reconcile Old and New Traditions," *Times Online*, 16 August 2003; http://www.timesonline.co.uk/tol/news/ world/article873733.ece, accessed 20 August 2007.

CHAPTER SIX

1. In the case of Israel, argues Yiftachel (2006), ethno-nationalism is the basis of a specific, late-modern form of colonial governance, which he subsumes under the term "ethnocracy."

2. Thus Adam Smith's (1904) well-known condemnation of joint stock companies for unnaturally constraining the workings of the free market: in *The Wealth of Nations* (book 1, chapter 7, para. 28) he rails against "the exclusive privileges of corporations" for raising market prices above "natural" levels and, thereby, for diminishing the "public opulence" (see also editor's introduction, para. 1.16). More recent theorists have had equally strong views, from those who dub the corporation an "accomplishment . . . beyond the power of any individual or any other type of organization in human history" (Brown 2003), through the likes of Noam Chomsky (2000:47), who followed John Dewey in seeing it as a form of "private power" that undermines democracy and freedom, to those who, after Ambrose Bierce's *Devil's Dictionary* (1911), deem it "an ingenious device for obtaining individual profit without individual responsibility."

3. *Santa Clara County v. Southern Pacific Railroad*, 118 US 394 (1886). This case, which arose out of a California law that taxed railroad property, is considered a turning point in the extension of Constitutional rights to juristic persons. While the court never actually ruled on the extension of that right to the railroad companies, a statement by Chief Justice Waite on the point was to influence later legal decisions: "The court does not wish to hear argument on the question whether the provision in the Fourteenth Amendment to the Constitution, which forbids a State to deny to any person within its jurisdiction the equal protection of the laws, applies to these corporations. We are all of the opinion that it does." This statement is recorded in the syllabus and case history above the opinion, but not in the opinion itself.

4. See Bleifuss (1998) and Korten (1996); also, "A Short History of Corporations," *New Internationalist*, July 2002; http://findarticles.com /p/articles/mi _m0JQP/is_2002_July/ai_89148684, accessed 7 August 2007.

5. See *West Coast Hotel Co. v. Parrish*, 300 US 379 (1937).

6. Cover copy for Westbrook (2007).

7. "Storm in a Coffee Cup," *Knowledge for Development*, 15 July 2004; http:// knowledge.cta.int/en/content/view/full/867, accessed 12 October 2007. See also David Brough and Reese Ewing, "Decaf Coffee Find Brews into Ownership Spat," *Reuters News Wire*, 13 July 2004. The story was printed in a number of places. For one on-line version, see http://abcnews.go.com/wire/ SciTech/reuters20040713_425.html, accessed 19 August 2006.

8. See, again, "Decaf Coffee Find Brews into Ownership Spat."

9. "Problem With Your Country's Image? Mr. Anholt Can Help," *Guardian*, 11 November 2006, 1–2 (emphasis added).

10. This passage, including the block quote, is excepted from Corporate Identity Documentation, a Web magazine "for designers interested in branding and corporate identity." See http://www.cidoc.net, under "Argentina National Brand," 30 July 2006, accessed 8 August 2006. Its given source is Guillermo Brea, but it also bears the signature of Robert Salzmer.

11. See "Brand the Beloved Country . . . A Design Indaba Project," *Design Indaba*, News, 2005; http://www.designindaba.com/news/news2005/article240406 .htm, accessed 5 June 2006.

12. See Brendan Boyle, "Leadership Endgame Destined for Stalemate," *Sunday Times*, 7 January 2007, 15–16.

13. This caricature is not all that fanciful. Across the world, if somewhat unevenly, the "corporate capture" of political parties has become a public preoccupation. In South Africa, for example, "ANC Inc." has appeared at the head of newspaper articles (e.g., Vicki Robinson, "Moves to Clamp Down on ANC Inc.," *Mail & Guardian*, 4–12 August 2006, 2), all the more so since the dealings of its investment company, Chancellor House Holdings, has come to light. This company, formed in 2003, had investments totaling R1.75 billion in late 2007. See, for example, Buddy Naidu, "New ANC Probes Old Guard's Shady Deals," *Sunday Times* (South Africa), 24 February 2008, 1; also Feinstein (2007).

14. The version of the cartoon that we saw was published in the *Sunday Times* (South Africa), 3 December 2006, Business Times, 8.

15. "A Proper Job Description for Mwai Kibaki," *Sunday Nation,* 29 December 2002; http://www.nationaudio.com/News/DailyNation/29122002/ Comment/Comment29123.html, accessed 27 July 2007. This statement was first drawn to our attention in 2005 by Sunkyo Im, then an undergraduate student at the University of Chicago.

16. See its Web site, http://www.heritagegb.co.uk, accessed 7 July 2006; note the "co," the designation of a *company*, rather than "gov," the e-moniker of state.

17. George Monbiot "Welcome to Britain plc," *Guardian Unlimited*, 9 September 2000, online edition; http://www.guardian.co.uk/imf/story/ 0,7369,370382,00.html, accessed 7 July 2006.

18. See Faisal Islam, "Whatever Happened to Big Economics," *Observer* (London), 3 June 2001, Business Section, 3.

19. See "Moves to Clamp Down on ANC Inc.," 2; specifically on Thabo Mbeki as "chief executive," see "Back to Work," editorial, *Cape Times*, 12 February 2007, 8.

20. There has been a great deal written about the third sector in the British press. For two examples, both highly informative—coincidentally, published on the same day in the same newspaper—see Patrick Butler, "Roles Fit For Heroes," *Guardian*, 25 July 2007, 3, and "Tough Choices For Charities on Commissioning," Jane Dudman, *Social Guardian*, 10. Our quotations in this paragraph are drawn from these two accounts.

21. The invasion of corporate-speak into the language of social relations and civic life is notable: we talk, unthinkingly, of domestic "partners," community "stakeholders," even criminal "firms" and "associates." Sports teams in the USA and beyond are now referred to as "franchises" and "brands." These days, Ivan Vladislavić (2006:164) notes of Johannesburg, street vendors

assume the attitude of "managers." Meanwhile, in Cape Town, *The Big Issue* (September 2007, 122[11]:cover), a local homeless magazine, enjoins readers to "Make Your Brand Do It." And *CNN* invites viewers across the world to "Take Your Seat in the Boardroom."

22. Andy Buckley and Arkady Ostrovsky, "Back in Business—How Putin's Allies Are Turning Russia into a Corporate State," *Financial Times*, 19 June 2006, 11.

23. Andrew E. Kramer, "Gazprom Reaps the Benefit of Friends in the Kremlin," *New York Times*, 23 September 2006, .B4.

24. J. F. O. McAllister, "Russia's New World Order," *Time*, 10 July 2006, 14–19.

25. See Peter Finn, "Kremlin Inc. Widening Control over Industry," *Washington Post*, 19 November 2006; http://www.washingtonpost.com/wp-dyn/content/article/2006/11/18/AR2006111801012.html, accessed 28 November 2006. The *New Yorker* also carried a story under the title "Kremlin, Inc." just two months later (Specter 2007); while it covered some of the same material, its central point was different, focusing on the question, "why are Vladimir Putin's opponents dying?"

26. For one widely syndicated account of Nashi, originally published by the *Times* (London), see "Putin's Sinister Summer Camp." We read it in the *Sunday Times* (South Africa), 29 July 2007, 20 (no author given). The quoted phrases are from this account.

27. First reported in Conal Walsh, "Putin Plan to Shut Out US Oil Giants: Kremlin Will Favour Norwegian Firms to Develop Barents Sea Field after Differences with Bush Scupper Russia's Bid to Join WTO," *Observer*, 23 July 2006, Business, 2.

28. This initiative, and reactions to it, were widely reported in the British press at the time. For two summary accounts, see Terry Macalister, "Britain Has 'Nothing to Fear' from Gazprom," *Guardian*, 17 July 2006, 21; and Hans Kundnani, "We're Not Putin's Policy Tool, Gazprom Tells Mps," *Guardian*, 19 July 2006, 22.

29. This was also widely reported in the world media. For one extensive account in the UK, see Terry Macalister, "FSA Sought Government's View on Whether to Allow Rosneft to Float," *Guardian*, 19 July 2006, 22; another is to be found in Peter Gumbel, "Crude Power," *Time*, 10 July 2006, 20–23.

30. See Carter Dougherty, "Europe Acts to Protect State-Run Interests: Officials Are Wary of Large Investments by China and Russia," *International Herald Tribune*, 14–15 July 2007, 1, 14.

31. Note, in this respect, the recent bailout of two major banks, UBS and Citigroup, by Singapore and Abu Dhabi, respectively. These bailouts, involving sovereign wealth funds and state corporations, were variably received. On one hand, Larry Summers, former US Treasury Secretary, expressed concern, referring to them—inappropriately, in our view—as "cross-border nationalizations"; see, for example, Floyd Norris, "A New Twist on Bailouts," *International Herald Tribune*, 14 December 2007, 14. On the other hand, the Swiss National Bank—USB is the largest finance house in Switzerland—openly

welcomed the Singaporean initiative; see Haig Simonian, "Central Bank Blessing for UBS Injection," *Financial Times*, 14 December 2007, 16. Recently, the USA has sought and won a commitment from both Singapore and Abu Dhabi to disavow "geopolitical goals" in their investment strategies; see, for example, Steven R. Weisman, "Sovereign Wealth Funds Accept U.S. Limits on Goals," *International Herald Tribune*, 22–23 March 2008, 15.

32. Andy Beckett, "Everything Must Go," *Guardian*, 4 July 2006, G2, 10. The quotations pertaining to the British economy in the next paragraph also come from this source, an exercise in forensic journalism which offers an excellent summary of debates on the topic to which we were witness in the UK in June–July, 2006.

33. "Everything Must Go," 10.

34. Notes Mark Gilbert,: "The latter example is . . . likely to set the blueprint for the future . . . Chinese companies, awash with cheap money from state-owned banks and backed by a $2 trillion economy, have the firepower to fund a global spending spree in consumer product companies, energy utilities, automakers—and financial services companies. The howls of protest that greet China's first attempt to buy a US or European bank will make the grousing over CNOOC seem mild." See "China Blamed for Currency Woes, Commodities, Missing Sock," 29 December 2005; Bloomberg.com; http://quote.bloomberg.com/apps/news?pid=10000039&refercolumnist_gilbert&sid=aC_fG4IOiWWk, accessed 15 August 2007.

35. For further detail, see the Tatarstan home page at http://www.tatar.ru and its various subsidiary pages, especially those on the local economy. The declaration of sovereignty is to be found at http://www.tatar.ru/index.php?DNSID=04bff57b51b8d6c78e1cbf90369faed9&node_id=150, accessed 7 August 2006; material on the attraction of foreign investment is summarized at http://www.tatar.ru/index.php?DNSID=04bff57b51b8d6c78e1cbf90369faed9&node_id=1335, accessed 7 August 2006. We were first made aware of the energy with which Tatarstan is seeking to build a sovereign economic identity, erected on a firm cultural and historical scaffolding, during a visit by John Comaroff to the Republic, in 2002, as a member of the National Academy of Sciences Committee on Conflict and Reconstruction in Multiethnic Societies.

36. Advertisement paid for by the Government of Ontario, *Economist*, 24–30 June 2006, between 42 and 43 (emphasis added).

37. For one example of the advertisement, see the *Mail & Guardian*, 21–27 July 2006, 4–5 (emphasis added). Meanwhile, Mpumalanga's neighbor, Limpopo, has established an organization named Trade and Investment Limpopo to market itself as a destination for both finance and industrial capital; see Wiseman Khuzwayo, "Limpopo's Prolific Growth of 6.3 percent Steals a March on Other Provinces in SA," *Sunday Independent*, Sunday Business Report, 6 August 2006, 3.

38. *Abdur Rehman Mubashir v. Syed Amir Ali Shah*, PLD 1978 Lahore 113. We were made aware of this case, and derive our summary of it, from the doctoral dis-

sertation research of Asad Ahmed (2006:chap. 3); all the page references in this paragraph are to Ahmed's study.

39. *Zaheeruddin v. The State* (1993; *Supreme Court Monthly Review*:1718); again, see Ahmed (2006:40–41).

40. For anthropological accounts of Islamic financial practices, especially with respect to banking, see Maurer (2005, 2006). On Sharia-compliant investment in South Africa, which has spawned an Accounting and Auditing Organisation for Islamic Financial Institutions, and which is making major inroads into the domain of SRI ("socially responsible investing), see Ashraf Mohamed, "Sharia-Compliant Unit Trusts Are Growing Rapidly," *Cape Times*, Business Report, 31 July 2007, 13.

41. Among them, Municipality, Inc. Brian Schwegler (2007:23) has described the striking case of Komárno and Komáron, twin cities separated by the Slovakia-Hungary border. Populated primarily by ethnic Hungarians, they appear to be evincing a shared urban *cultural* identity of their own. And to be commodifying it. Orthogonal to the nationalities in which it is embedded, that identity is expressing itself in efforts to "initiate trans-border cooperative cultural branding and tourism" based on a "consumer profile . . . [rooted in] Hapsburg nostalgia."

CHAPTER SEVEN

1. This view of Ethnicity, Inc., which treats it as a "concrete abstraction," a process at once general and specific, echoes Moishe Postone's (1993:127–28) profound reading of Marx's characterization of "the double character of commodity-producing labor"—and hence of commodification itself—at the heart of capitalism.

2. For a review of *The Realm of a Rain-Queen* (Krige and Krige 1943), that begins with an allusion to Haggard's "famous, fantastic story of 'She-who-must-be-obeyed,'" see Meek (1944:274–78).

3. Some dismiss entirely the usefulness of the idea of "ethnic conflict," noting that the causes of such conflict always lie in more basic political and economic factors; see, for example, Gilley (2004).

4. Much of this attention has grown out of the tendency to take as axiomatic that there has been a marked increase in ethnic violence since the end of the Cold War. But has there? The answer remains a subject of contention; see, for example, Huntington (1993); Kaplan (1994); and Wallensteen and Sollenberg (1995).

5. Rwanda Development Gateway, "Cultural and Heritage Tourism Vie for Top Slot in Rwanda"; http://www.rwandagateway.org/rubrique.php3?id _rubrique=65, accessed 22 August 2007. Unless otherwise noted, all the quoted phrases in this paragraph are from the same source.

6. This quotation is from Sandra Laville, "Two Years Late and Mired in Controversy: The British Memorial to Rwanda's Past," *Guardian*, 13 November

2006; http://www.guardian.co.uk/rwanda/story/0,,1946300,00.html, accessed 22 August 2007. For a scholarly account of Murambi School and the "politics of preservation," see Cook (2005b:298–302). Note that her eyewitness account differs in two respects from the others cited here: according to it, first, the bodies are *not* placed where they died (302), and, second, it was not children, but mothers clutching their offspring, whose arms were outstretched in self-protection (300).

7. See, again, "Two Years Late and Mired in Controversy."

8. Dr. Sean Gottschalk, personal communication, 23 August 2007.

9. In the wake of the attack, Uganda was estimated to have lost 90 percent of its foreign tourism. See Ross Herbert, "Guerrillas vs. Gorillas—Tourists Take on Ugandan Guerillas to See Endangered Gorillas," *Insight on the News*, Bnet Research Center, 9 August 1999; http://findarticles.com/p/articles/mi_m1571/is_29_15/ai_55426734, accessed 24 August 2007.

10. Ingrid Melander, "'Poverty Tourism' Injects Money into Townships: Foreign Visitor Boom," *Cape Times,* 24 August 2007, 9.

11. "German Travel Agents Robbed in South African Township," Bnet Research Center, December 2005; http://findarticles.com/p/articles/mi_kmafp/is_200512/ai_n15885592, accessed 12 October 2006.

12. Mark Banks, *Ek's a Doos from South Africa*, Baxter Theater, Cape Town, August 2003.

13. All the quoted passages in this paragraph are taken from Bocarejo's doctoral dissertation (2007); it is to her that we owe our familiarity with this case.

14. Herero women have sold themselves as ethnicized photographic objects, replete with their dolls, for several decades. A colleague from the University of the Witwatersrand has told us of similar sightings in Windhoek many years ago.

15. We visited this "graft market" on 27 August 2006. The three vendors to whom we spoke were all young men from Blaauwkrans. The manufacture of elephant dung paper appears to have been learned from an NGO that once sought to teach crafts to the local population but has since moved elsewhere.

Bibliography

ABU EL-HAJ, NADIA
n.d.   *Genetic Anthropology: The History of the Jews and the Making of a Discipline*. [In preparation.]

ADORNO, THEODOR W.
2006   Culture Industry Reconsidered. *The Adorno Reader*. Edited by Brian O'Connor. Oxford: Blackwell.

ADORNO, THEODOR W., AND MAX HORKHEIMER
1979   *The Dialectic of Enlightenment*. Translated by John Cumming. London: Verso. First edition, 1945.

AFRICAN STUDIES ASSOCIATION
2001   Special edition on ethnicity. *African Issues* 29, nos. 1–2.

AGAMBEN, GIORGIO
1998   *Homo Sacer: Sovereign Power and Bare Life*. Translated by Daniel Heller-Roazen. Stanford: Stanford University Press.

AHMED, ASAD
2006   "Adjudicating Muslims: Law, Religion, and the State in Colonial India and Post-Colonial Pakistan." Ph.D. dissertation, University of Chicago.

ALEINIKOFF, THOMAS ALEXANDER
2002   *Semblances of Sovereignty: The Constitution, the State, and American Citizenship*. Cambridge, MA: Harvard University Press.

ALEXANDER, CATHERINE
2004a   Review of *Who Owns Native Culture?* by Michael F. Brown, 2003. *POLAR* 27, no. 2:113–128.

2004b   The Cultures and Properties of Decaying Buildings. *Focaal—European Journal of Anthropology* 44:48–60.

ALLAHAR, ANTON
1994   More than an Oxymoron: Ethnicity and the Social Construction of Primordial Attachment. *Canadian Ethnic Studies* 26:18–34.

ANDERSON, BENEDICT
1983   *Imagined Communities: Reflections on the Origin and Spread of Nationalism.* London: Verso.

ANDREWS, LORI B., AND DOROTHY NELKIN
2001   *Body Bazaar: The Market for Human Tissue in the Biotechnology Age.* New York: Crown.

APPADURAI, ARJUN
1990   Disjuncture and Difference in the Global Cultural Economy. *Public Culture* 2:1–24.

ARKIN, KIMBERLY
n.d.   Clothing, Class, and Ethnic Ambiguity: Looking Jewish in Paris. Ms.

ASAD, TALAL, ED.
1973   *Anthropology and the Colonial Encounter.* London: Ithaca Press.

AZARYA, VICTOR
2004   Globalization and International Tourism in Developing Countries: Marginality as a Commercial Commodity. *Current Sociology* 52, no. 6: 949–967.

BANAJI, JAIRUS
1970   The Crisis of British Anthropology. *New Left Review* 64:71–85.

BANK, MARCUS
1996   *Ethnicity: Anthropological Constructions.* London and New York: Routledge.

BANKSTON, CARL L., III, AND JACQUES HENRY
2000   Spectacles of Ethnicity: Festivals and the Commodification of Ethnic Culture among Louisiana Cajuns. *Sociological Spectrum* 20:337–407.

BARTH, FREDERICK
1969   Introduction to *Ethnic Groups and Boundaries: The Social Organization of Cultural Difference.* Edited by Frederick Barth. Boston: Little, Brown.

BAYART, JEAN-FRANÇOIS

1993 *The State in Africa: Politics of the Belly*. New York: Longman.

2005 *The Illusion of Cultural Identity*. Translated by Steven Rendall, Janet Roitman, Cynthia Schoch, and Jonathan Derrick. Chicago: University of Chicago Press.

BEATTIE, JOHN

1964 *Other Cultures*. London: Cohen & West.

BENDA BECKMANN, KEEBET VON

1981 Forum Shopping and Shopping Forums: Dispute Processing in a Minangkabau Village. *Journal of Legal Pluralism* 19:117–159.

BENJAMIN, WALTER

1968 The Work of Art in the Age of Mechanical Reproduction. In *Illuminations: Essays and Reflections*. Edited by Hannah Arendt. New York: Schocken Books. First edition, 1936.

1978 Critique of Violence. In *Reflections: Essays, Aphorisms, Autobiographical Writings*. Translated by Edmund Jephcott and edited by Peter Demetz. New York: Schocken Books.

2002 *Selected Writings*, Volume 3, *1935–1938*. Translated by Edmund Jephcott, Howard Eiland, and others; edited by Howard Eiland and Michael W. Jennings. Cambridge, MA: Belknap Press of Harvard University Press.

BERGH, JOHAN S.

2005 "We Must Never Forget Where We Come From": The Bafokeng and Their Land in the 19th Century Transvaal. *History in Africa* 32:95–115.

BERMAN, BRUCE, DICKSON EYOH, AND WILL KYMLICKA

2004 Introduction to *Ethnicity and Democracy in Africa*. Edited by Bruce Berman, Dickson Eyoh, and Will Kymilicka. Oxford: James Currey; Athens: Ohio University Press.

BIERCE, AMBROSE

1911 *The Devil's Dictionary*. Reprinted as *The Unabridged Devil's Dictionary*. Edited by David E. Schultz and S. T. Joshi. Athens: University of Georgia Press, 2000.

BIOLSI, THOMAS

1992 *Organizing the Lakota: The Political Economy of the New Deal on the Pine Ridge and Rosebud Reservations*. Tucson: University of Arizona Press.

1995 The Birth of the Reservation: Making the Modern Individual among the Lakota. *American Ethnologist* 22, no. 1:28–53.

2005 Imagined Geographies: Sovereignty, Indigenous Space, and American Indian Struggle. *American Ethnologist* 32, no. 2:239–59.

BIBLIOGRAPHY

BLEIFUSS, JOEL
1998   Know Thine Enemy: A Brief History of Corporations. *In These Times*, February; www.thirdworldtraveler.com/Corporations/KnowEnemy_ITT .html.

BLU, KAREN
1980   *The Lumbee Problem: The Making of an American Indian People.* Cambridge: Cambridge University Press.

BOCAREJO, DIANA
2007   "Reconfiguring the Political Landscape after the Multicultural Turn: Law, Politics and the Spatialization of Difference in Colombia." Ph.D. dissertation, University of Chicago.

BOND, PATRICK
2006   *Talk Left, Walk Right: South Africa's Frustrated Global Reforms.* Second edition. Scottsville: University of KwaZulu-Natal Press. First edition, 2004.

BONIFACE, PRISCILLA AND PETER J. FOWLER
1993   *Heritage and Tourism in 'The Global Village.'* London and New York: Routledge.

BOURDIEU, PIERRE, AND JEAN-CLAUDE PASSERON
1977   *Reproduction in Education, Society and Culture.* Translated by R. Nice. London: Sage.

BOZZOLI, BELINDA
1991   *Women of Phokeng: Consciousness, Life Strategy, and Migrancy in South Africa, 1900–1983.* With the assistance of Mmantho Nkotsoe. London: James Currey.

BREUTZ, PAUL-LENERT
1953   *Tribes of the Rustenburg and Pilanesberg Districts.* Ethnological Publications, 28. Pretoria: Government Printer.

BRITTON, STEPHEN
1991   Tourism, Capital, and Place: Towards a Critical Geography of Tourism. *Environment and Planning D: Society and Space* 9, no. 4:451–478.

BROCH-DUE, VIGDIS, ED.
2005   *Violence and Belonging: The Quest for Identity in Post-Colonial Africa.* London: Routledge.

194

BROODRYK, JOHANN

2005   *Ubuntu Management Philosophy: Exporting Ancient African Wisdom into the Global World*. Randburg: Knowres Publishing.

BROWN, BRUCE

2003   *The History of the Corporation*, Volume 1. Sumas, WA: BF Communications.

BROWN, CAROLINE

n.d.   "Native, Inc.: A Geography of Alaskan Native Politics." Draft Ph.D. diss., University of Chicago.

BROWN, MICHAEL F.

1998   Can Culture Be Copyrighted? *Current Anthropology* 19, no. 2:193–222.

2003   *Who Owns Native Culture?* Cambridge, MA: Harvard University Press.

BROWN, WENDY

1995   *States of Injury: Power and Freedom in Late Modernity*. Princeton, NJ: Princeton University Press.

2003   Neo-liberalism and the End of Liberal Democracy. *Theory and Event* 7, no. 1:1–29.

BRUNER, EDWARD M.

1999   Abraham Lincoln as Authentic Reproduction: A Critique of Postmodernism. *American Anthropologist* 96, no. 2:397–415.

BUCK-MORSS, SUSAN

1989   *The Dialectics of Seeing: Walter Benjamin and the Arcades Project*. Cambridge, MA: MIT Press.

BUNN, DAVID

2001   Comaroff Country. *Interventions* 3, no. 1:5–23.

CAMERON, GREG

2004   The Globalization of Indigenous Rights in Tanzanian Pastoralist NGOs. In *Development and Local Knowledge: New Approaches to Issues in Natural Resource Management, Conservation and Agriculture*. Edited by Alan Bicker, Paul Sillitoe, and Johan Pottier. New York and London: Routledge.

CAMPISI, JACK

1991   *The Mashpee Indians: Tribe on Trial*. Syracuse: Syracuse University Press.

CASTELLS, MANUEL

2004   *The Information Age*, Volume 2, *The Power of Identity*. Second edition. Malden, MA: Blackwell.

CASTILE, GEORGE PIERRE

1996   The Commodification of Indian Identity. *American Anthropologist* 98, no. 4:743–749.

CATTELINO, JESSICA R.

2004   Casino Roots: The Cultural Production of Twentieth-Century Seminole Economic Development. In *Native Pathways: Economic Development and American Indian Culture in the Twentieth Century.* Edited by Brian Hosmer and Colleen O'Neill. Boulder: University of Colorado Press.

2005   Tribal Gaming and Indigenous Sovereignty, with Notes from Seminole Country. Special issue on Indigenous People of the United States, *American Studies* 46, nos. 3–4:187–204. Co-published in *Indigenous Studies Today* 1(Fall 2005–Spring 2006).

Forthcoming.   *High Stakes: Florida Seminole Gaming, Sovereignty, and the Social Meanings of Casino Wealth.* Durham: Duke University Press.

CAWTHORN, R. G.

1999   The Discovery of the Platiniferous Merensky Reef in 1924. *South African Journal of Geology* 102:178–183.

CHABAL, PATRICK, AND JEAN-PASCAL DALOZ

2006   *Culture Troubles: Politics and the Interpretation of Meaning.* Chicago: University of Chicago Press.

CHAMBERS, ERVE

2000   *Native Tours: The Anthropology of Travel and Tourism.* Prospect Heights, IL.: Waveland Press.

CHANOCK, MARTIN

2000   'Culture' and Human Rights: Orientalising, Occidentalising and Authenticity. In *Beyond Rights Talk and Culture Talk: Comparative Essays on the Politics of Rights and Culture.* Edited by Mahmood Mamdani. New York: St. Martin's Press.

CHENNELLS, ROGER

2006   *Report on the Land Rights of the!Khomani San: For the Commission on Restitution of Land Rights, Northern Cape.* Ms.

2007   *San Hoodia Case: A Report for* GenBenefit. Ms.

n.d.[a]   *Consulting with Indigenous Peoples' Organizations in Jamaica: A Report.* Ms.

n.d.[b]   Rastafarian Tabernacle Tales. Ms.

CHOMSKY, NOAM

2000   *Chomsky on MisEducation.* Edited by Donaldo Macedo. Lanham, MD: Rowman & Littlefield.

CLIFFORD, JAMES

1988   *The Predicament of Culture: Twentieth Century Ethnography, Literature, and Art.* Cambridge, MA.: Harvard University Press.

CLIFTON, JAMES A.

1977   *The Prairie People: Continuity and Change in Potowatomi Indian Culture, 1665–1965.* Lawrence: University of Kentucky Press.

COERTZE, ROELOF DEWALD

1990   *Bafokeng Family Law and Law of Succession.* Pretoria: SABRA. First edition, 1971 (in Afrikaans).

COFFEY, WALLACE, AND REBECCA TSOSIE

2001   Rethinking the Tribal Sovereignty Doctrine: Cultural Sovereignty and the Collective Future of Indian Nations. Special issue on "The State of Native America and Its Unfolding Self-Governance." *Stanford Law and Policy Review* 12, no. 2:191–221.

COHEN, FELIX S.

1941   *Handbook of Federal Indian Law.* Washington: U.S. Dept. of the Interior, Office of the Solicitor. [Reprinted as *Cohen's Handbook of Federal Indian Law*, 2005; Newark. NJ: LexisNexis.]

COHEN, ABNER

1974   Introduction: The Lesson of Ethnicity. In *Urban Ethnicity.* Edited by Abner Cohen. London: Tavistock.

COHEN, ANTHONY P.

1985   *The Symbolic Construction of Community.* London: Tavistock.

COHEN, ERIC

1983   Hill Tribe Tourism. In *Highlanders of Thailand.* Edited by J. McKinnon and W. Bhruksasru. Kuala Lumpur: Oxford University Press.

COLEMAN, ENID GABRIELLA

2005   "The Social Construction of Freedom in Free and Open Source Software: Hackers, Ethics, and the Liberal Tradition." Ph.D dissertation, University of Chicago.

COMAROFF, JEAN

1985   *Body of Power, Spirit of Resistance: The Culture and History of a South African People.* Chicago: University of Chicago Press.

COMAROFF, JEAN, AND JOHN L. COMAROFF

1991   *Of Revelation and Revolution*, Volume 1, *Christianity, Colonialism, and Consciousness in South Africa*. Chicago: University of Chicago Press.

2001   Millennial Capitalism: First Thoughts on a Second Coming. In *Millennial Capitalism and the Culture of Neoliberalism*. Edited by J. Comaroff and J. L. Comaroff. Durham: Duke University Press.

2002   Second Comings: Neo-protestant Ethics and Millennial Capitalism in South Africa, and Elsewhere. In *2000 Years and Beyond: Faith, Identity and the Common Era*. Edited by P. Gifford with D. Archard, T. A. Hart, and N. Rapport. London: Routledge.

2003a   Reflections on Liberalism, Policulturalism, and ID-ology: Citizenship and Difference in South Africa. *Social Identities* 9, no. 4:445–74.

2003b   Ethnography on an Awkward Scale: Postcolonial Anthropology and the Violence of Abstraction. *Ethnography* 4, no. 2:147–179.

2008   Nations With/out Borders: Neoliberalism and the Problem of Belonging in Africa, and Beyond. In *Border Crossings—Grenzverschiebungen und Grenzüberschreitungen in einer globalisierten Welt*. Edited by Shalini Randeria. Reihe Zürcher Hochschulforum Band 42. Zurich: vdf.

n.d.[a] *The Metaphysics of Disorder: Crime, Policing, and the State in a Brave Neo World*. [Volume in preparation.]

COMAROFF, JOHN L.

1996   Ethnicity, Nationalism, and the Politics of Difference in an Age of Revolution. In *The Politics of Difference: Ethnic Premises in a World of Power*. Edited by Edwin N. Wilmsen and Patrick A. McAllister. Chicago: University of Chicago Press.

2001   Law, Culture, and Colonialism: A Foreword. *Law and Social Inquiry* 26, no. 2: 101–110.

COMAROFF, JOHN L., AND JEAN COMAROFF

1997   *Of Revelation and Revolution*, Volume 2, *The Dialectics of Modernity on a South African Frontier*. Chicago: University of Chicago Press.

1992   *Ethnography and the Historical Imagination*. Boulder: Westview Press.

2004   Policing Culture, Cultural Policing: Law and Social Order in Postcolonial South Africa. *Law and Social Inquiry* 29, no. 3:513–546.

2006   Law and Disorder in the Postcolony: An Introduction. In *Law and Disorder in the Postcolony*. Edited by Jean Comaroff and John L. Comaroff. Chicago: University of Chicago Press.

COMAROFF, JOSHUA ADAM

2007   Terror and Territory: Guantanamo and the State of Contradiction. *Public Culture* 19, no. 2:381–405.

CONNOR, WALKER

1994 *Ethnonationalism: The Quest for Understanding.* Princeton, NJ: Princeton University Press.

COOK, SUSAN E.

2005a Chiefs, Kings, Corporatization, and Democracy: A South African Case Study. *Brown Journal of World Affairs* 12, no. 1:125–137.

2005b The Politics of Preservation in Rwanda. In *Genocide in Cambodia and Rwanda: New Perspectives.* Edited by S. E. Cook. Piscataway: Transaction Publishers.

n.d.[a] Caught in the Act: Implications of Communal Land Reform in South Africa. Paper presented at the annual meetings of the African Studies Association, New Orleans, November 2004. Ms.

n.d.[b] *Language, Ethnicity, and Nation in the New South Africa.* [Book ms in preparation.]

COOK, SUSAN E. AND REBECCA HARDIN

n.d. The Culture of Being Bafokeng. Ms.

COOMBE, ROSEMARY J.

1993 The Properties of Culture and the Politics of Possessing Identity: Native Claims in the Cultural Appropriation Controversy. *Canadian Journal of Law and Jurisprudence* 6, no. 2:249–285.

1998 *The Cultural Life of Intellectual Properties: Authorship, Appropriation and the Law.* Durham: Duke University Press.

1999 Intellectual Property, Human Rights, and Sovereignty: New Dilemmas in International Law Posed by the Recognition of Indigenous Knowledge and the Conservation of Biodiversity. *Indiana Journal of Global Legal Studies* 6, no. 1:59–116.

CORRIGAN, PHILIP R. D., AND DEREK SAYER

1985 *The Great Arch: English State Formation as Cultural Revolution.* Oxford: Blackwell.

DANIEL, YVONNE PAYNE

1996 Tourism Dance Performances: Authenticity and Creativity. *Annals of Tourism Research* 23, no. 4:780–797.

DARIAN-SMITH, EVE

2002 Savage Capitalists: Law and Politics Surrounding Indian Casino Operations in California. *Studies in Law, Politics, and Society* 26:109–137.

DÁVILA, ARLENE
2001   *Latinos Inc.: The Marketing and Making of a People.* Berkeley: University of California Press.

DELORIA, VINE, JR.
1979   Self-Determination and the Concept of Sovereignty. In *Economic Development in American Indian Reservations.* Native American Studies, University of New Mexico Development Series, 1. Edited by Roxanne D. Ortiz. Albuquerque: University of New Mexico Press.

DELORIA, VINE, JR., ED.
2002   *The Indian Reorganization Act: Congresses and Bills.* Norman: University of Oklahoma Press.

DERRIDA, JACQUES
1988   *Limited, Inc.* Evanston, IL: Northwestern University Press.
2002   Force of Law. In *Acts of Religion.* Edited by Gil Anidjar. New York: Routledge.

DE VILLIERS, BERTHUS
1999   *Claims and National Parks: The Makuleke Experience.* Pretoria: Human Science Research Council.

DIRLIK, ARIF
2000   Reversals, Ironies, Hegemonies: Notes on the Contemporary Historiography of Modern China. In *History After the Three Worlds: Post-Eurocentric Historiographies.* Edited by A. Dirlik, V. Bahl, and P. Gran. Lanham, MD: Rowman & Littlefield.

DOLGIN, JANET
1990   Status and Contract in Feminist Legal Theory of the Family: A Reply to Bartlett. *Women's Rights Law Reporter* 12:103–113.

DOMBROWSKI, KIRK
2001   *Against Culture: Development, Politics, and Religion in Indian Alaska.* Lincoln: University of Nebraska Press.
2002   The Praxis of Indigenism and Alaska Native Timber Politics. *American Anthropologist* 104, no. 4:1062–1073.

ESMAN, MARJORIE R.
1984   Tourism as Ethnic Preservation: The Cajuns of Louisiana. *Annals of Tourism Research* 11:451–67.

EVANS, GAVIN
2003   'Extinct' San Reap Rewards. In *Mail & Guardian Bedside Book 2003.* Edited

by Shaun de Waal and and Mondli Makhanya. Bellevue (South Africa): Jacana. Originally published in *Mail & Guardian*, 3–9 January 2003, 12.

FEINSTEIN, ANDREW

2007   *After the Party: A Personal and Political Journey Inside the ANC.* Johannesburg: Jonathan Ball.

FORTE, MAXIMILIAN C.

1998   Renewed Indigeneity in the Local-Global Continuum and the Political Economy of Tradition: The Case of Trinidad's Caribs and the Caribbean Organization of Indigenous People. *Issues in Caribbean Amerindian Studies,* Occasional Papers of the Caribbean Amerindian Centrelink, 1(2), September 1998–September 1999; www.centrelink.org/renewed.html.

FORTES, MEYER

1953   The Structure of Unilineal Descent Groups. *American Anthropologist* 55:17–41.

FOUCAULT, MICHEL

2004   *Naissance de la biopolitique: Cours au Collège de France, 1978–1979.* Édition tablie sous la direction de François Ewald et Alessandro Fontana, par Michel Senellart. Paris: Gallimard, Seuil.

FOX, KATE

2004   *Watching the English: The Hidden Rules of English Behaviour.* London: Hodder.

FRANK, THOMAS AND MATT WEILAND, EDS.

1997   *Commodify Your Dissent: Salvos from* The Baffler. New York and London: W.W. Norton & Co.

FRANZEN, JONATHAN

2001   *The Corrections.* New York: Farrar, Straus and Giroux.

GARLAND, ELIZABETH

1999   Developing Bushmen: Building Civil(ized) Society in the Kalahari and Beyond. In *Civil Society and the Political Imagination in Africa: Critical Perspectives, Problems, Paradoxes.* Edited by John L. Comaroff and Jean Comaroff. Chicago: University of Chicago Press.

GEERTZ, CLIFFORD

1963   The Integrative Revolution: Primordial Sentiments and Civil Politics in the New States. In *Old Societies and New States.* Edited by C. Geertz. New York: Free Press.

GEISMAR, HAIDY

2005   Copyright in Context: Carvings, Carvers, and Commodities in Vanautu. *American Ethnologist* 32, no. 3:437–459.

GHOSH, JAYATI

2006   The Economic and Social Effects of Financial Liberalisation. *New Agenda: South African Journal of Social and Economic Policy* 21 (1st Quarter):55–59.

GIBSON, JAMES L.

2004   *Overcoming Apartheid: Can Truth Reconcile a Divided Nation?* New York: Russell Sage; Cape Town: Human Sciences Research Council.

GILLEY, BRUCE

2004   Against the Concept of Ethnic Conflict. *Third World Quarterly* 25, no. 6:1155–1166.

GLAZER, NATHAN, AND DANIEL P. MOYNIHAN

1970   *Beyond the Melting Pot: The Negroes, Puerto Ricans, Jews, Italians and Irish in New York City.* Cambridge, MA: MIT Press.

1975   *Ethnicity: Theory and Experience.* Cambridge, MA: Harvard University Press.

GOOD, KENNETH

2003   *Bushman and Diamonds: (Un)Civil Society in Botswana.* Uppsala: Nordiska Afrikainstitutet, Discussion Paper 23.

GOODING, SUSAN S.

2006   Recognizing Indigenous America in Times of War. *Political Affairs.Net,* (June); www.politicalaffairs.net/article/view/3516/1/188, posted 25 May 2006.

GORDON, ROBERT J.

2002   "Captured on Film": Bushmen and the Claptrap of Performative Primitives. In *Images and Empires: Visuality in Colonial and Postcolonial Africa.* Edited by Paul S. Landau and Deborah D. Kaspin. Berkeley: University of California Press.

GRABURN, NELSON H. H.

1976   Introduction: Arts of the Fourth World. In *Ethnic and Tourist Arts: Cultural Expressions from the Fourth World.* Edited by Nelson H. H. Graburn. Berkeley: University of California Press.

GRAEBER, DAVID

2002   The Anthropology of Globalization (with Notes on Neomedievalism, and the End of the Chinese Model of the Nation-State). *American Anthropologist* 104, no. 4:1222–1227.

GRAHAM, LAURA R.
2005   Image and Instrumentality in a Xavante Politics of Existential Recognition: The Public Outreach Work of Eténhiritipa Pimentel Barbosa. *American Ethnologist* 32, no. 4: 622–641.

GRAY, PAULA
2003   People of the Dew. *Leadership* (August:10–16).

GREAVES, TOM, ED.
1994   *Intellectual Property Rights for Indigenous Peoples: A Sourcebook.* Oklahoma City: Society for Applied Anthropology.

GREENE, SHANE
2004   Indigenous People Incorporated? *Current Anthropology* 45, no. 2:211–236.

GREENWOOD, DAVYDD
1977   Culture by the Pound: An Anthropological Perspective on Tourism as Cultural Commoditization. In *Hosts and Guests: The Anthropology of Tourism.* Edited by Valene L. Smith. Philadelphia: University of Pennsylvania Press.

GULBRANDSEN, ØRNULF
1995   The King Is King by Grace of the People: The Exercise and Control of Power in Subject-Ruler Relations. *Comparative Studies in Society and History* 37, no. 3:415–444.

GUNN, MICHAEL
1987   The Transfer of Malagan Ownership on Tabar. In *Assemblage of Spirits: Idea and Image in New Ireland.* Edited by Louise Lincoln. New York: G. Braziller in association with the Minneapolis Institute of Arts.

HAGGARD, H. RIDER
1991   *She.* Edited by Daniel Karlin. Oxford: Oxford University Press (Oxford World's Classics). First edition, *She: A History of Adventure.* London: Longmans, Green, 1887.

HALL, STUART
1996   New Ethnicities. In *Stuart Hall: Critical Dialogues in Cultural Studies.* Edited by David Morley and Kuan-Hsing Chen. New York: Routledge.

HALTER, MARILYN
2000   *Shopping for Identity: The Marketing of Ethnicity.* New York: Schocken Books.

HAMILTON, CAROLYN A.

1998   *Terrific Majesty: The Powers of Shaka Zulu and the Limits of Historical Invention*. Cape Town: David Philip.

HANDLER, RICHARD, AND JOCELYN LINNEKIN

1984   Tradition, Genuine or Spurious. *Journal of American Folklore* 97, no. 2:273–290.

HARRIES, PATRICK

1987   'A Forgotten Corner of the Transvaal': Reconstructing the History of a Relocated Community through Oral Testimony and Song. In *Class, Community and Conflict*. Edited by Belinda Bozzoli. Johannesburg: Ravan Press.

HARVEY, DAVID

1989   *The Condition of Postmodernity: An Enquiry into the Origins of Cultural Change*. Oxford: Blackwell.

HARVEY, SIOUX

2000   Winning the Sovereignty Jackpot: The Indian Gaming Regulatory Act and the Struggle for Sovereignty. In *Indian Gaming: Who Wins?* Contemporary Indian Issues, 9. Edited by Angela Mullis and David Kamper. Los Angeles: UCLA American Indian Studies Center.

HEBDIGE, DICK

1979   *Subculture: The Meaning of Style*. New York: Methuen.

HENDRICKSON, HILDI

1996   Bodies and Flags: The Representation of Herero Identity in Colonial Namibia. In *Clothing and Difference: Embodied Identities in Colonial and Post-Colonial Africa*. Edited by H. Hendrickson. Durham: Duke University Press.

HEWISON, ROBERT

1987   *The Heritage Industry: Britain in a Climate of Decline*. London: Methuen.

HILLMAN, BEN

2003   Paradise under Construction: Minorities, Myths and Modernity in Northwest Yunnan. *Asian Ethnicity* 4, no. 2:175–188.

HITCHCOCK, ROBERT K., KAZUNOBU IKEYA, MEGAN BIESELE, AND RICHARD B. LEE

2006   Introduction: Updating the San, Image and Reality of an African People in the Twenty First Century. In *Updating the San: Image and Reality of an African People in the 21st First Century*. Edited by R. K. Hitchcock, K. Ikeya, M. Biesele, and R. B. Lee. Senri Ethnological Studies, 70. Osaka: National Museum of Ethnology.

HOBSBAWM, ERIC J.
1992   Ethnicity and Nationalism in Europe Today. *Anthropology Today* 8:3–8.

HOBSBAWM, ERIC J., AND TERENCE O. RANGER, EDS.
1983   *The Invention of Tradition.* Cambridge: Cambridge University Press.

HOLLOWELL-ZIMMER, JULIE
2001   Intellectual Property Protection for Alaska Native Arts. *Cultural Survival* 24, no. 4; www.culturalsurvival.org/publications/csq/ index.cfm?id=24.4.

HOWARD, PETER
2003   *Heritage: Management, Interpretation, Identity.* London: Continuum.

HORTON, SCOTT
2007   State of Exception: Bush's War on the Rule of Law. *Harper's Magazine* 315, no. 1886 (July): 74–81.

HUNTINGTON, SAMUEL P.
1993   The Clash of Civilizations? *Foreign Affairs* 72, no. 3:22–49.

IGOE, JIM
2006   Becoming Indigenous Peoples: Difference, Inequality, and the Globalization of East African Identity Politics. *Africa Affairs* 105, no. 420:399–420.

INTER-APACHE SUMMIT ON REPATRIATION
1995   Inter-Apache Policy on Repatriation and the Protection of Apache Cultures. Ms.

ISAACSON, RUPERT
2002   *Healing Land: A Kalahari Journey.* London: Fourth Estate.

JAY, ANTHONY
1971   *Corporation Man: Who He Is, What He Does, Why His Ancient Tribal Impulses Dominate the Life of the Modern Corporation.* New York: Random House.

JONES, PERIS SEAN
1999   'To Come Together for Progress': Modernization and Nation-Building in South Africa's Bantustan Periphery—The Case of Bophuthatswana. *Journal of Southern African Studies* 25, no. 4:579–605.

JUNG, COURTNEY
2001   *Then I Was Black: South African Political Identities in Transition.* New Haven: Yale University Press.

JUSDANIS, GREGORY
1998   Beyond National Culture. *Stanford Humanities Review* 6, no. 1; www
        .stanford.edu/group/SHR/6-1/html/jusdanis.html#042.

KAMPER, DAVID
2000   Introduction: The Mimicry of Indian Gaming. In *Indian Gaming: Who
        Wins?* Edited by Angela Mullis and David Kamper. Los Angeles: UCLA
        American Indian Studies Center.

KAPFERER, BRUCE, ED.
2005   *The Retreat of the Social: The Rise and Rise of Reductionism.* New York and Ox-
        ford: Berghahn Books.

KAPLAN, ROBERT D.
1994   The Coming Anarchy. *Atlantic Monthly* 273, no. 2:44–76.

KAUFMAN, STUART J.
2001   *Modern Hatreds: The Symbolic Politics of Ethnic War.* Ithaca: Cornell Univer-
        sity Press.

KEEFE, PATRICK RADDEN
2007   Letter from Jaipur: The Idol Thief. *New Yorker*, May 7, 58–67.

KELLY, JOHN D.
1999   The Other Leviathans: Corporate Investment and the Construction of a
        Sugar Colony. In *White and Deadly: Sugar and Colonialism.* Edited by Pal
        Ahluwalia, Bill Ashcroft, and Roger Knight. Commack, NY: Nova Science
        Publishers.

KELLY, JOHN D., AND MARTHA KAPLAN
2001   *Represented Communities: Fiji and World Decolonization.* Chicago: University
        of Chicago Press.

KENT, KATE PECK
1976   Pueblo and Navajo Weaving Traditions and the Western World. In *Ethnic
        and Tourist Arts: Cultural Expressions from the Fourth World.* Edited by Nel-
        son H. H. Graburn. Berkeley: University of California Press.

KENT, SUSAN
2002   Interethnic Encounters of the First Kind: An Introduction. In *Ethnicity,
        Hunter-Gatherers, and the "Other."* Edited by Susan Kent. Washington, DC:
        Smithsonian Institution Press.

KERSEY, HARRY A., JR.

1992 Seminoles and Miccosukees: A Century in Retrospective. In *Indians of the Southeastern United States in the Late Twentieth Century*. Edited by J. Anthony Paredes. Tuscaloosa: University of Alabama Press.

KIRSHENBLATT-GIMBLETT, BARBARA

1998 *Destination Culture: Tourism, Museums, and Heritage*. Berkeley: University of California Press.

2006 World Heritage and Cultural Economics. In *Museum Frictions: Public Cultures/ Global Tranformations*. Edited by Ivan Karp, Corrine A. Kratz, Lynn Szwaja, and Tomás Ybarra-Frausto. Durham: Duke University Press.

KNOPPERS, BARTHA MARIA

1999 Status, Sale and Patenting of Human Genetic Material: An International Survey. *Nature Genetics* 22:23–26.

KORTEN, DAVID C.

1996 *When Corporations Rule the World*. West Hartford, CT: Kumarian Press.

KRIEL, INGE

n.d. A Rich Nation of Poor People: Land and Ethnicity in a Village of the Royal Bafokeng Nation. Paper presented to the AEGIS Conference, Leiden, July 2007.

KRIGE, EILEEN JENSEN, AND JACOB DANIEL KRIGE

1943 *The Realm of a Rain-Queen: A Study of the Pattern of Lovedu Society*. London: Oxford University Press for the International African Institute.

KUPER, ADAM

1982 Lineage Theory: A Critical Retrospect. *Annual Review of Anthropology* 11: 71–95.

LATHRAP, DONALD W.

1976 Shipibo Tourist Art. In *Ethnic and Tourist Arts: Cultural Expressions from the Fourth World*. Edited by Nelson H. H. Graburn. Berkeley: University of California Press.

LAWRENCE, MICHAEL, AND ANDREW MANSON

1994 The 'Dog of the Boers': The Rise and Fall of Mangope in Botswana. Special issue on Ethnicity and Identity in Southern Africa, *Journal of Southern African Studies* 20, no. 3:447–461.

LEE, RICHARD B.

1992   The!Kung in Question: Evidence and Context in the Kalahari Debate. *Michigan Discussions in Anthropology* 10:9–16.

2002   Solitude or Servitude? Ju/'hoansi Images of the Colonial Encounter. In *Ethnicity, Hunter-Gatherers, and the "Other."* Edited by Susan Kent. Washington, DC: Smithsonian Institution Press.

LEE, RICHARD B., AND IRVEN DEVORE, EDS.

1968   *Man the Hunter.* Chicago: Aldine.

LEE, RICHARD B. AND MATHIAS G. GUENTHER

1993   Problems in Kalahari Historical Ethnography and the Tolerance of Error. *History in Africa* 20:185–235

1995   Errors Corrected or Compounded? A Reply to Wilmsen. *Current Anthropology* 36, no. 2:298–305.

LEMKE, THOMAS

2001   'The Birth of Bio-Politics': Michel Foucault's Lecture at the Collège de France on Neo-Liberal Governmentality. *Economy and Society* 30, no. 2:190–207.

LOWENTHAL, DAVID

1998   *The Heritage Crusade and the Spoils of History.* Cambridge: Cambridge University Press.

MACCANNELL, DEAN

1989   *The Tourist: A New Theory of the Leisure Class.* New York: Schocken Books.

MAFEJE, ARCHIE

1998   Anthropology and Independent Africans: Suicide or End of an Era? *African Sociological Review* 2, no. 1:1–43

MAGUBANE, BERNARD

1971   A Critical Look at Indices Used in the Study of Social Change in Africa. *Current Anthropology* 12, nos. 4–5:419–431.

MAMDANI, MAHMOOD

2000   Introduction. In *Beyond Rights Talk and Culture Talk: Comparative Essays on the Politics of Rights and Culture.* Edited by M. Mamdani. New York: St. Martin's Press.

2004   *Good Muslim, Bad Muslim: America, The Cold War, and the Roots of Terror.* New York: Pantheon Books.

MANSON, ANDREW AND BERNARD MBENGA

2003   "The Richest Tribe in Africa": Platinum-Mining and the Bafokeng in South

Africa's North West Province. *Journal of Southern African Studies* 29, no. 1:25–47.

MARX, KARL

1988   *Economic and Philosophical Manuscripts of 1844.* Translated by Martin Milligan. Great Books in Philosophy. [Published in one volume with the *Communist Manifesto*, Karl Marx and Frederick Engels.] Amherst, NY: Prometheus.

MATHERS, KATHRYN, AND LOREN LANDAU

2007   Natives, Tourists, and *Makwerekwere*: Ethical Concerns with 'Proudly South African' Tourism. *Development Southern Africa* 24, no. 3:523–537.

MAURER, BILL

2005   *Mutual Life, Limited: Islamic Banking, Alternative Currencies, Lateral Reason.* Princeton, NJ: Princeton University Press.

2006   *Pious Property: Islamic Mortgages in the United States.* New York: Russell Sage.

MAURER, JEAN-LUC, AND ARLETTE ZEIGLER

1988   Tourism and Indonesian Cultural Minorities. In *Tourism: Manufacturing the Exotic.* Edited by Pierre Rossel. Copenhagen: International Work Group for Indigenous Affairs.

MAUSS, MARCEL

1966   *The Gift.* Translated by Ian Cunnison. London: Cohen & West.

MAYBURY-LEWIS, DAVID, ED.

2002   *The Politics of Ethnicity: Indigenous Peoples in Latin American States.* Cambridge, MA: Harvard University Press.

MAZZARELLA, WILLIAM

2003   *Shovelling Smoke: Advertising and Globalization in Contemporary India.* Durham: Duke University Press.

2004   Culture, Globalization, Mediation. *Annual Review of Anthropology* 33: 345–67.

MBEMBE, ACHILLE

2001   *On the Postcolony.* Berkeley: University of California Press.

MCCRONE, DAVID, ANGELA MORRIS, AND RICHARD KIELY

1995   *Scotland the Brand: The Making of Scottish Heritage.* Edinburgh: Edinburgh University Press.

MCLAUGHLIN, ROBERT H.

2002   Rights, Remains, and Material Culture: Legal Pluralism in Native America. In *Truth Claims: Representation and Human Rights*. Edited by Mark P. Bradley and Patrice Petro. Rutgers: Rutgers University Press.

MCLUHAN, MARSHALL

1994   *Understanding Media: The Extensions of Man*. Cambridge, MA: MIT Press.

MCNEILL, FRASER, GEORGE

2007   "An Ethnographic Analysis of HIV/AIDS in the Venda Region of South Africa: Politics, Peer Education and Music." Ph.D. thesis, University of London.

MEEK, C. K.

1944   Review of *The Realm of a Rain-Queen: A Study of the Pattern of Lovedu Society*, by E. J Krige and J. D. Krige, 1943. *Africa* 14, no. 5:275–278.

MEZEY, NAOMI

1996   The Distribution of Wealth, Sovereignty, and Indian Culture through Indian Gaming. *Stanford Law Review* 48, no. 3:711–737.

MGOQI, WALLACE AMOS

n.d.   Who Is an African? Paper presented to the Harold Wolpe Memorial Trust, Centre for the Book, Cape Town, 29 June 2004; http://saqa.org.za/wolpe- new/dialogue2004/CT062004mgoqi_paper.htm.

MOKGATLE, NABOTH

1971   *The Autobiography of an Unknown South African*. London: C. Hurst & Company.

MOLOTLEGI, KGOSI LERUO

2007a   Message from *Kgosi*. In *Kgotha Kgothe 2007 Report*. Phokeng: Royal Bafokeng Nation.

2007b   Chairman's Message: To Our Stakeholders. *Royal Bafokeng Holdings Annual Review 2006*. Johannesburg: Royal Bafokeng Holdings.

2007c   Report from the Office of *Kgosi*: Overview. In *Kgotha Kgothe 2007 Report*. Phokeng: Royal Bafokeng Nation.

MONBIOT, GEORGE

2000   *Captive State: The Corporate Takeover of Britain*. London: Macmillan.

MONTESQUIEU, CHARLES DE SECONDAT

1989   *The Spirit of the Laws*. Translated and edited by Anne M. Cohler, Basia Carolyn Miller, and Harold Samuel Stone. Cambridge: Cambridge University Press.

MUEHLEBACH, ANDREA
2007   "Farewell Welfare? State, Labor, and Life Cycle in Contemporary Italy."
        Ph.D. dissertation, University of Chicago.

MULLIS, ANGELA, AND DAVID KAMPER, EDS.
2000   *Indian Gaming: Who Wins?* Los Angeles: UCLA American Indian Studies
        Center.

MUTWA, VUSAMAZULU CREDO
1966   *Indaba, My Children.* London: Kahn & Averill.

NEACSU, DANA
2006   Review of *Who Owns Native Culture?* by Michael F. Brown, 2003. *New York
        Law Journal,* 25 May:2; www.williams.edu/go/native/nylj-review.htm.

NGWENYA, THENGANI H.
2000   Orality and Modernity in Autobiographical Representation: The Case of
        Naboth Mokgatle's Life Story. In *Oral Literature and Performance in Southern
        Africa.* Edited by Duncan Brown. Athens: Ohio University Press.

NICKS, TRUDY
1999   Indian Villages and Entertainments: Setting the Stage for Tourist Souve-
        nirs. In *Unpacking Culture: Arts and Commodity in Colonial and Postcolonial
        Worlds.* Edited by Ruth B. Phillips and Christopher B. Steiner. Berkeley:
        University of California Press.

NIEZEN, RONALD
2003   *The Origins of Indigenism: Human Rights and the Politics of Identity.* Berkeley:
        University of California Press.

OAKLAND, JOHN
2006   *British Civilization: An Introduction.* Sixth edition. London: Routledge. First
        edition, 1989.

O'BRIEN, OONAGH
1990   Perceptions of Identity in North Catalonia. Special issue on "Family, Class
        and Nation in Catalonia," edited by Josep R. Llobera, *Critique of Anthropol-
        ogy* 10, nos. 2–3:3–10.
1993   Good to Be French? Conflicts of Identity in North Catalonia. In *Inside Euro-
        pean Identities.* Edited by Sharon Macdonald. Providence and Oxford: Berg.

OFFE, CLAUS
1993   The Rationality of Ethnic Politics. *Budapest Review of Books* 3, no. 1:6–13.

‡OMA, KXAO MOSES, AND THOMA, AXEL

2002 Will Tourism Destroy San Cultures? *Cultural Survival Quarterly* 26, no. 1:39–41; www.culturalsurvival.org/publications/csq/csq-article .cfm?id=1524.

OOMEN, BARBARA

2005 *Chiefs in South Africa: Law, Power and Culture in the Post-Apartheid Era*. New York: Palgrave.

OXFORD UNIVERSITY PRESS

1971 *The Compact Edition of the Oxford English Dictionary*, Volume 1. Oxford: Oxford University Press.

PAGE, MARTIN

1972 *The Company Savage: Life in the Corporate Jungle*. London: Cassell.

PAREDES, J. ANTHONY

1995 Paradoxes of Modernism in the South East. *American Indian Quarterly* 19, no. 3:341–60.

PATON, ALAN

1948 *Cry, The Beloved Country*. New York: Scribner's Sons.

PELEIKIS, ANJA

2006 Whose Heritage? Legal Pluralism and the Politics of the Past. A Case Study from the Curonian Spit (Lithuania). *Journal of Legal Pluralism and Unofficial Law* 53 no. 4:209–237.

PHILLIPS, RUTH B.

1999 Nuns, Ladies, and Queen of the Huron: Appropriating the Savage in Nineteenth-Century Huron Tourist Art. In *Unpacking Culture: Arts and Commodity in Colonial and Postcolonial Worlds*. Edited by Ruth B. Phillips and Christopher B. Steiner. Berkeley: University of California Press.

PHILLIPS, RUTH B., AND CHRISTOPHER B. STEINER

1999 Art, Authenticity, and the Baggage of Cultural Encounter. In *Unpacking Culture: Art and Commodity in Colonial and Postcolonial Worlds*. Edited by Ruth B. Phillips and Christopher B. Steiner. Berkeley: University of California Press.

PINEL, SANDRA LEE, AND MICHAEL J. EVANS

1994 Tribal Sovereignty and the Control of Knowledge. In *Intellectual Property Rights for Indigenous Peoples: A Sourcebook*. Edited by Tom Greaves. Oklahoma City: Society for Applied Anthropology.

PLAATJE, SOLOMON TSHEKISHO

1916   *Native Life in South Africa, Before and Since the European War and the Boer Rebellion*. London: P. S. King.

PLAMENATZ, JOHN PETROV

1976   Two Types of Nationalism. In *Nationalism: The Nature and Evolution of an Idea*. Edited by Eugene Kamenka. New York: St. Martin's Press.

POMERANZ, KENNETH

2000   *The Great Divergence: Europe, China, and the Making of the Modern World Economy*. Princeton, NJ: Princeton University Press.

POSEY, DARYL A.

1994   International Agreements and Intellectual Property Right Protection for Indigenous Peoples. In *Intellectual Property Rights for Indigenous Peoples: A Sourcebook*. Edited by Tom Greaves. Oklahoma City: Society for Applied Anthropology.

POSEY, DARYL A., AND GRAHAM DUTFIELD

1996   *Beyond Intellectual Property: Toward Traditional Resource Rights for Indigenous Peoples and Local Communities*. Ottawa: International Development Research Centre.

POSTONE, MOISHE

1993   *Time, Labor, and Social Domination: A Reinterpretation of Marx's Critical Theory*. New York: Cambridge University Press.

POVINELLI, ELIZABETH A.

1998   The State of Shame: Australian Multiculturalism and the Crisis of Indigenous Citizenship. *Critical Inquiry* 24, no. 2:575–610.

2001   Consuming Geist: Popontology and the Spirit of Capital in Indigenous Australia. In *Millennial Capitalism and the Culture of Neoliberalism*. Edited by J. Comaroff and J. L. Comaroff. Durham: Duke University Press.

2006   *The Empire of Love: Toward a Theory of Intimacy, Genealogy, and Carnality*. Durham: Duke University Press.

PRATT, MARY LOUISE

1992   *Imperial Eyes: Travel Writing and Transculturation*. New York: Routledge.

PROCTOR, RACHEL

2001   Tourism Opens New Doors, Creates New Challenges, for Traditional Healers in Peru. *Cultural Survival*, 24(4); www.cs.org/publications/csq/csq-article.cfm?id=1334.

PREMDAS, RALPH R., ED.

2000   *Identity, Ethnicity and Culture in the Caribbean*. St. Augustine, Trinidad: School of Continuing Studies, The University of the West Indies.

RAM, URI

2000   National, Ethnic or Civic? Contesting Paradigms of Memory, Identity and Culture in Israel. *Studies in Philosophy and Education* 19, nos. 5–6:405–422.

RAMUTSINDELA, MAANO F.

2002   The Perfect Way to Ending a Painful Past? Makuleke Land Deal in South Africa. *Geoforum* 33, no. 1:14–24.

2004   *Parks and People in Postcolonial Societies: Experiences in Southern Africa*. Dordrecht, Boston, and London: Kluwer.

RANCIÈRE, JACQUES

1999   *Disagreement: Politics and Philosophy*. Translated by Julie Rose. Minneapolis: University of Minnesota Press.

RANDERIA, SHALINI

2007   The State of Globalization: Legal Plurality, Overlapping Sovereignties and Ambiguous Alliances between Civil Society and the Cunning State in India. *Theory, Culture & Society* 24, no. 1:1–33.

RASOOL, CIRAJ

2006   Community Museums, Memory Politics, and Social Transformation in South Africa: Histories, Possibilities, and Limits. In *Museum Frictions: Public Cultures/Global Tranformations*. Edited by Ivan Karp, Corrine A. Kratz, Lynn Szwaja, and Tomás Ybarra-Frausto. Durham: Duke University Press.

REDDY, SITA

2006   Making Heritage Legible: Who Owns Traditional Medical Knowledge? *International Journal of Cultural Property* 13:161–188.

ROBINS, STEVEN

2001   NGOs, 'Bushmen,' and Double Vision: The ǂKhomani San Land Claim and the Cultural Politics of 'Community' and 'Development' in the Kalahari. *Journal of Southern African Studies* 27, no. 4:833–853.

2003   Whose Modernity? Indigenous Modernities and Land Claims after Apartheid. *Development and Change* 34, no. 2:1–21.

ROBINS, STEVEN AND KEES VAN DER WAAL

n.d.   'Model Tribes' and Traveling Models: The Makuleke Restitution Case in Kruger National Park. Ms.

ROSENTHAL, HARVEY D.
1990   *Their Day in Court: A History of the Indian Claims Commission*. New York: Garland.

ROYAL BAFOKENG HOLDINGS
2007   *Royal Bafokeng Holdings Annual Review 2006*. Johannesburg: Royal Bafokeng Holdings.

ROYAL BAFOKENG NATION
2007   *Kgotha Kgothe 2007 Report*. Phokeng: Royal Bafokeng Nation.

ROYAL BAFOKENG NATION, EXECUTIVE COUNCIL
2007   *Consolidated Report, 2002–2007*. Phokeng: Royal Bafokeng Nation.

ROYAL BAFOKENG NATION, LEGAL AND CORPORATE AFFAIRS DEPARTMENT
2003   *Submission by the Royal Bafokeng Nation In Respect of the Communal Land Rights Bill, 2003*; www.pmg.org.za/docs/2003/appendices/031114bafo keng2.htm.

SADR, KARIM
1997   Kalahari Archaeology and the Bushman Debate. *Current Archaeology* 38:104–112.

SAID, EDWARD W.
1993   *Culture and Imperialism*. New York: Vintage Books.

SANDERS, DOUGLAS
1989   The UN Working Group on Indigenous Populations. *Human Rights Quarterly* 11, no. 3:406–433.

SANGER, ANNETTE
1988   Blessing or Blight? The Effects of Touristic Dance-Drama on Village Life in Singapadu, Bali. In *Come Mek Me Hol' Yu Han': The Impact of Tourism on Traditional Music*. Edited by Olive Lewin and Adrienne Kaeppler. Kingston: Jamaican Memory Bank.

SCHILLER, FRIEDRICH
2004   *On the Aesthetic Education of Man*. Translated by Reginald Snell. Mineola, NY: Dover Publications. First edition, 1795.

SCHUTTE, GERHARD
2003   Tourists and Tribes in the New South Africa. *Ethnohistory* 50, no. 3:473–487.

SHAMIR, RONEN

2004   Between Self-Regulation and the Alien Tort Claims Act: On the Contested Concept of Corporate Social Responsibility. *Law and Society Review* 38, no. 4: 635–663.

SHANNON, P.

1995   Forging New Links. *New Zealand Business,* August:24–27.

SHWEDER, RICHARD A.

2003   The Gatekeepers: An Anthropologist is Skeptical about Extending the Logic of Group Rights to Music, Art and Origin Stories. Review of *Who Owns Native Culture?* by Michael F. Brown, 2003. *New York Times Book Review,* 14 September, 13.

SIDER, GERALD

2003   *Living Indian Histories: Lumbee and Tuscarora People in North Carolina.* Chapel Hill: University of North Carolina Press.

SIGALA, MARIANNA AND DAVID LESLIE

2005   Introduction: The Rationale and Need for This Book. In *International Cultural Tourism: Management, Implications and Cases.* Edited by Marianna Sigala and David Leslie. Amsterdam: Elsevier.

SILVERSTEIN, MICHAEL

1996   Indexical Order and the Dialectics of Sociolinguistic Life. In *Proceedings of the Third Annual Symposium about Language and Society,* Austin, Texas. Texas Linguistic Forum, 36. Edited by Risako Ide, Rebecca Parker, and Yukako Sunaoshi. Austin: University of Texas Department of Linguistics.

SMITH, A. B.

1996   The Kalahari Bushman Debate: Implications for Archaeology of Southern Africa. *South African Historical Journal* 35:1–15.

SMITH, ADAM

1904   *An Inquiry into the Nature and Causes of the Wealth of Nations.* Edited by Edwin Cannan. Fifth edition. London: Methuen. First edition, 1776.

SMITH, ANTHONY D.

1986   *The Ethnic Origins of Nations.* Oxford: Basic Blackwell.

SMITH, ROGERS, M.

1997   *Civic Ideals: Conflicting Visions of Citizenship in U.S. History.* New Haven: Yale University Press.

SOUTH AFRICA, REPUBLIC OF
2004   Broad-Based Black Economic Empowerment Act, no.53, 2003. *Government Gazette* (9 January 2004) 463, no.25899:1–6; www.dti.gov.za/bee/BEEAct-2003-2004.pdf.

SOUTH AFRICAN HUMAN RIGHTS COMMISSION
2004   *Report on the Inquiry into Human Rights Violations in the Khomani San Community.* Johannesburg: South African Human Rights Commission.

SPECTER, MICHAEL
2007   Kremlin, Inc.: Why Are Vladimir Putin's Opponents Dying. (Letter from Moscow.) *New Yorker,* January 29, 50–63.

SCHAPERA, ISAAC
1930   *The Khoisan Peoples of South Africa, Bushmen and Hottentots.* London: George Routledge and Sons.
1952   *The Ethnic Composition of Tswana Tribes.* Monographs on Social Anthropology, 11. London: London School of Economics.

SCHWEGLER, BRIAN A.
2007   "Confronting the Devil: Europe, Nationalism, and Municipal Governance in Slovakia." Ph.D. dissertation, University of Chicago.

SPILDE, KATHERINE A.
1999   Indian Gaming Study. In "Notes from Washington." *Anthropology Newsletter* 40, no. 4 (April):11, 16.

STALS, W. A.
1972   Die Kwessie van Naturelle-eiendomsreg op Grond in Transvaal, 1838–1884. *Archives Yearbook for South African History* 35, no. 2:1–84.

STAMATOPOULOS, ELSA
1994   Indigenous Peoples and the United Nations: Human Rights as a Developing Dynamic. *Human Rights Quarterly* 16, no. 1:58–81.

STARN, ORIN
2004   Review of *Who Owns Native Culture?* By Michael F. Brown, 2003. *American Ethnologist* 32, no. 1; www.aaanet.org/aes/bkreviews/result_details.cfm? bk _id=3106.

STEENKAMP, C. AND J. UHR
2000   *The Makuleke Land Claim: Power Relations and Community-Based Natural Resource Management.* Evaluating Eden Series, Discussion Paper no.18. London: International Institute for Environment and Development.

STEINER, CHRISTOPHER B.

1999   Authenticity, Repetition, and the Aesthetics of Seriality: The Work of Tour-
        ist Art in the Age of Mechanical Reproduction. In *Unpacking Culture: Art
        and Commodity in Colonial and Postcolonial Worlds*. Edited by Ruth B. Phil-
        lips and Christopher B. Steiner. Berkeley: University of California Press.

STRANGE, SUSAN

1986   *Casino Capitalism*. Oxford: Blackwell.

STRATHERN, MARILYN

1996   Enabling Identity? Biology, Choice and the New Reproductive Technol-
        ogies. In *Questions of Cultural Identity*. Edited by Stuart Hall and Paul Du
        Gay. London: Sage.

2001   The Patent and the Malanggan. *Theory, Culture & Society* 18, no. 4:1–26.

STRONG, PAULINE TURNER

2005   Recent Ethnographic Research on North American Indigenous Peoples.
        Annual Review of Anthropology, 34:253–68.

STRONG, PAULINE TURNER, AND BARRIK VAN WINKLE

1996   "Indian Blood": Reflections on the Reckoning and Refiguring of Native
        North American Identity. *Cultural Anthropology* 11, no. 4: 547–76.

SUNDER RAJAN, KAUSHIK

2005   Subjects of Speculation: Emergent Life Sciences and Market Logics in the
        United States and India. *American Anthropologist* 107, no. 1:19–30.

SWAIN, MARGARET BYRNE

1990   Commoditizing Ethnicity in Southwest China. *Cultural Survival Quarterly*,
        14, no. 1:26–30.

SYLVAIN, RENÉE

2005   Disorderly Development: Globalization and the Idea of "Culture" in the
        Kalahari. *American Ethnologist* 32, no. 3:354–370.

TALLBEAR, KIM

2007   Narratives of Race and Indigeneity in the Genographic Project. *Journal of
        Law, Medicine, and Ethics* 35, no. 3:412–424.

n.d.   Native-American-DNA.coms: In Search of Native American Race and Tribe.
        In *Revisiting Race in a Genomic Age*. Edited by Barbara Koenig, Sandra Soo-
        Jin Lee, and Sarah Richardson. Piscataway: Rutgers University Press. Forth-
        coming.

TALLBEAR, KIM, AND DEBORAH A. BOLNICK
2004   'Native American DNA' Tests: What Are the Risks to Tribes? *Native Voice*, 13–17 December.

TAMBIAH, STANLEY J.
1996   The Nation-State in Crisis and the Rise of Ethnonationalism. In *The Politics of Difference: Ethnic Premises in a World of Power*. Edited by Edwin N. Wilmsen and Patrick McAllister. Chicago: University of Chicago Press.

TAPELA, B. N., AND P. H. OMARA-OJUNGU
1999   Towards Bridging the Gap Between Wildlife Conservation and Rural Development in Post-Apartheid South Africa: The Case of the Makuleke Community and the Kruger National Park. *South African Geographical Journal* 81, no. 3:148–155.

TASSIOPOULOS, DIMITRI AND NANCY NUNTSU
2005   Cultural Tourism in South Africa: A Case Study of Cultural Villages from a Developing Country Perspective. In *International Cultural Tourism: Management, Implications and Cases*. Edited by Marianna Sigala and David Leslie. Amsterdam: Elsevier.

TAYLOR, CHARLES
1989   *Sources of the Self: The Making of Modern Identity*. Cambridge, MA: Harvard University Press.
1994   The Politics of Recognition. In *Multiculturalism: Examining the Politics of Recognition*. Edited byAmy Gutmann. Princeton, NJ: Princeton University Press.

TAYLOR, GRAHAM D.
1980   *The New Deal and American Indian Tribalism: The Administration of the Indian Reorganization Act, 1934–1945*. Lincoln: University of Nebraska Press.

TAYLOR, JULIE J.
2007   Celebrating San Victory Too Soon? Reflections on the Outcome of the Central Kalahari Game Reserve Case. *Anthropology Today* 23, no. 5:3–5.

THEAL, GEORGE M.
1893   *History of South Africa (1834–1854)*. London: Swan Sonnenschein.

TIEMESSEN, ALANA E.
2004   After Arusha: Gacaca Justice in Post-Genocide Rwanda. *African Studies Quarterly: The Online Journal for African Studies* 8, no. 1; www.africa.ufl.edu/asq/v8/v8i1a4htm.

TOFT, MONICA DUFFY

2003   *The Geography of Ethnic Violence: Identity, Interests, and the Indivisibility of Territory*. Princeton, NJ: Princeton University Press.

VANDERBILT, TOM

1997   The Advertised Life. In *Commodify Your Dissent: Salvos from* The Baffler. Edited by T. Frank and M. Weiland. New York and London: W.W. Norton.

VAN DER POST, LAURENS

1958   *The Lost World of the Kalahari*. New York: Morrow.
1961   *The Heart of the Hunter*. New York: Morrow.

VAN WYK, ILANA

2003   "'Elephants Are Eating Our Money': A Critical Ethnography of Development Practice in Maputaland, South Africa." M.A. thesis, University of Pretoria.

VENTER, ANDREW KARL

2000   Community-Based Natural Resource Management in South Africa: Experience from the Greater St Lucia Wetlands Region. Paper to the Second Pan-African Symposium on the Sustainable Use of Natural Resources in Africa, Ouagadougou (Burkina Faso), July 2000; www.iucn.org/themes/ssc/susg/docs/venter.PDF
2003   What Does the Wildlands Trust Do? *Wetlands Wire: Official Newsletter of the Greater St. Lucia Wetland Park Authority* 1, no. 1:13; www.lubombomapping.org.za/GSLWPA/Web/WW1/page13.htm.

VILJOEN, M. J.

1999   The Nature and Origin of the Merensky Reef of the Western Bushveld Complex Based on Geological Facies and Geological Data. *South African Journal of Geology* 102, no. 3:221–239.

VLADISLAVIĆ, IVAN

2006   *Portrait with Keys: Joburg and What-What*. Roggebaai, Cape Town: Umuzi.

WALLE, ALF H.

1998   *Cultural Tourism: A Strategic Focus*. Boulder: Westview Press.

WALLENSTEEN, PETER, AND MARGARETA SOLLENBERG

1995   After the Cold War: Emerging Patterns of Armed Conflict 1989–94. *Journal of Peace Research* 32, no. 3:345–360.

WALLERSTEIN, IMMANUEL

1972   Social Conflict in Post-Independence Black Africa: The Concepts of Race and Status Group Reconsidered. In *Racial Tensions in National Identity*. Edited by E. Campbell. Nashville: Vanderbilt University Press.

WATSON, LEO, AND MAUI SOLOMON

2001   The Waitangi Tribunal and the Maori Claim to Their Cultural and Intellectual Heritage Rights Property. *Cultural Survival* 24, no. 4; www
.culturalsurvival.org/publications/csq/csq-article.cfm?id'1119.

WEBER, MAX

1968   *Economy and Society: An Outline of Interpretive Sociology*. 3 Volumes. Edited by Guenther Roth and Claus Wittich. New York: Bedminster Press.

WESTBROOK, DAVID A.

2007   *Between Citizen and State: An Introduction to the Corporation*. Boulder, CO: Paradigm Publishers.

WHITE, HYLTON J.

1991   The Homecoming of the Kagga Kamma Bushmen. *Cultural Survival Quarterly* 17, no. 2; www.kaggakamma.co.za/en/history.html.

1995   *In the Tradition of Our Forefathers: Bushman Traditionality at Kagga Kamma: The Politics and History of a Performative Identity*. Cape Town: University of Cape Town Press, in association with the Centre for African Studies.

WILDER, GARY

2005   *The French Imperial Nation-State: Negritude and Colonial Humanism between the Two World Wars*. Chicago: University of Chicago Press.

WILLCOCK, JOHN W.

1827   *The Law of Municipal Corporations*. London: William Benning.

WILMSEN, EDWIN N.

1989   *Land Filled with Flies: A Political Economy of the Kalahari*. Chicago: University of Chicago Press.

1993   On the Search for (Truth) and Authority: A Reply to Lee and Guenther. *Current Anthropology* 34, no. 5:715–721.

2008   The Structure of San Property Relations: Constitutional Issues and Interventionist Politics. In *Paradoxical Conjunctions: Access to Rural Resources in a Transnational Environment*. Edited by Bertram Turner and Melanie Wiber. *Anthropologica*, 49. [In press.]

WILMSEN, EDWIN N., AND JAMES R. DENBOW

1990   Paradigmatic History of San-Speaking Peoples and Current Attempts at Revision. *Current Anthropology* 31, no. 5:489–524.

BIBLIOGRAPHY

WILSON, RICHARD A.

1997   Human Rights, Culture and Context: An Introduction. In *Human Rights, Culture and Context: Anthropological Perspectives*. Edited by R. Wilson. London: Pluto Press.

WOOD, ROBERT

1998   Tourist Ethnicity: A Brief Itinerary. *Ethnic and Racial Studies* 21, no. 2: 218–241.

WORGER, WILLIAM H.

2000   Review of *Terrific Majesty: The Powers of Shaka Zulu and the Limits of Historical Invention*, by Caroline A. Hamilton, 1998. *Journal of American History* 87, no. 2:635.

XIE, PHILIP FELFAN

2003   The Bamboo-beating Dance in Hainan, China: Autheniticity and Commodification. *Journal of Sustainable Development* 11, no. 1:5–16.

YIFTACHEL, OREN

2006   *Ethnocracy: Land and Identity Politics in Israel/Palestine*. Philadelphia: University of Pennsylvania Press.

YOUNG, CRAWFORD

1993   The Dialectics of Cultural Pluralism: Concept and Reality. In *The Rising Tide of Cultural Pluralism: The Nation-State at Bay?* Edited by C. Young. Madison: University of Wisconsin Press.

ŽIŽEK, SLAVOJ

n.d.   Move the Underground: What's Wrong with Fundamentalism, Part 2; www.lacan.com/zizunder.htm.

Index